A Grand Bargain
for
Education Reform

A Grand Bargain

for

Education Reform

New Rewards and Supports
for New Accountability

Edited by
THEODORE HERSHBERG
CLAIRE ROBERTSON-KRAFT

Harvard Education Press
Cambridge, Massachusetts

Library of Congress Control Number 2009925547

Paperback ISBN 978-1-934742-24-2
Library Edition ISBN 978-1-934742-25-9

Published by Harvard Education Press,
an imprint of the Harvard Education Publishing Group

Harvard Education Press
8 Story Street
Cambridge, MA 02138

Cover Design: schwadesign, inc.

The typefaces used in this book are Adobe Garamond and Adobe Stone Sans

*Dedicated to the memory
of John Grossman*

———————

Contents

Foreword

To those of us who have worked in the school reform arena for the past several decades, it is a given that today's educational system has not kept pace with changes in society. As a nation, we have invested what must surely be many billions of dollars in trying this quick fix, that silver bullet, this bright idea, yet none has had much success in raising student achievement.

In this extremely timely volume, Ted Hershberg and Claire Robertson-Kraft at Operation Public Education (OPE), and their colleagues, set forth a detailed agenda that eschews the concept of a magic solution in favor of a comprehensive approach that focuses on what we all now know is key—the development of highly effective, not simply highly qualified, teachers.

In practice, this means putting into place a system that combines incentives for performance with necessary supports to be certain that teachers have the knowledge and tools to see to it that every child has the opportunity to learn.

While we acknowledge the importance of highly effective teachers, we have historically lacked the systems for attracting, recognizing, rewarding, and retaining the best. We need thoughtful ways to measure and reward exemplary practice. We also need a range of new supports—not simply individual accountability—to help educators improve their instructional capacity in the classroom and at the school level. This volume provides valuable practices to meet these requirements.

Educators are awash in a sea of data yet all too often lack the information necessary to help them become more effective. We need solid indicators of those aspects of schooling we value most so that we can provide feedback in ways that improve practice. We also need training to help teachers, principals, and district and state leaders use the data to improve student learning. The OPE framework offers many useful examples.

This volume is a call to action. It is a call for all districts to reexamine current practices in light of what is best for all students. It is a call to establish a culture of evidence so sorely needed within the education sector. I applaud OPE, and the extraordinary collaborators brought together for this volume, for the boldness of the vision they have set forth. May their voices be joined by other bold reformers as together we reshape our nation's schools to prepare our students for college and career success.

CHRISTOPHER CROSS
Chairman, Cross & Joftus, LLC
January 2009

Preface

The comprehensive framework for school reform presented in these pages is the product of Operation Public Education, or OPE, as it has come to be known. OPE was established following a frustrating experience with the Southeastern Pennsylvania Standards Consortium—thirty-one suburban Philadelphia school districts organized by the Center for Greater Philadelphia at the University of Pennsylvania. Launched in 1996, well in advance of No Child Left Behind, with support from the William Penn Foundation, The Pew Charitable Trusts, and local corporations, the Consortium set out to have school districts across the region adopt uniformly high academic standards while it coordinated the districts' collaborative work in meeting them. Three years and several million dollars later it became clear that at most two districts had fully committed themselves to the goal.

In the spring of 2000, the Annenberg Foundation was preparing to publish a report describing the results of its $500 million gift to eighteen school systems across the nation. As the report made clear, much useful knowledge was learned through the Annenberg Challenge,[1] but there was some disappointment that the investment had not leveraged greater systemic change. At a Foundation-sponsored seminar, I was invited to speculate on the reasons why this was the case. Based on my experience with the Standards Consortium, I suggested that absent new rules and incentives under which the public schools would operate, fundamental change would remain elusive. When the Foundation asked what the Center would do with a grant, my response was that it would design a new reward structure for public schools that aligned the interests of teachers and administrators with the goal of significant increases in student achievement.

OPE was created later that year with funds from the Annenberg Foundation and renewed support from the William Penn Foundation. We built our comprehensive framework through two basic activities. We visited states such as North Carolina, Ohio, and Tennessee, where innovative reform efforts were under way. And we invited leading reformers from the ranks of teachers, administrators, and school board members who were engaged in cutting-edge reform in their communities to come to Pennsylvania and share their ideas and programs with local educators. Because we were not burdened by the need to reach consensus among multiple education stakeholders, when all the travel and seminars were completed, we selected practices that supported each other and had been shown individually to improve instruction and raise student achievement. Taken together, the framework represents a comprehensive rather than a piecemeal approach to school reform.

In 2003, OPE asked six members of the Teacher Union Reform Network (TURN), each a president or former president of their respective local, to vet an early version of the framework during a daylong conference at Penn. Attendees included Bonnie Cullison, Montgomery County, Maryland; Roger Erskine, Seattle; John Grossman, Columbus; Louise Sundin, Minneapolis; Randi Weingarten, New York City; and Becky Wissink, Denver. Rob Weil and Richelle Patterson attended from the national office of the American Federation of Teachers. On several other occasions, Adam Urbanski, a cofounder of TURN, offered valuable comments on the framework.

We adopted several of their key suggestions, including peer review and shared decision making. Although no formal vote on the framework was sought or taken, the meeting ended with a sense that while the reforms were controversial and would face considerable political obstacles at both the local and state levels, OPE had developed a fair and teacher-friendly approach that would likely lead to increased student achievement. None of these committed union leaders is responsible for the framework in its current form, but we are grateful for their candid advice and counsel.

The framework was then converted to legislative language in a rewrite of the law governing Pennsylvania's public schools and introduced in the state House of Representatives. When strong opposition from the state's teachers unions and unwillingness by Democrats and Republicans in the General Assembly to compromise on an approach requiring "investment with accountability," OPE had to decide whether to close down or learn whether the sweeping reforms it proposed merited introduction outside Pennsylvania. To answer this question, advice was sought from prominent educators who subsequently agreed to serve on our national advisory board.

OPE's national advisory board was formed in 2003 and chaired by Christopher Cross, the former president of the Council on Basic Education and president of the Maryland State Board of Education. Its founding members included Dan Challener, president, Chattanooga Public Education Foundation; John Deasy, superintendent, Santa Monica-Malibu Unified School District; Jim Geringer, former governor of Wyoming and former chair of the Education Commission of the States; John Grossman, the former longtime president of the Columbus Education Association; Gerry House, president, Institute for Advanced Achievement; Walter

Hussman, publisher, *Arkansas Democrat Gazette;* Timothy Kremer, executive director, New York State School Boards Association; C. Kent McGuire, dean of the school of education at Temple University; Margaret Raymond, director, CREDO, Hoover Institution, Stanford University; Howard Wainer, Distinguished Research Scientist, National Board of Medical Examiners; and Randi Weingarten, president of the United Federation of Teachers. Our board's support and encouragement is one of the major reasons that OPE exists today. Representing significantly different points of view, its members share a deep commitment to high-quality public education, and OPE is grateful for the time and energy they have given us.[2]

Our advisory board counseled against compartmentalizing the framework because its comprehensive quality was what made it so attractive, and they urged us to introduce the framework to national audiences. With renewed funding from the Annenberg Foundation and new support from the Carnegie Corporation, The Pittsburgh Foundation, and area corporations, OPE spent several years introducing its framework to diverse education constituencies and writing about it in national education journals.[3] Over this time, we elaborated the framework and refined its individual components.

I was joined in developing the first draft of the framework by two remarkably gifted colleagues: Ian Rosenblum, at the time a recent graduate of the University of Pennsylvania and currently a senior member of the public policy team working for Pennsylvania's governor Ed Rendell; and Virginia Adams Simon, a former director of admissions at the Baldwin School who earned her mid-career doctorate in education at Penn while engaged in the design process, and now a lecturer in education policy at the University of California, Davis; she also authored one of the chapters in this volume. Our collaboration was as delightful as it was challenging, and Rosenblum and Adams Simon deserve enormous credit for the inventiveness and wisdom of their contributions.

Others who have contributed significantly to OPE since 2000 include Barbara Lea-Kruger, who served initially as director of development and communications and later as associate director; Carla Mosley, senior administrator, who organized our outreach activities and kept the project on track; and Stephanie Levin and Farah Dilber, senior research associates, who ably provided background research on a broad range of issues. Their efforts helped both to improve the framework and to introduce it to audiences nationwide. Many students at the University of Pennsylvania helped with a wide array of research and clerical tasks, and I especially want to thank Ashley Cash, a most capable undergraduate dedicated to public school reform.

The funding provided by the foundations already mentioned is gratefully acknowledged, but two individuals—Gail Levin, president of the Annenberg

Foundation, and Dan Fallon, former director of the education programs at the Carnegie Corporation—deserve special mention because of their early personal support and encouragement of our efforts. Our greatest debt is to the Bill & Melinda Gates Foundation, whose support made possible the description of the framework in book-length format. The Gates Foundation is also underwriting the elaboration of the framework so practitioners and researchers will have access to Web-based links to additional resources and tools for each component.

The nationally prominent educators who contributed chapters describing their respective component in the OPE framework (their bios appear at the close of this volume) merit special recognition. They are unrivaled in their understanding of the ingredients for reform, and we are delighted they agreed to share their considerable expertise with us.

I am pleased to acknowledge the contributions of Claire Robertson-Kraft, the coeditor of this volume. A 2004 graduate of the University of Pennsylvania, her passion for and commitment to public education reform grew during three years with Teach For America—two as a teacher in the Houston Independent School District and one as a supervisor of corps members in elementary and special education. In just over a year's time after joining OPE, she mastered the array of issues embedded in the framework and brought brilliance and energy to the task of completing this volume.

This volume is dedicated to John Grossman, a good friend, wonderful colleague, talented educator, and passionate union leader, who died while the manuscript was being completed. A member of OPE's national advisory board, John's courageous spirit and enterprising leadership was an inspiration to us all.

Douglas Clayton, director of the Harvard Education Publishing Group, recognized the potential of this project at the outset, remained a steadfast advocate throughout the process of bringing it to completion, and offered much valuable advice along the way. We are grateful for this support because none other than President Barack Obama recently called for teacher performance pay and a means for dismissing ineffective teachers.[4] This makes *A Grand Bargain for Education Reform* very timely indeed because it provides for these in ways that both innovative and fair, but as the following pages demonstrate, our comprehensive framework for school reform does far more.

On a personal note, I am grateful to my wife, Betsy, who despite frequent setbacks along the way urged me not to give up on our school reform framework, and I thank her and my children, Dan and Jessica, for indulging me on countless occasions over the last decade to ramble on about the possibilities of value-added assessment in transforming public education.

Finally, in reading this volume, please note that the editors' introductions to each chapter appear in italics to distinguish them from the author(s)' prose. Readers can find additional resources for each component in the framework at http://www.operationpubliced.org.

THEODORE HERSHBERG
Philadelphia
May 2009

PART I

Introduction

CHAPTER ONE

Overview of the OPE Framework

THEODORE HERSHBERG
CLAIRE ROBERTSON-KRAFT

*We are fooling ourselves if we believe that tweaking tax rates, training, or
trade agreements will turn this tide. The global information economy is here.
It is brutal and unforgiving . . . The only way to ensure we remain a world
economic power is by elevating our public schools—particularly the teachers
who lead them—to the top tier of American society.*

—Louis Gerstner, former chairman of IBM
and chairman of The Teaching Commission[1]

The dawn of the twenty-first century is not a time for complacency. The challenge
is to educate our nation's youth to enter a fiercely competitive global economy that
rewards high cognitive abilities. The data are undeniably clear in demonstrating
that our students are falling behind those of other nations, that current teachers
are dissatisfied and leaving their classrooms in record numbers, and that the best
and brightest of our college graduates are opting not to join the teaching profession at the very moment when research has made clear they are by far the most important factor in student learning.

Despite enormous financial investment and the efforts of educators over the
last three decades, our schools continue to underserve the large majority of their
students. Ending this failure will require a significant improvement in the quality
of classroom instruction. The central argument of this book is that this is most
likely to be accomplished by changing the system in which our educators work.
Enormously successful in the industrial economy, our public schools were not designed to educate all our children to the levels demanded in a knowledge economy.

The key change for public education is not whether school boards are elected or
appointed or whether schools are large or small, but the need for a new strategy for
human capital development—that is to say, a new way to evaluate, compensate, remediate, and provide professional development for our teachers and administrators.

3

Retaining, supporting, and attracting the most able to the teaching profession will require a transformed school system, one that will make teaching a more financially rewarding and intellectually satisfying experience.

The framework developed by Operation Public Education (OPE) begins with an essential realignment so that the interests of individual educators are tied to student learning results and all educators are provided additional assistance to upgrade their instructional expertise. It is designed around these two separate but indispensably linked parts: The New Reward Structure and Support for Educators. In this realigned system, new forms of accountability are introduced, but they go hand in hand with access to new forms of professional development to help educators succeed in their instructional tasks. This is not about getting tough with teachers and administrators—it's about creating a system where appropriate responsibility is paired with necessary support.

This volume has three purposes. The first is to encourage educators and policy makers to become familiar with the core themes advanced in these pages— how to align the goal of increased student achievement with new rewards through both positive and negative incentives, and how to support educators in their efforts to improve the quality of classroom instruction. Even though they may not adopt any of the specific components as they are described here, we hope that this book will help districts and policy makers create new human capital development strategies and fashion the specifics of reform for the culture and practice of their districts.

The second is to showcase the framework's individual components as part of a "tool kit," whose valuable practices work effectively when used alone or in combination. While the description of the framework that follows was deliberately constructed to illustrate how each component could fit into an overall design, this is not an all-or-nothing approach. Districts do not have to adopt the overall framework; indeed, most are likely to choose a subset of the components that support one another and best fit within their own reform efforts. To maximize usefulness, each author has been asked to write a how-to essay. In addition to providing an overview of the component, each chapter concludes with concrete action steps and guidelines for managing the process of implementation.

The third is to interest school districts in piloting the framework in its entirety. Different approaches are being advanced to ensure that American students are able to meet the demanding academic standards of the twenty-first century, but the contributors to this volume believe that success is more likely to come through comprehensive rather than piecemeal reform. Districts adopting the framework will require especially progressive leadership and access to appropriate resources from the public and private sectors to fund its final design and implementation. In the best circumstances, these pilots will go forward with support and encouragement from their national and state teachers unions.

In short, the book can be read as a general guide to reform in which districts align new rewards and new supports according to their own designs, as a collection of complementary reforms from which districts will choose and modify, and as a specific framework for comprehensive reform to be piloted.

While it is hoped that the OPE framework will be widely read by policy makers interested in transforming the nation's public schools, classroom teachers remain at the heart of this work. If the reforms advocated here are welcomed by the millions of women and men who labor daily in our schools to educate our children, by mid-century the teaching profession will be among the most highly regarded in the knowledge economy.

As the education crisis worsens, state legislatures, perhaps even the federal government, may impose change through top-down command and control. But we believe strongly that the best chances for success lie with progressive educators and union leaders who willingly work together as equal partners in reform.

THE NEW REWARD STRUCTURE

The National Commission on Teaching and America's Future documents the fact that teacher attrition has grown by 50 percent over the past ten years.[2] Approximately one in three teachers leaves the profession in the first three years of service. While this is not very different from turnover in other professions, the attrition rate increases to 46 percent in the first five years and these rates are a third higher in urban districts.[3] But finding high-quality replacements is problematic because with gender discrimination in the workforce greatly diminished, women of talent have been flocking to other professions. Teachers accounted for just under a third of all professional women in 1972, but fewer than one-seventh in 2004.[4] To reduce attrition and reverse this trend, we must develop a more attractive system for prospective and current teachers.

Aligning the System

Today's system of public education is largely unchanged from the nineteenth century. It socialized millions of immigrants and rural migrants for success in an industrial economy by teaching them to respect authority, develop a work ethic, and repeat monotonous tasks; it provided universal basic literacy; and it prepared the top one-fifth of our students for higher education. Our schools were enormously successful in these tasks, and there is no way to understand the emergence of America as a twentieth-century industrial superpower without acknowledging the key role schools played. Our schools and the workforce needs of the factory economy were perfectly aligned.

To meet the new demands presented by a complex democracy and a competitive global economy, schools must now graduate their students able to use technology, think critically, solve problems, and learn on their own throughout their lives. These new goals go well beyond socialization and credentialing. Our schools must now educate all the children, not simply the top fifth, and educate them to meet far more challenging academic standards. Aligning our system of public education—actually, realigning is more accurate—means linking the new goals with incentives made possible by new approaches to evaluation and compensation.

In introducing school-based accountability, No Child Left Behind broke new ground, but it did not go far enough. A single score for a school obscures the most effective and least effective teaching by expressing all performance as a single average. This is unfortunate, because using new growth models we are now able to measure the effectiveness of individual teachers, and we've learned that the quality of instruction varies more within schools than between schools and districts. Whether corrections are made in the law's reauthorization or simply adopted by states and districts as a fully complementary reform, it is time to introduce accountability at the level of individual teachers and administrators.

The introduction of individual-level accountability, moreover, addresses several key issues. With new value-added methodologies providing an empirical component in teacher evaluation, we can identify the most effective teachers, pay them higher salaries, and enable them to advance faster in their careers. These changes will help attract to our schools more of the most talented college graduates while keeping more of our most able current educators in their classrooms. We can also identify the least effective teachers, provide them with an opportunity to improve, and dismiss those who fail to do so despite the provision of key supports.

The logic of the OPE framework is that significant increases in student achievement will not emerge until our reward structures directly support our new educational goals. This belief can be illustrated by an analogy to higher education. The reward structures of our nation's leading research universities can be succinctly summarized in three words: publish or perish. One does not get hired at these institutions, granted tenure, and promoted to full professor without producing high-quality research. But what would happen to the productivity of the faculties at the University of Pennsylvania, Stanford University, and Harvard University, for example, if next year these institutions announced that compensation would henceforth be based on years of service? That is a rhetorical question: to ask it is to answer it. Whatever can be said about the reward structures—they are good because research is their raison d'être or they are bad because they ignore teaching—these structures are perfectly aligned with their stated goals. Faculty advance in their careers only if they produce high-quality research.

An anecdote simultaneously reveals the shortcomings of the current public school system and highlights the value of new reward structures. Cheryl Lemke, former director of information technology for the Illinois Department of Education, delivered a 2006 keynote address at a statewide conference of Indiana educators. The National Science Foundation, she reported, had developed a multimedia module for teaching middle school science at the cost of $17.5 million. Research shows that if this module is used, students are three to four times as likely to master the curriculum, but despite its effectiveness, the group monitoring usage reported that few school districts had adopted it. After sharing this unfortunate fact, Lemke paused and then asked, "Can we call this malpractice?"[5]

The same question could be asked about great volumes of best practices that go unused. To be sure, individual educators at some schools are actively engaged in searching for what works, but they do so in spite of rather than because of existing reward structures. Would not the interests of students and the nation as a whole be better served if the administrators and teachers in every district saw their own interests tied to increased student learning, and therefore assigned staff to scour the Internet for curriculum that would lead to such positive results in their classrooms and schools?

A grade school physics lesson provides a useful image. After iron filings of different shapes and sizes are scattered across a sheet of cardboard, a magnet is drawn slowly along the underside. The filings quickly arrange themselves on the path traveled by the magnet. It's time to develop a reward structure that will similarly align the interests of teachers and administrators around the common goal of increasing student achievement. For example, persuading district-level decision makers who hold ideological positions on whole language or phonics to adopt research-based methods to teach reading is currently a very difficult undertaking, but tie student learning results to evaluation and compensation and educators will be far more willing to find out what actually works best.

Indeed, it is this alignment—and the system of new supports that will accompany it—that is missing from America's system of public education. As long as the nation's schools were successful in meeting their historic goals, it did not matter how educators were evaluated and compensated. But with the nation's new and dramatically elevated goals, it matters a great deal.

K–12 has always been an input-based system. The days and hours that teachers and administrators work have long been purchased on an annualized basis, but they are not connected to outputs in the form of student learning results. Teacher compensation follows the single-salary schedule, with increases driven essentially by longevity. Everyone knew there were "good" and "bad" teachers, but it was neither possible nor desirable to identify them objectively because outputs were always measured solely in terms of achievement.

Since achievement, a point on a vertical scale at a single moment in time, is best predicted by family income—schools in wealthy suburban communities always have high test scores and schools in poor urban communities always have low test scores—there was no way to tie teaching and learning together in a system of accountability that wasn't deeply biased.

But there is another way to express student learning, known as growth. It can be thought of as the progress students make over the course of the school year regardless of the achievement level at which they started in the fall. Datasets can now track individual students over time and match their scores in all tested subjects with the teachers who taught them. And unlike achievement, student learning results measured in terms of growth are best predicted by the quality of instruction.

As a result, an empirical component, both accurate and fair, is finally available for use in teacher evaluation and compensation. Sophisticated growth or value-added models are very good at identifying the most effective and least effective educators in schools, and the data they provide can become part of the evaluation criteria for the large majority of teachers and all administrators. How the value-added estimates are calculated and used are critically important issues that will be addressed later.

The Empirical Evidence for Differentiating Teacher Compensation

Recent research provides compelling evidence for ending a compensation system based on longevity and a salary schedule that pays teachers the same regardless of their effectiveness in promoting student learning.

A review of the literature undertaken by the National Center for Teacher Quality (NCTQ) finds little evidence to support "compensation packages that raise salaries equally for each year of service without regard to other considerations."[6] Most research finds the benefits of experience—growing effectiveness in improving student learning—ending after a couple of years or as many as four or five years in the classroom.[7] "A few years of experience make a teacher more effective," the NCTQ report concludes, adding, "After that it's unclear." With teacher productivity, on average, peaking early in a career, the typical salary schedule driven by longevity is indefensible. If this pattern were widely understood, the taxpaying public would not tolerate it.[8]

Value-added studies done in Tennessee and elsewhere demonstrate the impact of instruction on student learning, revealing considerable variability in teacher effectiveness. In two large metropolitan districts with hundreds of classrooms, researchers set out to examine how the quality of the teacher sequence affected student performance. All students who began third grade at the same level of math achievement were followed through fifth grade, and their scale scores on the Terra Nova math test were recorded at the end of fifth grade.

As measured by value-added, the researchers found very different achievement levels for these students, depending on the quality of the teachers who taught them math in third, fourth, and fifth grades. As expected, students in the wealthier of the two districts (system A) always had higher absolute test scores than their counterparts, but there were striking differences that were attributable to the teacher sequence. Students in both districts with three consecutive teachers drawn from the top third of the teacher pool (ranked by their value-added scores) scored fifty percentile points higher than those who had teachers drawn from the bottom third of the teacher pool (see figure 1.1). In other words, students who started at the same level of math achievement had very different outcomes, depending on the quality of the teachers who instructed them in math.[9]

FIGURE 1.1
The importance of the teacher sequence

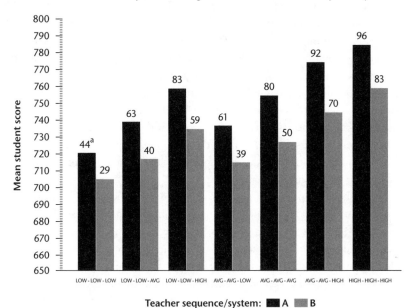

Cumulative effects of teacher sequence on fifth-grade math scores for two metropolitan systems

Teacher sequence/system: ■ A ■ B

[a] University of Tennessee Value-Added Research and Assessment Center November 1996.

The Dallas Independent School District replicated this study and found similar effects related to the teacher sequence. The fact that a different test and a different value-added model were used but produced comparable results—the hallmark of scientific rigor—has persuaded even skeptics that the teacher effect is real and statistically valid.[10]

In another groundbreaking study, June Rivers demonstrated the powerful impact that instruction has on student learning.[11] Rivers ranked all students in these same large metropolitan Tennessee school districts at the end of fourth grade, dividing them into quartiles. She then asked what the probabilities were for the typical student in each quartile to pass the high-stakes exam required for graduation, which is given for the first time in ninth grade. In the example used here, the results are for the bottom quartile, but the patterns she found were the same in each quartile.

Because each student had four teachers in fifth through eighth grades before taking the exam, Rivers identified all teachers in these grades and divided them into quartiles as well, based on their value-added scores. If a typical bottom-quartile student had four teachers drawn from the bottom 25 percent of the teacher pool, the chances of passing the test were less than 15 percent.

Explanations for this result typically rely heavily on factors beyond the school. Some observers cite difficult socioeconomic circumstances. Others point to inherent ability: some children have it, others don't. The excuses usually conclude with a sad inevitability: "It's most unfortunate, but these are the 'bottom of the barrel' kids." "You can bring the horse to water," we are told, "but you can't make it drink." These explanations share a deeply flawed conclusion: the fault lies with the students rather than with the quality of instruction they received.

However, despite being hobbled by nurture or nature, if these same students had four teachers drawn from the middle 50 percent of the teacher pool, their chances of passing increased to 38 percent. And if they were fortunate enough to have had four teachers drawn not from the exceptional top 1 percent or 5 percent of the teacher pool but from the top 25 percent, their chances of passing the test improved to 60 percent.

Why should top-quarter teachers measured by value-added be paid more than their colleagues? They deserve greater compensation because they confer considerable benefits on their students. In a recent study, Thomas Kane, Jonah Rockoff, and Douglas Staiger described these benefits as three times the advantage of having an experienced versus an inexperienced teacher and more than ten times the advantage of having a certified rather than a noncertified teacher.[12]

Studies like these reveal the enormous power of effective teaching. Students otherwise deemed hopelessly low achievers or academic failures can perform at much higher levels—if they receive high-quality instruction. These results make it demonstrably difficult to defend a compensation system that pays all teachers the same regardless of their effectiveness with students.

Arguments Against the Use of Student Learning Results in Evaluation and Compensation

The arguments put forward to oppose the inclusion of student learning results in evaluation and compensation can be straightforwardly addressed:

It cannot be done fairly. Aware of James Coleman's and Christopher Jencks' conclusions that family income is the primary factor in explaining student achievement, many educators believe there is no fair way to compensate teachers using student-learning results.[13] This is true if the evaluation is based on absolute achievement—a test score on a vertical scale at a single moment in time. But if the measure is growth—the progress students make over the course of the school year—then the effectiveness of instruction can and should become an important component of evaluation.

Teachers shouldn't be judged by test scores alone. Agreed, but value-added assessment can make an important empirical contribution to teacher evaluation and compensation. As recent reports from RAND, the National Association of State Boards of Education, and the Educational Testing Service (ETS) make clear, value-added can be used to identify the highest and lowest performers but should never be used as the sole or principal criterion of teacher effectiveness.[14] Value-added scores should be used as part of a balanced system with multiple measures that include sophisticated teaching frameworks to guide observation, as well as appropriate safeguards, such as review panels composed of teachers and administrators, to ensure fair treatment for individual educators.[15]

Differentiated pay fosters competition rather than collaboration. When the comparison pool is sufficiently large—a big city, a county, or a grouping of small districts of similar demographics—teachers within schools are unlikely to see themselves as competitors. But another approach eliminates competition entirely by establishing an externally defined growth standard. North Carolina uses the 1996 statewide average; Tennessee uses one set from 1998. Despite arguments that pay for performance unavoidably creates a "Darwinian competition," the use of an external growth standard means that teachers compete with themselves—not with each other—to surpass this benchmark.[16]

Evaluation and compensation should be done on a schoolwide rather than on an individual basis. As already noted, studies have shown that the variation in the quality of instruction is much greater within schools than between schools.[17] Schoolwide scores are simply averages that ignore the most and least effective instruction. Paying bonuses to everyone in a school means rewarding ineffective teaching as well as minimizing the district funding available for outstanding teaching. Group awards can play a valuable role in promoting collaboration, but they should accompany rather than preclude evaluation and compensation at the individual level.

There are ways to spend the money that will reap far better long-term results than compensation reform. Value-added research, replicated in different settings by different investigators, has shown that the proportion of the variance in student gain scores accounted for by teacher quality is many times greater than race, income, class size, and gender.[18] Because good teaching profoundly influences student learning, we should be concentrating our resources on professional development to improve instruction and on new systems of evaluation and compensation to measure and reward it.

It will cost too much. Critics argue that even if philanthropy provides the funds to launch these reforms, there is no way to sustain the support. While taxpayers almost everywhere resist substantial new investments in the status quo, Denver voters several years ago approved a $25 million surcharge on their real estate taxes to support a system of differentiated compensation for the city's teachers. The Denver case strongly suggests that if you offer citizens something innovative, voters will respond positively. A strategy of "investment with accountability" can be a powerful tool for uniting educators, policy makers, business leaders, and the general public around a school reform agenda.

If you want to invest in teachers, increase salaries for everyone. The case can be made that starting pay for teachers should be increased, but only if it is part of the quid pro quo of investment with accountability. If the goal is to improve the quality of classroom instruction, compensation reform should focus on raising the effectiveness of all teachers: more days for professional development, multiyear mentoring for new teachers, and full-time instructional coaches drawn from the ranks of the highly effective to help teachers, especially those who are struggling, to improve their craft.

Current test results cannot be used in high-stakes personnel decisions. There is little evidence to support the contention that current tests are not "good at identifying the best teachers."[19] Despite their acknowledged shortcomings, current tests can be used to accurately distinguish three levels of instruction (highly effective, effective, and ineffective) as long as they meet three criteria: they satisfy the requirements of statistical reliability, are strongly correlated with the standards being taught in schools, and have sufficient "stretch" at each end of the scale—that is, they allow differentiation in the degree of success and failure, respectively, among the highest- and lowest-scoring students. That is not to say that the interests of the nation will not be better served by more rigorous, internationally benchmarked national standards and markedly improved assessments that measure higher-order thinking skills. It is encouraging to observe that these goals are being pursued in a cooperative effort by governors in upwards of thirty states.[20] This movement is both welcome and timely because the inclusion of student-learning results in educator evaluation and compensation will significantly increase the attention paid to the high-stakes assessments states have developed as mandated by federal law. "We do not need to abandon either the principle of accountability or the fill-in-the-bubble format," argues E. D. Hirsch. "Rather, we need to move from teaching to the test to tests that are worth teaching to."[21]

Tying student-learning results to educator compensation will unavoidably lead to wide-scale cheating. There is little systematic evidence on the extent of cheating by educators—either in response to the accountability provisions in NCLB or to pay-for-performance systems. Whatever the actual patterns, a genuine concern remains that once student-learning results are tied to both evaluation and compensation, educators will have a marked incentive to cheat. While the worry is real, the reality is that statistical systems can detect cheating by identifying scores outside expected ranges, in much the same way the IRS identifies taxpayers whose expense-to-income ratios exceed established parameters.

Framework Components for the New Reward Structure

Previous attempts at merit pay have failed for several valid reasons. They were considered highly subjective when based solely on observation, particularly when teachers distrusted the judgment of administrators.[22] Those that relied on student achievement scores, which are strongly influenced by family income, were unfair. Finally, by whatever measure districts ranked teachers, they were typically competing with each other for a fixed number of dollars set aside in advance by the school board. When these quota systems were introduced, teachers often expressed fear that introducing rewards would engender competition rather than promote collaboration.

OPE's approach to a new reward structure is very different from previous attempts at merit pay. It is not a limited bonus for which teachers compete or something tacked onto the existing salary schedule but a whole new way of thinking about compensation that draws on a teacher's entire evaluation, including observation, rather than on test scores alone. The OPE framework incorporates the following components as the foundation of the new reward structure.

Evaluating Educators. Evaluation is based on multiple measures. It is a balanced approach, using both empirical data from value-added assessment and observational data from the many components used in sophisticated frameworks.

- *Value-added assessment provides the empirical component in teacher and administrator evaluation.* The revolution in measuring student learning results—using growth rather than achievement to provide an empirical component in the appraisal of instruction—is the keystone of the OPE framework. Value-added assessment provides the empirical portion in teacher evaluation by aggregating student scores in individual classrooms, and in administrator evaluation by aggregating student scores in individual schools and districts into three categories: highly effective, effective, and ineffective. Student performance data do not bias the results because value-added scores (growth) rather than absolute test scores (achievement) are used. Chapter 3, "Choosing a Value-Added Model" by William Sanders and June Rivers, explains the key principles that school districts must consider when choosing among competing models.

- *Sophisticated frameworks are utilized to evaluate teacher actions.* Observation is carried out using sophisticated protocols instead of subjective judgments. Rubrics are provided to differentiate four levels of performance: unsatisfactory, basic, proficient, and distinguished. This approach is more robust than an administrator's visit to a classroom several times over the course of a year that results in a rating, most often without consequence, of satisfactory or unsatisfactory. In chapter 4, "Teacher Evaluation," Charlotte Danielson describes how the observation portion of evaluation can be conducted using this comprehensive approach.

- *Administrators are evaluated through a comprehensive portfolio process.* The interests of all members of the school team are aligned; administrators as well as teachers have an equal stake in the learning outcomes of the students in their classroom, school, or district. Chapter 5, "Administrator Evaluation" by John Deasy, describes a new balanced approach to administrator evaluation that draws on the standards established by the Interstate School Leaders Licensure Consortium (ISLLC) and the Framework for Teaching and includes an innovative set of reflective exercises that supports administrator self-improvement.

Compensating Educators. With a new way to evaluate educators, districts need to develop a means for translating these results into a system that replaces the single-salary schedule. The compensation system in the OPE framework is designed to attract the best young talent, allow highly effective teachers to achieve high salaries, reach these levels faster, and establish a clear performance link between pay and student learning gains. It promotes collaboration and incentivizes both individual and group improvement.

- *Teacher and administrator compensation reflects performance and rewards improvement.* Teachers and administrators compete only with themselves and not with each other in climbing a career ladder. The ladder (1) separates base pay from variable pay; (2) provides incentives for individual performance and performance as a member of a group (e.g., the school); and (3) includes steps for increasing compensation within rungs; however, it ties these raises not to longevity as in traditional salary schedules but to maintaining student growth at rates commensurate with the requirements of each rung. Chapter 6, "Compensation" by Marc Wallace, describes this approach and outlines general principles for reforming compensation systems.
- *All educators are included in the new system.* All educators, regardless of subject taught or specialist function, are included in the compensation system; while they cannot be treated the same way, a fair system should provide everyone with an opportunity to earn additional pay. In chapter 7, "Compensating Educators in the Absence of Value-Added Assessment," Virginia Adams Simon discusses the options available for compensating teachers and other professional staff who fall into three groupings in which the empirical component derived from value-added assessment is not available for evaluation: kindergarten through second grade, nonacademic core subjects (e.g., music, art, physical education, etc.), and specialists (e.g., librarians, nurses, guidance counselors, social workers, etc.).

Figure 1.2 provides a visual representation of the OPE Career Ladder and its distinctive features are discussed here.

Number of rungs. The minimum number of rungs required is three because value-added models are statistically accurate in identifying the "tails" of the teacher distribution, hence the designation of highly effective for the best and ineffective for the worst performers. These models do not differentiate reliably among the large majority of teachers in the middle of the distribution; as a result, all those in the effective range are treated the same. Because the goal is to maximize compensation for top performers, a fourth rung is recommended, the requirements for which opinions differ.

FIGURE 1.2
Teacher career ladder

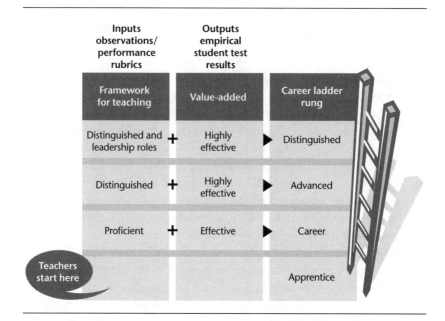

Moving up the career ladder. In the OPE system, teachers begin their careers as Apprentices. In as few as three years—the minimum necessary to provide statistically valid value-added estimates—they can move up to Career status. Teachers not meeting their input and output requirements can be dismissed at this point, but they may be given up to five years if additional time will enable them to succeed. Teachers can remain at the Career level for the duration of their career as long as they are rated proficient in their observations and have effective value-added scores. Although they are encouraged to move up the ladder, they are not required to do so.

To move up to Advanced status, teachers must receive the highest input (distinguished) and output (highly effective) ratings. That is to say, they must meet the highest standards measured by the performance rubrics and succeed in helping their students achieve empirical growth rates at the highest statistically defined levels. To reach the Distinguished rung—the top rung of the ladder—OPE recommends that teachers meet all the requirements for Advanced status and hold one of several leadership roles, e.g., mentor, coach, team leader, or content specialist.[23]

Teachers would be tenured when they reach the Career rung of the ladder. But while tenure provides appropriate protection from political abuses, in the OPE framework it does not protect teachers who are rated ineffective and unable to improve their instructional practices during the remediation process discussed in chapter 12.

Maintaining performance. The system also provides incentives to keep teachers performing at the level of mastery required at their rung through mandatory remediation, by dividing salary into base pay and variable pay (both individual and group), and making variable pay as well as step-based pay dependent on maintaining appropriate classroom effectiveness (see chapter 6).

Funding. The career ladder can be funded with or without additional monies. When new funds are available, Career teachers earn as much as they did in the old compensation system, but Advanced and Distinguished teachers can earn substantially more. When additional funds are unavailable, the OPE framework would include a grandfather clause that offers all current teachers the option of choosing to remain under the same compensation system with which they began their careers. All teachers who enter the profession after the OPE system is in effect would fall under the new compensation system. Veteran teachers would, however, be subject to the new evaluation system regardless of the compensation system they choose.

In districts with collective bargaining, negotiations would establish the starting salary in terms of absolute dollars; they could also lead to increases in the mandated percentage minimums that are specified for moving up the rungs in the OPE career ladder.

To create a symmetrical system that promotes increased student learning and aligns the interests of all educators, administrators must be held accountable as instructional leaders. The OPE system has designed an administrator evaluation system and career ladder similar to that for teachers (see figure 1.3). Half of every administrator's evaluation would be based on observed practices and performance rubrics, as described in chapter 5. The other half of the evaluation would be based on student growth results for their designated area of responsibility. For instance, principals would be rated based on the aggregate results of their buildings, superintendents on the aggregate results of their districts, and all other administrators on the building or buildings for which they have responsibility. Administrators' compensation would also be tied to this evaluation through a career ladder consisting of three rather than four rungs; these are classified as Associate, Career, and Distinguished.

FIGURE 1.3
Administrator career ladder

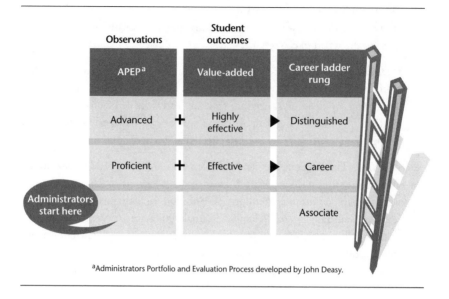

^aAdministrators Portfolio and Evaluation Process developed by John Deasy.

Administrators would begin their careers as Associates. As was the case with teachers, in as few as three years they can move up to Career status by meeting the requirements of the rung—effective value-added scores for the school and a proficient rating on the performance rubric. To move up to Distinguished status, administrators must receive the highest input (advanced) and output (highly effective) ratings. In other words, they must meet the highest standards measured by the performance rubrics and succeed in helping the students in their school or district achieve empirical growth rates at the highest statistically defined levels.

The purpose of the OPE framework's New Reward Structure, in sum, is to align the interests of all teachers and administrators with the new goal of significant increases in student learning. As the data on teacher effectiveness make clear, raising student achievement requires a direct focus on the classroom where learning actually takes place, and value-added assessment provides us for the first time with a tool to render a fair and objective evaluation of classroom instruction. For this reason, value-added can be the foundation for a system of accountability that holds individual teachers and administrators responsible for student learning results. Let's be clear—no educator should ever be evaluated solely on the basis of a single measure, not even one as powerful as value-added, but educator evaluations should be linked at least in part to student results. The New Reward Structure will provide districts with concrete guidelines for designing new systems for educator evaluation and compensation

SUPPORT FOR EDUCATORS

The Human Capital Development Challenge: Knowledge and Skill Requirements for Twenty-First-Century Classrooms

Pay for performance, while necessary, is far from sufficient. Alone it will not, and cannot, result in significantly higher achievement for *all* students because it does not provide other critical system changes designed to improve the instructional effectiveness of *all* teachers. To think otherwise is to believe that all teachers know what to do and how to do it and have been withholding their expertise, waiting for higher pay. The reality is that many teachers need additional time and support in order to improve.

Pay for performance is the right prescription, but it is a long-term solution. In the short run, some teachers may work harder in response to the incentive of higher pay. But pay for performance is primarily designed to persuade more of our top college graduates each year to opt for a career in teaching and to keep more of our most able educators from leaving the classroom. In the meantime, much more must be done to help current teachers develop the requisite knowledge and skills needed to help their students meet the more demanding standards and challenging curricula of the twenty-first century.

The realities of the global economy have placed additional demands on schools. In the old system, teachers were responsible for determining academic accomplishment in their classrooms, and students were sorted by ability along a bell-shaped curve. In order to graduate, students needed only to meet expectations set out by individual teachers, and many were just passed through the system on the basis of social promotion. Those who achieved at high levels were placed on the path to higher education; the others were instructed with a watered-down curriculum. In the standards-driven world, all children should be held to high expectations. Not only does every student deserve a rigorous education, the new economy also demands that they receive one. Though it will not be easy, educating all children to high levels is possible if teachers and administrators in our twenty-first century schools master an expanded base of knowledge and important new skills.

Replace Ability-Based Notions with an Efforts-Based Theory of Learning. Educators will need to replace ability-based notions that dominate the thinking of too many who work in our schools with an effort-based theory of learning: intelligence is not fixed, but must be viewed as malleable. Students are not simply born smart— they get smart with appropriate resources and high-quality instruction.[24] Research shows that all children can achieve at high levels, regardless of their genetic predispositions or socioeconomic circumstances, provided they are given high-quality instruction and appropriate resources.[25]

Eliminate the Bell-Shaped Curve. There is no place in a standards-driven school system for a bell-shaped curve. All students, except the most seriously disadvantaged, should be expected to meet rigorous, internationally benchmarked standards. To do so, some students will require additional resources and more time—evenings, weekends, summer school—but sustained effort and high-quality instruction will help them succeed. This is not to deny that ability is differentially distributed—it is. Standards can be thought of as the floor, while the ceiling is as high as individual students can reach. While some students are working to meet proficiency, other students can be pursuing advanced mastery.

Embrace a Problem-Solving Pedagogy. Educators will need to be proficient in using a problem-solving pedagogy in the classroom. Memorization will always have its place in the learning process, but research has documented that student understanding deepens when knowledge is applied in meaningful ways.[26] In order to develop higher-order thinking capacity and take ownership over their learning, students must do more than mechanically apply a set of skills. Teachers must encourage them to go beyond a search for the right answer and explore the different approaches taken to reach a specific conclusion.

Differentiate Instruction. Educators will have to learn how to differentiate instruction; one-size-fits-all cannot suffice in an era in which no child can be left behind and children have many different styles of learning. Students have different readiness levels, interests, and learning profiles, and effective instruction must accommodate these needs by differentiating the content focus, process requirements, and end products of learning.[27]

Employ Data-Driven Decision Making. In order to appropriately differentiate instruction, teachers must master data-driven decision making. Instead of relying on anecdotal evidence, high-quality formative assessments can provide teachers with a detailed picture of individual student need. Educators need not become psychometricians, but they must be familiar with how to interpret data and utilize the results to design appropriate student interventions. Using data as their guide, effective teachers will need to know where their students are, create a clear vision for where they need to be, and develop academic trajectories for each student to achieve success.

Develop Student-Centered Classrooms. Data should become the ultimate motivator for teachers and for students. If used appropriately, assessment will foster students' engagement in their own learning process by teaching them to monitor and take ownership over their progress toward a set of goals. Research has confirmed that students learn best when they are engaged in purposeful, active, and inquiry-based learning, so teachers must design student-driven environments, where the learner is central to the process.[28]

This is the human capital development challenge now facing public education. Implementing this new knowledge consistently will be difficult for educators because improving instructional practice requires more than merely changing a teacher's way of thinking. Converting new beliefs into action will necessitate multiple opportunities and sustained support over time. But investing in professional development without first creating the incentives, both positive and negative, for all educators to master what they are being taught is to permit the status quo to remain firmly in place. While we must provide additional compensation for our best performers, we must at the same time provide extensive support for all our teachers.

In effect, public education would be offering a new "social contract" to its teachers and administrators that parallels what is now accepted practice in the corporate world. Employees are no longer guaranteed jobs that persist over an entire career. Their value to their employers is a function of how effectively they develop the skills demanded by a rapidly changing business environment. In the new contract, the employer would be responsible for publicizing the available positions, describing the skills and knowledge they require, and offering courses—either in-house or at nearby colleges and universities—that provide appropriate training and education. The employee's responsibility would be to learn about the new opportunities and master the skills and knowledge necessary to succeed.

In the new social contract in public education, school districts would be responsible for providing their faculties and staffs with appropriate forms of professional development, and educators would be responsible for mastering these new offerings so their instructional practices could meet the human capital development challenge. When reward structures are aligned so that it is in the direct interest of every adult working in our public schools to master the knowledge and skill requirements for twenty-first century classrooms, the goal of all students achieving at high levels comes into reach.

Framework Components for Support for Educators

Research has shown that while districts often devote significant resources—in terms of both time and money—to supporting educators, the various efforts do not always address a district's most important priorities or incorporate best practices of staff development. Far too often, districts have not identified how new programs align with existing professional development initiatives, especially those that may overlap in terms of content and focus. Further, professional development is typically viewed as separate from teacher evaluation and compensation systems, rather than as a reinforcing system where all resources are viewed as investments in developing teacher capacity.[29]

To avoid these pitfalls, districts should ensure that they devise support strategies that align with teacher, student, and school needs. Schools should be reorganized to promote higher levels of teaching and learning excellence. Teachers should be aware of how new best practices can be incorporated into current curriculum requirements, and necessary supports should be in place to ensure effective implementation. Finally, educators should be provided with the time they need to sustain learning communities and the data and resources necessary to continually explore their professional practice. Though much still remains to be learned about professional development, the following components serve as the foundation for the OPE support structure.

Using Data to Drive Instruction. The adoption of higher standards has placed growing pressure on teachers to increase student achievement. This trend will require a significant upgrade in how we test our students and the kinds of support we give our educators to ensure they can be effective in utilizing data to drive instructional practice. Student data should also be used to gauge progress and gaps in educator knowledge and skill and to differentiate support based on need. In the framework:

- *An integrated assessment system informs instruction and increases student motivation.* To succeed in helping all students meet high standards, teachers will need high-quality assessment data that allow them to gauge students' readiness levels and monitor progress over the course of the year. Chapter 8, "Integrated Assessment" by Margaret Jorgensen, Claire Robertson-Kraft, and Theodore Hershberg, discusses the need for an assessment system that purposefully links high-quality summative exams—that is, exams that measure higher-order thinking skills—with frequent formative assessments. Equally important, the chapter discusses "assessment *for* learning," the important steps teachers can take to help their students become active agents in their own learning process.
- *Value-added data guides school and classroom improvement.* Equipped with value-added data, discussed in chapter 3, teachers, principals, district admin-

istrators, and school board leaders will learn the extent to which schools and classroom teachers are effective in raising performance and can use this information to guide improvement decisions. In chapter 9, "Value-Added as a Diagnostic," Joel Giffin, Claire Robertson-Kraft, and Theodore Hershberg describe the vital role that value-added assessment can play in improving instruction and highlight how it served as part of a broader reform effort that made Maryville Middle School the most academically successful school in Tennessee. This discussion of how data were used to drive instruction is a persuasive example of how the value-added methodology can contribute to increased student learning.

- *High-quality training maximizes the usefulness of value-added data.* Educators will benefit from high-quality training, which not only introduces them to the new metrics but helps them understand how to integrate what they have learned into their specific classroom and school context. Based on the extensive experience of Battelle for Kids, chapter 10, "Value-Added Training" by James Mahoney, Michael Thomas, and Jacquelyn Asbury, documents the rigorous professional development process teachers and administrators can undergo to understand how the growth metric differs from the achievement metric they have used exclusively in the past, how value-added data can be used for purposes of accountability, differentiated compensation, and school improvement, and how value-added reports can be institutionalized so they undergird their efforts to improve instructional practice.

Professional Development. Since data are driving the decision-making process, professional development should directly align with both student and teacher needs.[30] Sufficient ongoing support—people, time, and money—should be in place to ensure that educators make use of this valuable information over the course of their careers.

- *Multiyear mentoring replaces sink-or-swim induction process.* High-quality and comprehensive induction programs for new teachers can increase teacher effectiveness. In chapter 11, "Mentoring and New Teacher Induction," Ellen Moir and Patricia Martin describe the content and principles of the New Teacher Center's successful multiyear mentoring program for new teachers, which has been shown to increase student achievement and to lower districts' costs by reducing attrition.
- *Peer assistance and review programs provide ongoing support and a means for fairly dismissing ineffective teachers.* Teachers who need or want assistance should have access to high-quality support. This system's primary purpose

should be to improve instructional effectiveness, but it should also provide a mechanism for fairly dismissing teachers who demonstrate inadequate progress. In chapter 12, "Peer Assistance and Review," John Grossman and Claire Robertson-Kraft discuss the PAR process used in Columbus, Ohio.

- *A strategic review allows districts to reallocate limited professional development resources to the most important priorities.* Value-added training, peer assistance and review, multiyear mentoring and coaches are not inexpensive elements in a district's budget. However, before the question, how much will this cost? can be answered, districts need to determine how much they are currently spending on all their professional development activities. Chapter 13, "Strategic Professional Development Review" by Regis Shields and Karen Hawley Miles, describes a methodology developed by Education Resource Strategies to identify and classify total spending. With this information in hand, district leaders can redeploy available resources and learn the extent to which expanded professional development programs add new costs to the budget.

Restructuring Schools to Provide Additional Time and Support

Richard Elmore describes public education as consisting of two "loosely coupled" parts: a "core" (teachers and students) and an "administrative superstructure" (school boards, superintendents, principals, etc.).[31] The culture of the core socializes teachers to believe that when they close the door to their classroom, what goes on between them and their students is personal, intimate, and, above all else, private. This is as it should be. Indeed, it is the responsibility of the administrative superstructure to buffer the core from outside interference. The unintended consequence of this culture, however, is the isolation of the teacher, and isolation, as Elmore explains, is the enemy of learning.

To successfully implement a new approach to support, schools need to end the isolation of teaching by ensuring ample time and effective structures for teachers to engage in collaborative learning. Instead of the typical professional development sessions where teachers attend prearranged workshops, they should be directly involved in learning communities designed to target their knowledge/skill deficiencies and meet the needs of their students. Teachers should be aware of how new best practices can be incorporated into current curriculum requirements, and necessary supports should be in place to ensure effective implementation.

Districts should create time and space within every school to achieve these ends. Working collaboratively throughout the school year, teachers need support to use rich formative assessment data to improve the quality of their instruction. Creating such a climate will mean changing the existing school calendar to allow sufficient time for teachers to reflect on and explore their craft.

BENEFITS OF THE FRAMEWORK

If implemented, the strategic investments and organizational changes provided by this new approach to supporting educators promise a daily experience that is far more intellectually stimulating and emotionally satisfying for educators than that provided by the current system. Accompanied by the new reward structure, these supports should help to attract, nurture, and retain high-quality teachers and administrators and, in turn, increase student achievement by creating a new pathway to deliver what most teachers have long wanted—improved school leadership, better working conditions, more valid evaluation, meaningful professional development, higher student achievement, and increased salaries. The framework:

- *Allows teachers to rise as fast as their talent and efforts permit.* The framework calls for a career ladder—with compensation built into its rungs—so that teachers compete only with themselves and never with each other as they progress in their career. In most states and districts it now takes teachers up to twenty-five years to reach the top of the salary scale. Under the OPE framework, teachers who succeed in the classroom could earn the maximum pay in one-third of the time.
- *Creates a more attractive environment in which to work.* In the OPE framework, teachers will spend more time working with each other on ways to improve the quality of their instruction and increase student achievement. When teachers are engaged in joint study to these ends, they are no longer isolated, schools become learning communities, and the profession provides greater satisfaction as educators see the results of their efforts in higher student achievement.
- *Provides new opportunities for leadership.* In the current system, teachers who are looking for leadership opportunities have limited options. Under the OPE framework, teachers seeking higher salary and greater prestige will not have to leave the classroom for positions in the administration. They are provided multiple opportunities for both growth and leadership, as well as higher pay, by becoming coaches, mentors, content specialists, and team leaders.
- *Establishes a fair evaluation system.* Currently, most teachers are judged by their superficial behaviors rather than by what they know and how much they help their students achieve. By analogy, imagine if we were judging auto mechanics by the tools they own and the organization of their garage, rather than by how well the cars run after leaving the shop. Of course, we may give our mechanics some credit for having the right equipment and behaving in a professional manner, but the real question is how well their work holds up over time.
- *Gives teachers far more flexibility in the classroom.* Because there is no individual-level accountability for ends in the current system, the focus must necessarily

be on means. When teachers cannot be held directly responsible for student learning results (outputs), they are often required to follow strict curricular and pedagogical scripts (inputs). Since the OPE framework measures how successful teachers are in increasing student achievement, they should be provided with more freedom to decide how best to achieve the desired outcomes.

Joint decision making is at the core of the OPE framework; it provides teachers with equal ownership over the process of change. In chapter 2, "Professional Unionism," Julia Koppich and Brad Jupp establish a foundation for the cooperative labor-management relations required for schools to succeed in the difficult and complex task of transforming themselves. The goal is not to replace the union's long-standing "industrial" focus on the material well-being of its members; indeed, in the OPE framework, collective bargaining is modified but it remains in place. It continues to be the means for setting starting salaries, determines whether the minimum percentage increase set by the framework for each rung of the career ladder should be accepted or exceeded, and defines the meaning of "significant" as it applies to bonuses and/or higher salaries provided to educators in hard-to-staff and hard-to-serve positions. Rather than discard the current industrial model, as the OPE example illustrates, professional unionism expands it to respond to the relentless pressure teachers are under to increase student achievement by offering them the support necessary to improve instructional effectiveness.

The OPE framework has never been implemented. That is why no claims can be made about the degree to which student learning results will increase if a district embraces the reforms in their entirety. Nonetheless, when they are combined, it is reasonable to expect two sorts of benefits. The first should come from the synergies that emerge when the components are used in combination with one another—as systems theory posits, "The whole is greater than the sum of its parts." The second should come as a result of realigning the system so that the goal—increased student achievement—is tied to the interests of teachers and administrators, aided by a new system of supports.

These potential benefits can be illustrated with the example of value-added assessment. This new way of expressing student learning results traces individual students over time and provides educators with powerful diagnostic information at the classroom, grade, school, and district level. Yet experience from Tennessee and Pennsylvania makes clear that by itself, the introduction of value-added methodology did not lead to substantial increases in student learning. To improve the likelihood that students will achieve at higher levels, districts must ensure that professional development accompanies the introduction of value-added assessment. Additionally, attaching both positive and negative consequences to student learning results should incentivize educators to master the training offered by the state and individual districts. When individual components such as value-added assessment are accompanied by appropriate professional development, and when everyone's interests—the classroom teacher, the principal, the administrators responsible for providing the training, and the superintendent—are served by making effective use of the new methodology, OPE contends that student achievement will increase substantially.

CONCLUSION

The framework for school reform described here may initially alarm some readers because of its controversial subject matter: it breaks from the single-salary schedule, holds educators accountable for student learning, and puts teachers in charge of evaluating their colleagues. As its details are introduced, however, readers should keep in mind that its central goal is to improve the quality of instruction. Against the changes required by this new system, enormous benefits would accrue to educators and, through them, to their students and the nation as a whole. These can be thought of as two indispensably important quid pro quos, each part of a *grand bargain for education reform.*[32]

An Expanded Role for Teachers in Return for Individual Responsibility for Student Learning

In return for accepting the framework's individual-level accountability, teachers would win an expanded role in their schools: peer review, a key part in the process of remediating their struggling colleagues, and equal say in major issues that affect their classrooms. Once the classroom rather than the bargaining table becomes the venue in which teacher career success is determined, administrators can no longer impose on them professional development, curricula, or assessments not mandated by the state.

New Investment in the Public Schools in Return for Adopting the Framework

In return for accepting the framework with individual-level accountability for educators, the public sector—federal, state, or local government—would increase its investment in the schools by providing funds for the additional compensation and expanded professional development necessary to sustain the reforms over time.

These quid pro quos penetrate the catch-22 that characterizes much of the ongoing debate between educators and elected officials with responsibility for funding schools. "We cannot raise student achievement to meet the new standards without additional resources," educators contend. "We are not going to invest any more money in the public schools," elected officials respond, "until they can show better results." The way out of this conundrum is the strategy of investment with accountability. If the education establishment is willing to offer as collateral its accountability as individuals, then the public sector should be willing to invest the necessary new funds. The result will be a school system with genuine integrity, where student learning is central to all decision making and educators are at the vanguard of change.

We know the status quo is failing the large majority of our students. Developing a new and better school system is not merely something that should be done— it *must* be done if America is to remain a stable and successful middle-class society offering real opportunity for all its citizens. Change is always difficult, and systemic change even more so. People will certainly disagree about what the new system should look like, but we are certain that this is not the time to allow the perfect to drive out the good.

What is most important about a *Grand Bargain for Education Reform* is the challenge of creating a "New Deal" for teachers. Although the OPE framework offers one systemic example, we are buoyed by other exciting experiments now under way across the country. This volume should be understood as part of this effort to rethink public education. It is our hope that it will catalyze reform—both sweeping and modest—by equipping districts with the knowledge, skills, and tools they need to implement change.

CHAPTER TWO

Professional Unionism

JULIA E. KOPPICH
BRAD JUPP

It is appropriate to open with a discussion of professional unionism because its philosophy lays the foundation for all that follows. The challenge of educating all students to unprecedented high levels of achievement means changing the work of teaching and changing the school as a workplace. It also means changing the way unions represent teachers, and the way teachers unions and school districts conduct their business. Above all else, reform requires teachers and administrators to work as partners.

The industrial model of union-management relations now common in most school systems emerged nearly fifty years ago. It assumes that labor and management are fundamental adversaries, and that collective bargaining is the primary means to resolve the conflict between them. Under the industrial model, teaching is a largely uniform type of work, and collective bargaining agreements seek to establish uniform conditions for the teaching workforce. The industrial model has been enormously successful in improving the pay, benefits, working conditions, and job security of teachers. But if our public school systems are to advance, unions must take the lead in improving the quality of education.

Trust and shared power lie at the heart of the model of professional unionism promoted by Operation Public Education (OPE). In a professional model, unions collaborate with school districts to redefine the work of teaching, create standards for educator performance, and ensure that their members excel in increasing student learning. These changes expand rather than discard the current "industrial" union model. In this chapter, Julia Koppich, an education consultant who works closely with teachers unions and coauthor of United Mind Workers, *and Brad Jupp, currently senior academic policy advisor to the superintendent of the Denver Public Schools and a key architect of Denver's Professional Compensation System for Teachers, or ProComp, while a member of the Denver Classroom Teachers Association, discuss the central elements of a professional union model and provide recommendations for implementing these changes.*[1]

INTRODUCTION

At the moment when the standards movement merged in state legislatures with the accountability movement, the policy landscape that shapes our public school systems shifted irreversibly; we entered an era where results matter in public education. Although the broader public may not fully agree about how to measure school performance, it expects its schools to be successful and demands measurable evidence of that success. The OPE framework offers considerable potential for helping school districts create and maximize this type of performance culture.

School districts and teachers unions must recognize that they have entered into a new era where student performance matters at every level of operation: district, school, and classroom. Together they must create a workplace culture where improving student performance is the focus of school improvement efforts.

This goal will require a breakthrough in labor-management relations—a partnership between a reform-minded administration and union leadership. Without such a partnership, the terms and conditions for advancing our schools will be set on an uneven foundation. If they are to make this breakthrough, labor and management will have to enter into a unified effort to improve student learning at the classroom level in every school and across our school systems. This means that unions must quickly adapt to changing times or perhaps face irreversible decline.

This chapter (1) offers both union and district leaders perspective on the key differences between (and principles of) industrial and professional models of unionism; (2) presents the challenges unions face as they seek to remold themselves into the professional model; and (3) makes recommendations for building successful union-management partnerships in the service of educational improvement.

INDUSTRIAL TO PROFESSIONAL UNIONISM: KEY PRINCIPLES AND BENEFITS

Collective bargaining agreements are instruments of politics and policy. These legally binding pacts, the products of negotiations between a local school board and the teachers union elected by teachers in a school district, considerably shape the operation of the local school district, the distribution of education resources, and the structure of teachers' work.

Shaped by experience, the exigencies of changing times, and shifting policy tastes and preferences, two types of bargaining and two types of contracts have emerged. As illustrated by figure 2.1, traditional contracts reflect industrial-style collective bargaining, while reform contracts represent a shift to professional unionism.[2]

FIGURE 2.1
Traditional versus reform bargaining

Traditional (industrial) bargaining	Reform (professional) bargaining
• Separation of labor and management	• Blurred labor-management distinctions
• Adversarial negotiations	• Collaborative negotiations
• Positional bargaining	• Interest-based bargaining
• Limited scope of negotiations	• Expanded scope of negotiations
• Protection of individual interests	• Protection of teachers and teaching

Industrial Unionism

As industrial bargaining became more widespread among teachers in the 1960s and 1970s, teacher unionism came to be identified by three hallmarks:

1. *Separation of Labor and Management.* Traditional contracts draw clear lines of distinction between labor and management roles, specifically delineating the jobs administrators should do from the jobs teachers should do. Union and management are assumed to have different, and often conflicting, interests. Thus, the responsibilities each assumes are placed in separate and distinct spheres of work.

2. *Adversarial Labor-Management Relations.* Traditional labor-management bonds are shaped by adversarial relationships. The tenor of discussions can often be shrill and angry, as union and management vie for the more powerful negotiating hand, while negotiations are played out as a zero-sum game. Labor relations are permanently contested, and an us-versus-them mentality permeates the relationship.

3. *Limited Scope of Bargaining.* Collective bargaining laws specify those issues that are mandatory, permissive, and prohibited subjects of bargaining. Delineating the scope of negotiations—what can be, must be, and is barred from bargaining—represents an effort to balance employees' interests in negotiating working conditions with the impact of any issue on managerial prerogatives and public policy.[3] Traditional contracts maintain a limited scope of bargaining, typically staying within the commonly understood meaning of the conventional negotiations triumvirate of wages, hours, and working conditions.

Traditional agreements reinforce a basic assumption of collective bargaining. The system restricts teachers' voices to the conditions of work while management maintains control over the conduct and content of it. In traditional or industrial bargaining, in other words, the union represents employees' economic and day-to-day work concerns; management, acting for the school board, is responsible for making educational policy.

Traditional contracts center on protecting and expanding the rights of individual teachers.[4] They are about monetary benefits and workplace conditions. In this bargaining tradition, the contract documents how teachers as solitary practitioners interact with the system that employs them. It is not a professional compact reflecting how the work of teaching gets done.

Industrial union contracts often contain similar provisions district-to-district, but they can also include a fair amount of variation, including the nature of a district's labor-management relations (more or less adversarial), the substance of preceding contracts (or past practice), state and local contexts, and the personalities and priorities of participants in the negotiations process.[5]

An enduring result of industrial-style bargaining is that many contracts have come to embody the cumulative scar tissue of past battles.[6] As unions and management have struggled for influence and authority, they often have built up an ongoing history of failed issues, lasting antagonisms, and nagging contract-to-contract dilemmas.[7]

The Emergence and Key Principles of Professional Unionism

In the decade between 1983 and 1993, some local unions (for example, Minneapolis, Cincinnati, Toledo, Rochester, Columbus, and Montgomery County, Maryland) began to adopt innovative approaches to labor-management relations and enlarged the content of their contracts to encompass more reform-oriented issues. They began to take on the coloration of what would come to be called professional unionism.

Professional unionism is premised on the idea that labor and management share interests and responsibilities for improving education.[8] Initially, union and management engaged together in fledgling efforts to transform industrial unionism, with negotiated programs around teacher evaluation, professional development, shared school-based decision making, and budget development.[9]

As professional unionism matured, a small number of districts and unions began to venture into other policy-rich territory. Seniority, a bulwark of industrial unionism, often was eliminated as the principal criterion for voluntary transfers. A few unions and districts began to edge away from the traditional single-salary schedule, on which teachers were paid exclusively on the basis of years of experience and college credits earned, and began to offer additional dollars, for example, to teachers who earned advanced certification through the National Board for Professional Teaching Standards.

Those union locals that have moved toward professional unionism have found that engaging in it requires accepting four requisite principles:

1. *Both union and management must accept that change is mandatory.* Both sides must understand that change is inevitable and that if they do not choose to shape the change, it will be thrust upon them.[10] Unions such as the Rochester Teachers Association and the Cincinnati Federation of Teachers understood that continuing to do business as usual was not sufficient. These locals, among others, actively worked toward a more professional conception of a teaching career as part of building a culture of educational improvement.

2. *Teachers must have the flexibility, within accepted bounds of professional practice, to experiment in the name of educational improvement.* This principle requires union and management to keep typical local politics at bay as much as possible, creating a zone of tolerance and a cushion for change.[11] Unions, such as the Toledo Federation of Teachers and the Columbus Education Association, made the move toward professional unionism and put in motion programs such as peer assistance and review, which challenged the industrial notion of teacher unionism and did not, at their inception, have a proven track record. Yet these and other programs, such as Cincinnati's career-in-teaching program and Montgomery County's teacher-directed staff development teacher program (a joint effort of Montgomery County Public Schools and the Montgomery County Education Association), were viewed by both the union and district as having the potential to improve teacher quality and student achievement.

3. *Union and management must engage with each other collaboratively.* Both sides must be able to move beyond the partisan anger that often characterizes labor-management relations and find a means of replacing conflict with co-operation.[12] The pioneers of professional unionism adopted collaborative labor relations in which union and management seek common ground in the name of education improvement instead of the constant warfare that previously characterized contract development.

4. *Both sides must believe in an expanded role for teachers.* A centralized web of controlling rules, whether a function of the district bureaucracy or the union's centralized contract, is not conducive to professional unionism.[13] Those who venture into professional unionism blur the line between what is traditionally "management work" or "labor work." In Montgomery County, for example, teachers took on numerous leadership roles (e.g., peer evaluators, school-based staff developers). Likewise, Cincinnati's career-in-teaching program created one of the first negotiated career ladders for teachers, which offered job options that did not require them to leave teaching for administration.

Given the new demands of the school system, industrial-style bargaining is limited, and professional unionism must take hold. Industrial unionism gave teachers organizations the wherewithal to respond to teachers' concerns about essential matters of wages, hours, and working conditions. However, industrial bargaining fails to recognize teachers' expertise as professionals, their need and desire to exercise professional judgment in the performance of their duties, the interests they legitimately share with management, and the obligation to involve them in significant decisions about policies affecting their professional lives.[14] If the hallmarks of industrial unionism are separation of labor and management, adversarial union-management relations, and a limited scope of bargaining, professional unionism is something of its mirror opposite.

Professional union contracts blur the lines of distinction between teachers and administrators and between union and management, emphasizing the collective nature of education work. District and union assume joint custody for education improvement as they consider what makes sound educational sense for the school system and its students.[15] Professional unions engage in a different kind of bargaining—collaborative bargaining. Collaborative negotiation's functional slogan is, "Hard on the problem, not hard on each other." In collaborative bargaining, union and management break away from their traditional adversarial contract stances and seek mutual ground for common understanding and agreement.[16]

Unions that adopt a professional mode also expand, with their school districts, the scope of negotiated agreements. Interestingly, those unions that have moved toward professionalism have widened the boundaries of negotiations while operating under the same collective bargaining laws as traditional agreements, thus illustrating the remarkable elasticity of the legal scope of negotiations.

Traditional industrial-style contracts assume all teachers are the same, thus they apply a districtwide template to teacher working conditions. Contracts negotiated by professional unions, on the other hand, begin to acknowledge that teachers are different one from another—that they have differing levels of knowledge and skill, as well as differing professional aspirations. No longer simply a statement of the accrued rights of individual teachers, the contract comes to be a document that speaks both to teachers' individual interests and to the profession's public responsibility.[17] To be sure, professional union contracts continue to maintain teachers' due-process rights, but they also focus much more fundamentally than do industrial-style contracts on protecting and enhancing the quality of teaching.

As union and management come to accept that the real product of labor-management cooperation is meant to be education improvement, they must also recognize that the improvement is stymied if the topics of conversation—the scope of bargaining—are limited.

Moving from industrial to professional unionism requires accepting a new conception of collective bargaining and a shift in the expectations for negotiated agreements. Professional union contracts acknowledge the shared labor-management nature of education work, sanction labor-management cooperation, and expand the scope of bargaining to include a broader swath of education policy directly related to improving the quality of teaching and, by extension, the level of student learning.[18]

Collaboration between labor and management should establish shared ownership of the broad mission of our public schools—improvement in student learning and the closing of achievement gaps. In the long run, the goodwill and power created by this shared effort will lead to improved wages, benefits, and working conditions. These are just causes that labor should be able to embrace with ease. From this starting point, it is possible to imagine a shift in attitudes led by professional teachers unions to advocate for their members, as well as for the academic expectations of the communities they serve. This change would create a fundamentally different approach to labor-management practice, as well as a fundamentally different body of demands made by teachers unions.

CHALLENGES

Unions that want to change from industrial to professional unionism have a difficult task. They must persuade longtime members that a new way of doing business does not mean abandoning traditional union values or issues, and at the same time convince newer members that the union is an important vehicle for career advancement and education improvement. This is not an easy sell, even in the places where it is most consistent with reality.[19]

Teachers unions face a dilemma, balancing what is essentially a bifurcated membership as some members cling to traditional unionism and others—those who represent the future of the union—seek change. These organizations must sustain and build an organization that simultaneously meets the needs and professional aspirations of veteran and novice teachers.

Adopting and implementing this more widely encompassing agenda will also require unions to attend to the very real dilemmas of organizational capacity building. A 1999–2003 study of six union locals (Albuquerque, Denver, Montgomery County, Minneapolis, Seattle, and Syracuse) was funded by the federal government under the auspices of the Teacher Union Reform Network (TURN). This study sought to understand the challenges these organizations, all of which desired to move toward professional unionism, faced. Among the findings:

- Union staff jobs have changed little, even as the union has changed, often creating a mismatch between staff role and member needs.[20] Unions found they must rethink the role of staff as more than grievance handlers, turning staff interests and responsibilities to the expanded union agenda. A number of locals, especially NEA locals that did not hire their own staff but had staff assigned by the state affiliate, found it particularly difficult to secure staff with a broader conception of their roles.

- Union budgets tend to be constructed based on preexisting categories rather than on programmatic needs.[21] Few union locals engage in zero-based budgeting. Instead, they tend to use the categories they have always funded—the same staff positions with unchanging job descriptions and working committees—rather than reexamining the way union dollars are allocated and the needs of a changing organization.

- School-based union representatives, the "face" of the union at the school, have an incomplete understanding of the role of a professional union.[22] These representatives often are comfortable with the role of problem-solver (or, more likely, being the person who "takes on" the principal) but less comfortable with furthering the union's agenda on professional issues and education improvement. Some local unions tried a system of dual representation—one school representative for traditional issues and one for professional issues—but this created a more bifurcated union and was abandoned.

- Communication between the union and its members is often less effective than it needs to be, particularly as the organization seeks to assume new roles. Communication outlets, when limited to traditional house organs that stick to traditional industrial union issues, fail to paint a picture for their members of the expanding role of the organization or the emerging opportunities for professional members. One of the best examples of change in this arena is the monthly newsletter of the Albuquerque Teachers Federation. This publication has been transformed by the current union leadership into a communiqué dedicated almost exclusively to professional issues.

To be sure, moving from industrial unionism to professional unionism can be difficult and painful. Union leaders must unlearn some old habits and learn new ones. They must see with fresh eyes the issues that ultimately will make or break their organizations in the future. And they must accomplish all of this while balancing the needs and interests of an increasingly diverse and shifting membership. Whether the newer generation of teachers coupled with more open-minded union leadership will provide the canvas on which a new form of unionism can be painted remains an open question. But there is reason for hope, as progressive union leaders have begun to incorporate aspects of professional unionism into their practice. The following recommendations are based on their experiences.

Recommendations

Ground the Union in a Confident Belief in Effective Teaching. Teachers unions working under the industrial model assumed the following position: that the impact teachers make on the lives of their students cannot be measured and that too many factors influencing student learning, such as poverty and parental engagement, are out of a teacher's control. New practice must begin with the expectation that the impact of teaching on student learning is measurable and that we can use judgments about teacher performance to inform decisions about levels of teacher pay and employment. Union leaders would be right to insist that principals and peers use information about student learning in fair ways when evaluating teachers, setting pay rates, granting tenure, and dismissing teachers. They should also demand better and more diverse assessments of student learning—assessments that represent the impact of the teacher with greater precision. In turn, district leaders should engage union members, especially instructional leaders in their ranks, in practical discussion of measuring student learning. Application of value-added measures, as well as more practice-driven methods of measuring teacher impact on student learning at the classroom level, will work only if the measures are credible. Unions and districts operating under the professional paradigm would begin work in this field immediately.

Embrace the Policy Premises of the Standards and Accountability Movement. The last twenty years of school reform have worked forward from two simple premises: (1) the public should expect schools to accelerate student learning toward a standard for what all students can know and do, and (2) there should be a simple set of incentives, including rewards and sanctions, that support schools and educators as they strive to meet those expectations. Throughout this period, teachers union leaders, clinging tightly to the industrial model of unionism, have repeatedly placed themselves on the wrong side of these premises, trying to claim that they are in the grip of unfair policy makers and simple-minded school district leaders who want to speed up the assembly lines in their classrooms. This posture has placed union leaders in the outrageous position of saying they cannot expect schools to improve academic performance, and that teachers, already overburdened, will not respond to new incentives. New practice would begin by acknowledging the importance not only of high expectations for students, but also of aligned incentives. Union leaders would then be in a position to demand a rich package of incentives, including improved job quality and career opportunity for teachers, in exchange for accepting the responsibility of meeting high expectations. A district seeking to advance along this avenue could begin by exploring with its union the differentiation of job responsibilities, even compensation, for teachers with track records of results. Teacher leadership is much talked about separately by both labor and management. It is a natural starting point for the conversation.

Make a Strength of the Diverse Beliefs of the Membership. Stand By Me, the report of the Public Agenda Foundation, demonstrates that one thing uniting all teachers is their willingness to join an organization that has influence over the policies that shape their careers. In most states, teachers unions are the dominant force for fulfilling that interest. Beyond that, though, the report shows that union members are not monolithic in their beliefs about school reform or what unions should do in response to it. Teaching is astonishingly varied work, done by an astonishingly heterogeneous workforce. In the face of this diversity, professional union leaders would give up clannish and parochial notions of workplace solidarity. They would begin a practice that addresses the variety of jobs and the diverging views and aspirations of their members. In turn, they would demand far more competitive wages for teachers in hard-to-serve schools and hard-to-staff assignments. Moreover, they would demand richer models of professional participation, at both the school and district level, for instructional leaders in their ranks. School district leaders may take an easy first step along this path by introducing differentiated pay for teachers in hard-to-serve schools and hard-to-fill assignments, and by differentiating responsibilities for teachers, especially at the school level.

Construct a Results-Oriented Relationship with the School District. A professional teachers union would seek an alliance with its school district and embrace this call for change in partnership. The professional union would then establish a new labor-management relationship grounded in results—not only student learning outcomes, but also successfully implemented instructional reforms led by members of the workforce they represent. Professional union leaders would demand member engagement and expect quick decisions with district and community leaders. Their members would inform implementation with feedback to advance practice. They would oppose promiscuous changes and the program du jour approach to education reform, knowing that it is effective teaching, not new textbook packages, that advances student learning. Executed well, this practice would open new seats at new tables for the union's members and expand the influence of practicing professionals. From this results-oriented participation, unions would want to take part in the discussion of district-level performance targets, in establishing and measuring progress toward performance expectations, in district and school decisions about curriculum and professional development, in selection of principals and faculty members, and even in decisions to dismiss underperforming teachers and principals.

Create New Possibilities for the Role of Collective Bargaining in Public School Districts. Collective bargaining is the cornerstone in the architecture of industrial teacher unionism. The collective bargaining agreement between the school district and the teachers is a powerful policy-making tool. Usually two or three years in duration, these agreements become very conservative and hold tightly to powerfully defined rules. In this era of urgent change, collective bargaining agreements invest great power in past decisions to shape present practice. Professional union leaders are in a position to establish a new practice of collective bargaining that embraces the reforms of the standards and accountability movement and advances the interests of the members they represent. Similarly, school district leaders should rid themselves of the prejudice that collective bargaining will always be an impediment and begin imagining ways to use collective bargaining to the shared advantage of the union and the district.

New practices of collective bargaining are emerging. One promising practice is that of thin contracts—contracts that resist a centralized, one-size-fits-all rule. Under a thin contract (or, as Kerchner, Koppich, and Weeres call it, a compact), very little would be governed by centrally determined rules; for example, teacher transfer, compensation, and benefits. School leadership teams would make decisions about working conditions based on student achievement goals and write them into school-based compacts. Because decisions would vary from school to school based on student needs, so too would working conditions.

No union has yet tried to negotiate a compact, but some have made substantial efforts to extend the practice and function of collective bargaining. The agreement between the Minneapolis Public Schools and the Minneapolis Federation of Teachers, for example, centers largely on improving the quality of teaching through professional development and multiple means of measuring student success. In Minneapolis, the collective bargaining agreement is a record of decisions made jointly by labor and management to support critical portions of the reform agenda they codevelop. This work has the effect of creating shared ownership by labor and management of important change initiatives.

Another promising practice is the living contract, or a contract not bound by rigid multiyear decision-making cycles. In Rochester, New York, for example, the Rochester Teachers Association (an AFT local) and management share the ability to make adjustments to the labor agreement in real time, not in awkward three-year cycles. In so doing, the teachers and the board retain ownership of the agreement as a critical policy lever but create new agility to respond to emerging conditions and issues.

When creating its Professional Compensation System for Teachers, or Pro-Comp, the Denver Classroom Teachers Association—an affiliate of the National Education Association (NEA)—asked its members to ratify a separate agreement with a longer, nine-year cycle for change than its master agreement. This was a strategic response to teachers union members' concerns that ProComp, including its rich $25 million revenue stream provided by a property tax increase, could be hijacked by management and directed to other purposes. At the same time, the Pro-Comp agreement provided for periodic negotiations within the longer nine-year arc, so that labor and management could make agreed-upon adjustments to a system that both parties knew to be a work in progress.

These and other practices show great potential, even if that potential is, at the moment, largely unfulfilled. It is the potential of a profession seizing control of its own best hopes—to advance the causes of students, teachers, schools, and public education in the name of taking greater responsibility for improving student learning.

CONCLUSION

OPE is proposing a grand bargain, where in exchange for accepting individual-level accountability for improving student learning, teachers acquire greater annual and career earnings potential, as well as new authority and responsibility. Through a modified peer-review process, teachers are responsible for observing and evaluating their colleagues. Moreover, the OPE framework provides teachers with an equal say with school management in all major decisions affecting their classrooms, such as curriculum, professional development, and assessment not mandated by the state. The various components bring together much of what is needed to take steps toward a labor-management partnership dedicated to establishing a performance culture in a school district. Even so, the OPE framework leaves union leaders much to do, and those seeking to advance this approach will assume a seat at the founder's table.

It is wrong to think that it will be easy for a teachers union to accomplish this shift in attitudes and practices. The union will have to leap over the decades their colleagues have invested in resisting, even obstructing, the standards and accountability movement. Nevertheless, for the union that does, the possibilities are immense. Public expectations of our schools are growing, not diminishing. Policy leaders are becoming even more demanding. The moment belongs to the professional unions that are ready to change labor-management relations and redefine the quality of work for their members.

PART II

The New
Reward Structure

CHAPTER THREE

Choosing a Value-Added Model

WILLIAM SANDERS

JUNE RIVERS

Value-added assessment is likely to be recognized as an extraordinarily important breakthrough in the methodology of education research because it provides an alternative to measuring student learning results solely in terms of achievement. Absolute achievement, or a score on a vertical scale at a single moment in time, is best predicted by family background, but growth or the value-added progress made by individual students from year to year is best predicted by the quality of instruction. Value-added models thus provide a much fairer way to measure the performance of schools and individual educators. They also provide uniquely valuable diagnostic data to help individual teachers improve the quality of their instruction and individual students raise the level of their academic achievement.

Skepticism about value-added models has diminished over the last half-dozen years in light of new empirical research.[1] Nonetheless, some concerns remain. For example, can the "teacher effect" (the impact of instruction) and the "classroom effect" (a teacher working in a specific environment with a particular group of students) be treated as one and the same? How should the impact past teachers had on student scores be weighted in developing an estimate for the current teacher? With these and other questions, it is important to keep in mind that the research shows that sophisticated value-added models are accurate in identifying the most effective and least effective performers.[2] They are less useful for making fine distinctions among the large majority of teachers found between these extremes. The use of value-added assessment in the Operation Public Education (OPE) framework is entirely consistent with the research; the top performers are rewarded and the lowest performers undergo remediation. In sum, value-added assessment needs only to be accurate at the tails of the distribution, and that is how it is used in the framework.

Before adopting a value-added model, districts need to know whether it operates with appropriate precision and minimal bias across a host of complex statistical challenges. While simple-and-transparent growth models enjoy the benefit of allowing teachers to calculate their own scores, these "pretest, posttest" approaches, which subtract last year's score from this year's score and attribute the entire difference to the teacher, will not generate stable evaluations of instructional effectiveness. More robust, value-added models offer a far more reliable way to evaluate teachers by using multiple years of data and by estimating how much of the difference between projected and actual scores for each student can be attributed to the student and to the teacher. Other selection considerations for a district include learning whether the value-added model is user friendly, available online, and has the capacity to make projections about educational outcomes for individual students, an important feature to help educators undertake appropriate academic interventions.

Regardless of the model selected, the value-added scores for teachers should never be used as the sole or principal criterion in evaluation. The OPE framework ensures that value-added estimates are part of a balanced system, with multiple measures and appropriate human safeguards. In the following chapter, William Sanders and June Rivers of the SAS EVAAS group at SAS Institute, Inc., provide districts with guidelines for choosing an appropriate value-added model.

INTRODUCTION

Few would disagree that there is more emphasis now than ever before on improving academic achievement for all students. Two of the major reasons cited for this heightened concern are the call for more equitable opportunities for individuals regardless of ethnicity and the need to maintain economic competitiveness within an increasingly challenging world economy. Educators are struggling with the following questions: how can the level of academic achievement of all students be raised, and how can the responsibility for their success or failure be appropriately attributed to schools, districts, teachers, families, and the students themselves?

While there continue to be divergent views as to how these questions should be addressed, some consensus has emerged around the standards movement, which embodies the concept of a stair-step approach to curricula and assessment. To define specific goals for each grade level, states and districts ask, what should students know and be able to do at particular grade levels? As a result, testing regimes have been created that purport to measure the percentage of students within grades who are at mastery, proficient, basic, and below basic levels. When the results of these tests are presented, it becomes obvious that differences among schools and districts are strongly related to socioeconomic measures of the student population.

It is certainly true that considerable bias is introduced if student achievement levels are purported to be a direct indicator of student learning. But there is another way to measure student learning: growth—the progress students make over the course of the school year, regardless of the achievement level at which they started in the fall.[3]

The differences between these two measures are clarified in the four-cell matrix displayed in figure 3.1. Proficiency (achievement at a single moment in time), high and low, is tracked on the vertical axis, while growth, high and low, is tracked on the horizontal axis. The bottom left cell represents schools that are clearly not serving the needs of their students, providing them with appropriate levels of neither proficiency nor growth.

Schools represented in the top right cell are the best performers. They are doing what all schools should ideally do: providing their students with both high proficiency and high growth. The fact that No Child Left Behind (NCLB) does nothing to promote these results confirms that it is focused primarily on closing the minority-majority achievement gap. This is an important and admirable national goal, and history undoubtedly will view NCLB as a vital piece of civil rights legislation. But succeeding only in closing the achievement gap is akin to winning the battle and losing the war. In the fiercely competitive global economy, the nation must not lose sight of the need for incentives for all schools to provide high achievement and high growth for their students.

The top left cell represents schools whose students are meeting proficiency targets but where little growth is occurring. Most often found in affluent communities, where high test scores go hand-in-hand with family income, these schools have been called slide-and-glide schools because they appear to be resting on the laurels of their students. Schools need to be held accountable for providing their students with the annual growth to which they are entitled.

FIGURE 3.1
Rating schools by proficiency and growth

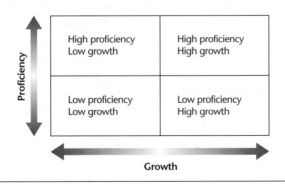

The bottom right cell represents schools, disproportionately found in poor communities, that provide their students with high growth but still fall short of meeting proficiency targets. Unlike the schools represented in the bottom left cell, these schools have succeeded in academically "stretching" their students, but given how far behind students were when they entered school, these schools have not yet been able to raise them to proficiency. Nevertheless, these schools are clearly helping students improve their academic performance. Growth measures recognize this effort and encourage educators and students to continue working hard to reach proficiency targets.

When consequences are attached to test results (e.g., retention of students in grade, mandatory summer school, etc.), political pressure often builds to lower the height of the "step," to diminish the role of the tests, or to eliminate the tests all together. Eventually and invariably, these arguments distill into debates over how academic achievement is to be measured and what the proper role of standardized testing is within the total framework of student assessment.

The use of value-added assessment, or student academic growth, can eliminate much of this debate. Progress rates are more important than attainment levels because they push teachers to help all students achieve their maximum potential, regardless of individual starting points. If students enter schools with relatively high attainment levels yet have schooling experiences that retard their academic growth, their achievement levels will atrophy over time. Conversely, if students enter schools with relatively low attainment levels but have a sequence of high-growth years, their relative attainment levels will rise substantially.

Much recent research has indicated that the rate of student progress is in fact primarily determined by the effectiveness of schooling.[4] These more recent research findings have been made possible by the creation and availability of large longitudinal databases, which trace the same students over time. These analyses have yielded results and interpretations that often are in opposition to previous research findings that came from cross-sectional analysis. The general conclusions from the older studies were that student achievement is primarily determined by socioeconomic factors and that differences in school effectiveness play only a minor role in the ultimate achievement for students. In contrast, recent research, which utilizes various approaches to educational value-added assessment, has documented the importance of schooling effectiveness on the rate of student academic progress.

OVERVIEW OF VALUE-ADDED METHODOLOGY

Value-added assessment is not a test—no more classroom time is spent assessing students—but a new way of looking at the results that come from tests so that we can determine whether the students in a classroom, school, or district are achieving sufficient academic growth each year. This is possible because datasets can now be created to track individual students over time and match their scores in all tested subjects with the teachers who taught them.

Value-added assessment is often confused with simple growth because the words themselves make it is easy to think about this growth as the "value" that is "added" over the last year. But high-quality value-added assessment provides a way of isolating the impact of instruction on student learning. Its great advantage is its ability to separate the annual academic growth of students into two parts: that which can be attributed to the student, and that which can be attributed to the teacher, school, or district. Because individual students rather than cohorts are traced over time, each student serves as his or her own baseline or control, and this can capture students' inputs into education (see figure 3.2).

While value-added assessment is statistically and computationally complex, it is relatively easy to grasp at the conceptual level: Test scores are projected for students and then compared to the scores they actually achieve at the end of the school year. Classroom scores that exceed projected values at statistically significant levels indicate effective instruction. Conversely, scores that are below projections at statistically significant levels suggest that the instruction was ineffective.

Value-added is fair to students because their projected scores are based only on their performance on previous standardized tests. Because it does not consider students' race or socioeconomic background, low-income children are not expected to do poorly and high-income students are not expected to do well. But it is also fair to educators precisely because the use of students' past performance as

FIGURE 3.2
Each child serves as his or her own statistical control

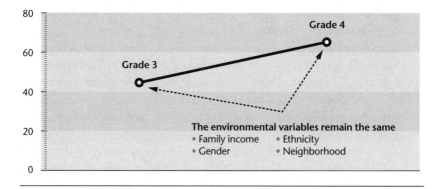

the baseline score inherently takes into account family and neighborhood characteristics that so strongly influence absolute test scores.

The value-added calculation is concerned not with the score on an achievement test by itself but with the difference between this actual score and the projected score. Because the key measurement is between these two measures rather than on the absolute score alone, value-added levels the playing field across schools with students of very different socioeconomic backgrounds.

KEY CHARACTERISTICS OF A VALUE-ADDED MODEL

In value-added modeling efforts ranging from simple to complex, the objective is to use longitudinal data at the student level to measure the impact of educational entities—districts, schools, and classrooms—on the rate of student academic progress. However, the results from these various approaches are not equivalent, especially at the classroom level. The remainder of this chapter will discuss the essential principles and data requirements for an effective system, compare the advantages and disadvantages of various approaches to value-added assessment, and share views on how value-added assessment can offer a paradigm shift for the way schooling is planned and delivered to increase student achievement.

Statistical Reliability

Some approaches to value-added assessment are simple and transparent. While these approaches have the advantage of allowing teachers to calculate their own growth scores, they can result in erratic and specious representations of a teacher's impact on student learning. To meet statistical reliabilities, districts must choose a value-added model that responds to the following issues and concerns:

- *Students with incomplete records.* Because many students are transient, they have incomplete assessment records. To provide fair determinations of teacher and school quality, value-added methodology must have a way to incorporate students with incomplete records into the analyses.
- *Measurement error in test scores.* Accurate conclusions about teacher and school effectiveness cannot be drawn from a single test. A single year's performance is a limited measure of a student's general level of achievement because any single test has measurement error. As a result, value-added models that rely on multiple test scores are more desirable than those that rely on one previous test score.
- *Appropriately modeled educational inputs.* The methodology used must be sufficiently sophisticated to protect against inappropriate testing practices or improprieties in test administration.

Practical Application

Additionally, given the complexity of school organization, the contribution of each teacher for each student for each grade and subject must be accurately linked to student test records. In order to address these challenges, high-quality value-added assessment systems must develop methods for responding to the following:

- *Pullout programs for support beyond standard delivery of instruction.* Many students receive additional support during the school day from a variety of specialists. Without a way to acknowledge the existence of these influences on student growth, teachers may receive an unfair advantage.
- *Organization of classrooms.* Since classrooms are organized in a variety of different ways—self-contained, team teaching, departmentalized instruction, etc.—the model must have a way to approach this problem, for both statistical and practical reasons. One possible option is to assign various proportions of student growth to multiple teachers.

Subsequent research will determine whether separate weights for each of these considerations is necessary—some researchers believe that simpler models will produce comparable results—but the political value of not including this information is clear. Until research demonstrates otherwise, educators will be more likely to embrace the new methodology if they believe they are being held accountable only for the students for whom they had instructional responsibility. In an already complex statistical approach to evaluation, it would be wise to incorporate student-roster information that teachers believe is important.

CHOOSING A VALUE-ADDED MODEL

Various attempts to measure student academic progress using longitudinal test data have been developed and implemented. These attempts range from simplistic models with inelaborate computational procedures to mixed model methods with intense computing requirements. Collectively, these various approaches have been placed under the banner of value-added assessment (or sometimes generally under the label of growth models). However, all of these models are not equivalent in providing reliable and comparably unbiased estimates of schooling effects, especially at the classroom level.

Class Average Gain (comparison of average gain between tests)

With this approach, each student's previous score for a subject is subtracted from the current score to obtain a gain, and then a simple average gain for the class is calculated. This is the simplest possible value-added model. However, this is one of the least desirable of all of the value-added approaches for a number of reasons.

First, not every student will have a gain because the previous year's score may be unavailable. For the two districts analyzed in a previous study, 11 percent to 12 percent of the students did not have a gain score due to unavailable data.[5] Also, these students are generally not a random selection from the class, which may bias the results. Second, for appropriate interpretation of the results, the tests have to be scaled in such a manner that the differences between scores (the gains) are meaningful and consistent for all students, which is often not the case. For these reasons, simple gain approaches to value-added assessment are not the most accurate way to measure teacher and school effectiveness.[6]

Analysis of Covariance (ANCOVA, with only the previous score as a predictor)

With this approach, the current score is predicted using the previous year's score through a simple regression model. Because this model uses the same data as the class average gain approach (current score and previous score), it also suffers from the problems due to missing test scores. However, in this approach, the scaling of the tests is no longer an issue, which is an advantage over the class average gain approach.

However, there is another major problem with this approach that has to be considered so that severe bias in the results will not give rise to faulty interpretations—the problem due to errors of measurement in the predictor variable (i.e., the previous test score). A student's predicted score is biased if it is based on only one previous score. The consequence of this bias is that classrooms with higher-achieving entering students will appear to be more effective than they really are, while classrooms with lower-achieving entering students will appear to be less effective. Like simple gain approaches to value-added assessment, this process is one of the least desirable for measuring teacher and school effectiveness.[7]

Analysis of Covariance (ANCOVA, using many previous scores as predictor variables)

To dampen the errors of measurement problem to the point that they are no longer of statistical concern, at least three previous scores need to be available for each student. However, this requirement creates another challenge. Most commercially available statistical software will only use the data for each student who has complete data over the span of grades and subjects. For the two districts in the previously mentioned study, six scores were used as predictors of the current score: the math, reading/language, and science test scores from the previous year and from two years previous. As a consequence, results from 21 percent to 24 percent of the students were discarded due to missing data. The result is that the selection bias often cited as a concern with value-added models will indeed be a reality. Student selection bias refers to the situation in which data from certain types of students are excluded because of missing data elements.

Univariate Response Model

Conceptually, this model is the same as the previous one—it uses multiple prior scores as predictors, but the dependent variable is a current test score.[8] Unlike the models described earlier, this approach does not discard students who do not have all scores; rather, it includes any student who has at least three prior test scores (three scores being the minimum required to mitigate the measurement error problem). This is accomplished by creating pseudo-classification groups based on students' pattern of prior test scores. For example, those students with no missing data would be in one group, those students who missed the tests one year earlier would be in another group, etc.[9]

With this process, the classroom effects can then be estimated without a substantial loss of information. As for the two districts in the study previously cited, only about 8 percent to 10 percent of the students were omitted due to missing data. This procedure offers much flexibility, particularly in estimating schooling effects in high school when end-of-course tests are not on the same scale as the elementary tests.

Multivariate Response Models

This modeling approach simultaneously utilizes test scores for each student over all grades and subjects.[10] This analytical approach has advantages over the others.[11] First, regarding missing test scores, all data from each student are used no matter how sparse or complete. Second, the model mitigates the impact of measurement error in much the same way the multiple-predictor ANCOVA model does, but with the possibility of using even more data for each student. Third, the concern about student selection bias is greatly reduced.[12] Fourth, due to the layering (the fact that each student's score is linked not only to the current teacher but to all previous teachers), this model offers additional protection from other interference.[13]

Multivariate mixed models are among the best that have been developed to date. They have been found to be robust under simulated data conditions, as well as in real-world applications. They give conservative results, thus minimizing the likelihood of both false positives and negatives for teacher effects.

Even when more sophisticated models are deployed, some analysts have introduced various socioeconomic measures (e.g., free and reduced-price lunch, ethnic designation, ELL status, etc.) directly into these models either at the individual student level or at the group level. Since the value-added methodology already accounts for these variables by tracing the same student over time, statistically controlling again for them amounts to "double adjusting." It is strongly recommended that this not be done. First, at the student level it has been found that the inclusion of these socioeconomic measures is not necessary.[14] At the group level, if these measures are included and if there is a relationship between teacher assignment and teacher effectiveness, there is a great risk in over adjustment, resulting in hiding serious inequities in teacher assignment to schools serving students with high needs. For example, consider the urban teacher-assignment practice of disproportionately placing beginning teachers in inner-city schools, year after year. The low value-added scores in these schools and classrooms reflect the minimum impact that, on average, new teachers have on student learning. Double adjusting, in other words, shifts the "blame" from the teacher to the students. This is a clear example of why this practice may hide influences that policy makers need to address.

Table 3.1 summarizes the comparisons and relative advantages and disadvantages of the models described on the previous pages.

The models discussed in table 3.1 are meant to be illustrative of the complex statistical issues involved in the process of choosing an appropriate value-added model. The list is not exhaustive; other models may be responsive to the criteria outlined previously.

IMPLEMENTATION GUIDELINES

Before a state or district can implement value-added assessment, the following elements need to be in place: (1) each student and teacher must be assigned a unique individual identifier; (2) teacher IDs should be linked to the students they taught, along with their students' annual scores on the high-stakes summative exams; and (3) assessments need to be closely aligned with the standards and curricula, have appropriate stretch at the ends of the distribution, and be available in fresh, nonredundant, and equivalent forms. Overall, this last element guarantees that when these conditions are met, the test cannot be "gamed"—that is to say, no advantage would be given to a teacher's students if they practiced using the previous year's test.

Because of NCLB, all states will likely have the historical data necessary to meet these basic assessment conditions in grades 3–8. However, because annual testing is not required in high school by federal law, assessments that meet the requirements listed above do not always exist for grades 9–12. Ideally, states should create end-of-course exams for all high school subjects and grade levels so that the comparison pool would be sufficiently large. However, when this is not the case, districts interested in using value-added analysis at the high school level must create these exams themselves.

TABLE 3.1
Summary of comparisons among value-added models

Model	Advantages	Disadvantages
Class average gain	• Simple to calculate.	• Only students with previous and current scores contribute to the calculations, resulting in unstable estimates. • Tests must be on the same scale.
ANCOVA, one previous score	• Simple model to fit with most commercially available software. • Does not require the previous test scores to be on the same scale as the current score.	• Only students with previous and current scores contribute to the calculations. • Severe bias results because only one test is used to predict current performance.
ANCOVA, for students with six previous scores	• Simple model to fit if software with mixed-model capability is available. • Does not require the previous test scores to be on the same scale as the current score. • Dampens the error of measurement by using multiple tests for each student.	• Severe loss of information due to the fact that many students will not have a complete testing history, which raises a concern about student-selection bias.
Univariate Response Model (URM)	• Does not require the previous test scores to be on the same scale as the current score. • Uses all data for each student if at least three prior test scores are available. • Minimizes the concern about student selection bias. • For classroom-level analysis can accommodate team teaching, departmentalized instruction, and self-contained classrooms.	• Most commercially available software with mixed-model capability can be used, but extensive programming is necessary. • Computer resources necessary for computations are not trivial.
Multivariate Response Models (MRM)	• Uses all data for each student. • Minimizes the concern about student selection bias because data from all students are included in the analysis. • Uses past, present, and future data for each student. • Provides protection against non-educational interferences that could provide influences on student achievement not attributable to educational intent (e.g., tornado alert, an individual failing to follow the testing rules, etc.). • For classroom-level analysis; can accommodate team teaching, departmentalized instruction, and self-contained classrooms.	• Even though the statistical methodology and theory on which this approach is based are published, at the present time commercially available software is not generally available to accommodate the calculations. • Does require that the test data within a grade and subject meet a requirement that the expected amount of progress be consistent over the entire range of student achievement. If this condition is not met with the scale scores coming directly from a test supplier, then data transformations are necessary to ensure this condition.

Once assessments are created, there are major challenges to overcome in the construction of a longitudinal database that will ensure that accurate matches result when individual student records are merged over time—numeric IDs may be miscoded, names may change, etc. If subsequent value-added estimates at the classroom level are desired, then the linking of individual teacher IDs to an individual student's test records becomes a huge challenge. To accommodate policy requirements regarding the inclusion or exclusion of an individual student's record for the value-added estimation process at the classroom level, information on the student's dates of attendance within the classroom and on the percentage of instructional effort provided by each teacher to each student must be accurately maintained.

EDITORS' NOTE

The following section is written by the editors and discusses how the results from value-added assessment are used in the OPE framework.

Distinguishing Between Levels of Instruction

OPE recommends the use of value-added assessment to create three levels of teacher, school, and district effectiveness: (1) highly effective—those in which the students are being stretched so that (in a statistically significant sense) they experience more than expected growth annually; (2) effective—classrooms, schools, or districts where students on average are receiving expected growth in a year; and (3) ineffective—those where they are losing ground, meaning students' achievement levels fall below projections based on the capacity they demonstrated in past years.

When using multivariate mixed-model methods, the process would work as follows: each teacher would get a value-added estimate with a standard error that is a function of (1) the number of data points for each student and (2) the number of students he or she taught. For teachers who teach multiple subjects, a composite effect can be calculated for an overall estimate. Adjusting these estimates with further standard error produces a tradeoff: it increases the probability that the classification of teachers is correct while it decreases the number of teachers in the category. OPE applies an additional 2.0 standard errors to the bottom of the distribution to identify ineffective teachers, and an additional 1.5 standard errors to the top of the distribution to identify highly effective teachers. We apply standard errors in this differentiated manner because we want to be more certain when the consequence of an error is mandated remediation than when the consequence of an error is the payment of additional salary.

Individual teacher estimates would then be used to create a teacher distribution, which can be compared to a growth standard. There are at least two distinct ways that this standard can be set—an external growth standard or the district average.

External Growth Standard. To utilize an external growth standard, one option would be to pick an anchor year (e.g., the state's average growth in 2005) and compare each teacher's estimates in subsequent years to that external standard. Use of this standard eliminates the complaint that the model will create competition because all teachers compete only with themselves, not each other, to exceed this standard.

District Average. This process would work the same as the external growth standard, except that instead of choosing an anchor year from the past, teachers' estimates would be compared to the average district growth in that subject area/grade level for that year. Although this could lead to competition when carried out within a single school or among a small number of teachers, it is highly unlikely to be the case when the comparison pool consists of thousands of teachers, e.g., a large school district or a grouping of many smaller districts. In settings like these, collaboration among teachers to improve instructional practice should not be undermined.

High Schools and End-of-Course Exams. To distinguish between levels of teacher effectiveness at the high school level, end-of-course exams (EOCs) are required. With these exams in place, projections are made for individual students, based on the assumption that a student is in the average classroom in the average school of the population of interest (in this case, the district). Because of (1) the types of tests administered in grades 9–12 and (2) the different times in the academic schedule when students take various high school subjects, either the district average can be used when creating the teacher distribution or larger comparison pools can be used if EOCs are developed by the states.

Determining school effectiveness parallels the teacher assessment process previously outlined. Because more data are available at the school level, school effects will have smaller standard errors than teacher effects. As a result, there will be greater variation in the distribution of schools falling into the three categories of effectiveness.

OPE uses these three categories of teacher and school effectiveness to (1) reward and remediate teachers and administrators based on school performance,

continued

and (2) provide bonuses for all teachers in the building to encourage collaboration. For more detail on utilizing value-added as the basis of a new reward structure, refer to chapter 6.

While value-added assessments are currently provided for statewide use in Tennessee, North Carolina, Ohio, and Pennsylvania, in the latter two states data are not being collected at the classroom level. This is most unfortunate, because research has shown that the variation in the quality of instruction is much greater within schools than between schools and districts.[a] States using value-added assessment to grade only the performance of schools are ignoring this finding and thus eliminating the possibility of identifying, rewarding, and learning from outstanding performers. Perhaps more important, districts also lose the ability to identify educators who are not providing adequate classroom instruction. Tennessee data make clear that while struggling students are found in all types of classrooms, they are found disproportionately in the classrooms of ineffective teachers. When districts, in an effort to meet their annual yearly progress goals, focus only on remediating their struggling students rather than on the teachers who are providing them ineffective instruction, scarce resources are being devoted to the symptoms rather than to their underlying causes.

When states fail to collect value-added data at the classroom level, they also prevent educators from using the information for diagnostic purposes. Tennessee data make clear that students taught by ineffective teachers two or three years in succession never reach the levels of academic accomplishment that better instruction would have provided. Without classroom-level data, students suffer permanent harm because principals do not have the necessary information about individual classrooms to redeploy their teachers.

Promoting Data-Driven Decision Making

In addition to selecting a model that accurately identifies highly effective, effective, and ineffective instruction, OPE believes it is imperative for districts to choose a value-added system that provides reports at three levels: classroom, school, and district. Although the calculation of value-added scores is complex, districts should develop efficient and user-friendly systems for reporting results so that they are easily understood by practitioners.

For example, in the figure "Sample district or school value-added report for math," provided by the EVAAS system, the application of traffic light shading to the results makes the reporting more comprehensible—green (labeled G) shading indicates that the district met the growth standard; yellow

Sample district or school value-added report for math

Estimated mean NCE gain

Grade	3	4	5	6	7	8	Mean NCE gain over grades relative to	
Growth standard		0.0	0.0	0.0	0.0	0.0		
State 3-yr-avg.		1.2	3.6	0.2	1.5	2.4	**Growth standard**	**State**
2005 mean NCE gain		–1.4 R*	4.0 G	–0.6 R	–0.2 Y	0.4 G	0.4	–1.3
Standard error		0.4	0.4	0.4	0.3	0.3	0.2	0.2
2006 mean NCE gain		1.9 G	4.1 G	–0.5 R	0.5 G	1.7 G	1.5	–0.2
Standard error		0.4	0.4	0.4	0.3	0.3	0.2	0.2
2007 mean NCE gain		0.8 G	2.9 G	–0.4 R	1.4 G	1.1 G	1.2	–0.6
Standard error		0.4	0.4	0.4	0.3	0.3	0.2	0.2
2-yr-avg. NCE gain		0.4 G	3.7 G	–0.5 R*	0.6 G	1.1 G	1.0	–0.7
Standard error		0.3	0.2	0.2	0.2	0.2	0.1	0.1

Legend

G—Estimated mean NCE gain equal to or greater than growth standard.

Y—Estimated mean NCE gain below growth standard, but by less than one standard error.

R—Estimated mean NCE gain below growth standard by at least one, but less than two, standard errors.

R*—Estimated mean NCE gain below growth standard by at least two standard errors.

Source: Copyright © 2008 SAS Institute Inc., Cary, NC, USA. All Rights Reserved.

(labeled Y) indicates that the student progress was below the state growth standard but within 1.0 standard error; pale red (labeled R) indicates that the student progress was more than 1.0 standard error below the growth standard but less than 2.0 standard errors below; and dark red (labeled R*) appears if the estimated mean gain is more than 2.0 standard errors below the growth standard—evidence of the severest student progress retardation attributable to schooling.

Examples of these reporting features and how they can be used to drive instruction are discussed in greater detail in chapter 9 of this volume.

[a] William L. Sanders and Sandra P. Horn, "The Tennessee Value-Added Assessment System (TVAAS): Mixed-Model Methodology in Educational Assessment," *Journal of Personnel Evaluation in Education 8* (1994): 299–311.

CONCLUSION

The philosophy of value-added assessment—that each student, regardless of where they enter school, deserves expected growth in a year—ensures fairness and redresses much of what is wrong in current practice. Value-added assessment represents a paradigm shift in the way we think about education. It is a move away from blaming students, teachers, and administrators, and toward improving accountability in the educational community such that all students, regardless of achievement level, make a reasonable amount of progress each year. Most important, it is a shift toward improving the postsecondary education and career options for every student in a competitive, twenty-first century economy. The impact of statistical questions about value-added models that remain unanswered must be weighed against the pressing need for a new reward structure.

In sum, value-added assessment provides three crucially important benefits. Its rich diagnostic information helps educators use data to drive pedagogical decisions and differentiate instruction. It is a far fairer way to measure the performance of schools than absolute test scores. Finally, value-added assessment can serve as the basis for a new system of individual-level accountability for teachers and administrators. Value-added is the single most powerful tool available to educators for measuring student progress and the effectiveness of instruction and instructional programs. Without it, we will continue to work in the dark, tinkering at the edges of the system and ignoring what has always mattered most: good teaching.

CHAPTER FOUR

Teacher Evaluation—
Performance Frameworks

CHARLOTTE DANIELSON

No educator should ever be evaluated solely on the basis of a single measure. Unfortunately, most observation practices currently in place do not usually reveal enough information about the quality of instructional practice.[1] For example, in many school districts, someone, usually an administrator, observes teachers in their classroom a few times a year and provides a rating of satisfactory or unsatisfactory.

Effective teaching is much more complex than these simple evaluation systems reveal. To raise student achievement, teachers must set goals for student performance, invest students in their learning, and plan purposefully. They also must execute lessons effectively in order to meet students' diverse needs, manage time and resources, and fulfill a range of professional responsibilities. To reflect this complexity, districts should design a multidimensional comprehensive framework through which educators can develop a shared understanding of what constitutes excellent instructional practice. A strong framework for teaching provides novice teachers with a road map for instructional excellence, enables all teachers to assess their practice and identify areas for improvement, and allows for a standardized observation mechanism to evaluate teacher performance.

A growing number of school districts across the nation have begun to rely on more sophisticated approaches, such as Charlotte Danielson's framework for teaching. This comprehensive and coherent framework identifies those aspects of a teacher's responsibilities that have been documented through empirical studies and theoretical research as promoting improved student learning. Though more evidence needs to be gathered to substantiate the link between comprehensive frameworks like Danielson's and student achievement, several studies have found that teachers who received higher ratings on their evaluation went on to produce greater gains in student test scores.[2] Below, Danielson explains how districts can create a comprehensive framework for teaching and how this framework can be utilized to evaluate practice and accelerate improvement.

INTRODUCTION

In the Operation Public Education (OPE) framework, teachers are designated as highly effective, effective, or ineffective. This determination can be accomplished through one of two general approaches, which depend on either inputs (that is, what teachers do) or outputs (that is, the results teachers achieve with students). The OPE framework uses both approaches, and success on both is essential if teachers are to advance in the career and compensation structure.

There are important trade-offs between the two approaches. Basing evaluation decisions on measures of student learning is, on its face, the most direct approach to ascertaining teacher quality—what results do they achieve with their students? Granted, some practical challenges are inherent in this method—namely, that the assessments themselves must be valid and available for all teachers. But if those challenges can be overcome, there are clear advantages to this approach.

On the other hand, while an indirect measure of teacher quality, basing evaluations of teacher performance on what teachers do has one enormous advantage: the results provide guidance for the teacher on how his or her performance could be improved. The evaluation process itself becomes an assessment of need, and both teachers and their supervisors can use the results of the evaluation to guide future learning. Basing teacher evaluation only on the results they achieve with students does not carry this benefit. This chapter will explore the key principles and challenges involved in evaluating teacher performance based on their actions (inputs to the act of teaching) and provide districts with concrete recommendations for moving forward.

PURPOSES OF AN EVALUATION SYSTEM

Two principal purposes of any system of teacher evaluation focused on inputs are quality assurance and professional learning. Quality assurance is vital; public schools are, after all, public institutions. They take public money, thus the public has a right to expect good (or at least competent) teaching. And for the purpose of rewarding excellent teaching with salary bonuses, this function is essential. However, most educators also recognize that with an activity as complex as teaching, it is not sufficient to simply inspect teaching; an evaluation system should, if possible, cultivate and develop good teaching.

Some individuals regard the two fundamental purposes of teacher evaluation as being in conflict with one another. The first, quality assurance, requires that a system be robust, valid, reliable, and defensible (professionally and, if necessary, legally). These are rigorous demands, unyielding in the need for objectivity and personal interaction. Without such assurances, the validity of evaluation decisions could be dismissed or regarded as entirely idiosyncratic or, worse, the result of favoritism and corruption.

The second purpose of evaluation—namely, to promote professional learning—suggests a softer approach that depends on the establishment of trust. However, the professional learning purpose of a system of teacher evaluation need not depend (at least not solely) on the relationship between the teacher and the evaluator. It can be embedded in the system itself. Thus, a well-designed system of teacher evaluation will include activities for teachers that are known to promote learning—self-assessment, reflection on practice, and professional conversation. If such practices are embedded in a robust system of teacher evaluation, that system can achieve both of its purposes: to determine the quality of teaching (for the purpose of performance awards) and to promote the learning of teachers to support ongoing professional development.

DEFINING GOOD TEACHING: A FRAMEWORK FOR TEACHING

Any system of teacher evaluation must be grounded in a clear definition of good teaching that is accepted by everyone who will participate in implementing the system. It's impossible to evaluate practice or to offer suggestions for how it could be improved if one has not even defined it. School administrators have been heard to remark, "I can't tell you what good teaching is, but I know it when I see it." This attitude is indefensible, since the first rule of valid assessment is that the person being evaluated must understand the criteria on which performance will be judged.

Several requirements govern the development, or choice, of a set of evaluative criteria. The framework for teaching will be referenced as one example for how these requirements can be met.[3]

Research-Based Definitions

A viable definition of good teaching, one that can serve as the foundation of a consequential system of teacher evaluation, must be grounded in solid research. It must be possible to claim that the skills and educational practices embedded in the definition will, if followed, result in enhanced student learning.

This is not a simple matter. Research design is determined by clear outcomes, measures of those outcomes, and control of other variables that might influence the outcomes. Unfortunately, none of these conditions is routinely met in educational research. But in spite of limitations and caveats, it's important that any definition of teaching be grounded as far as possible in solid research. The framework for teaching is so grounded, based where possible on empirical research, and where that is not available, on the theoretical research from learning, motivation, and cognition.

Reflecting a Professional View of Teaching

No one can deny the importance of the work of teaching. Teachers are, after all, collectively charged with preparing the next generation of a nation's citizens, to instill in them a love of learning and the skills to be lifelong learners. Furthermore, the work itself is highly complex, requiring making hundreds of decisions daily. Any definition of good teaching, then, must respect this complexity, and an evaluation system based on such a definition must include procedures through which teachers can demonstrate their skill in making sound decisions.

Clear Performance Standards

Despite its inherent complexity, a good definition of teaching must include clear performance standards. Granted, teaching requires highly sophisticated skills; there are many moving parts to any instructional interaction between teacher and students. But educational research offers educators reasonably clear findings as to the impact of different actions on student learning, and a coherent definition of teaching, particularly when it is used to make high-stakes decisions regarding teachers, must be grounded in this research.

The framework for teaching provides one such example of a research-based definition of good teaching. It divides the complex work of teaching into four domains and twenty-two components (summarized below). Each component is further divided into anywhere from two to five smaller elements. Additionally, it describes all of teaching, not merely the interaction between teacher and students in the classroom. Classroom performance is generally, and rightly, considered to be at the heart of teaching. However, much of the important work of teaching, such as planning lessons, maintaining accurate records, communicating with families, and collaborating with colleagues, takes place behind the scenes. Skill in these areas is essential to good practice; therefore, a definition of teaching and the procedures to evaluate it should recognize the entire scope of the work.

> Domain One: Planning and Preparation
> a. Demonstrating knowledge of content and pedagogy
> b. Demonstrating knowledge of students
> c. Setting instructional outcomes
> d. Demonstrating knowledge of resources
> e. Designing coherent instruction
> f. Designing student assessments

Domain Two: Classroom Environment
  a. Creating an environment of respect and rapport
  b. Establishing a culture for learning
  c. Managing classroom procedures
  d. Managing student behavior
  e. Organizing physical space

Domain Three: Instruction
  a. Communicating with students
  b. Using questioning and discussion techniques
  c. Engaging students in learning
  d. Using assessment in instruction
  e. Demonstrating flexibility and responsiveness

Domain Four: Professional Responsibilities
  a. Reflecting on teaching
  b. Maintaining accurate records
  c. Communicating with families
  d. Participating in a professional community
  e. Growing and developing professionally
  f. Showing professionalism[4]

Levels of Performance

For some time, educators and policy makers, in recognition of the importance of having clear standards of practice to guide both teacher preparation and evaluation, have promulgated lists of the qualities of good teaching. However, it's not sufficient to simply list the components. For example, practitioners would agree that good teaching requires establishing an environment of respect and rapport. But this is not an act of teaching that can be evaluated as a dichotomous judgment. Such an environment is neither present nor absent—it is present *to some degree.* Performance in all aspects represents a continuum, from very poor to excellent.

Thus, in order to truly operationalize the components of good teaching, it's necessary to create levels of performance that describe, in language easily accessible to practitioners, how a classroom looks (what the students are doing, what the teacher is doing, the nature of the interactions, etc.) when the teacher is performing at each level of performance.

It should be noted that these are levels of performance of teaching, not of teachers. While performance is to some degree stable (it gradually improves with growing expertise), it is not absolutely the same from one day to the next. Thus, when one comments about a teacher's performance, it is grounded in evidence from a single lesson or as an amalgam of a number of lessons. But it is the teacher's performance that is being evaluated, not the teacher as a person.

The framework for teaching is organized into four levels: unsatisfactory, basic, proficient, and distinguished. An example of a component and its accompanying levels of performance is provided in table 4.1.

PROCEDURES AND INSTRUMENTS FOR TEACHER EVALUATION

Many issues need to be resolved in determining the procedures in an evaluation system. They are briefly described next.

Observations of Teaching

How Many Observations of Teaching Should There Be? State statutes or other negotiated agreements typically specify the minimum number of classroom observations,

TABLE 4.1
Levels of performance for questioning and discussion techniques

Element	Unsatisfactory	Basic	Proficient	Distinguished
Quality of Questions	Teacher's questions are virtually all of poor quality, with low cognitive challenge, single correct responses, and asked in rapid succession.	Teacher's questions are a combination of low and high quality, posed in rapid succession. Only some invite a thoughtful response.	Most of teacher's questions are of high quality. Adequate time is provided for students to respond.	Teacher's questions are of uniformly high quality, with adequate time for students to respond. Students formulate many questions.
Discussion Techniques	Interaction between teacher and students is predominantly recitation style, with the teacher mediating all questions and answers.	Teacher makes some attempt to engage students in genuine discussion rather than recitation, with uneven results.	Teacher creates a genuine discussion among students, stepping aside when appropriate.	Students assume considerable responsibility for the success of the discussion, initiating topics and making unsolicited contributions.
Student Participation	A few students dominate the discussion.	Teacher attempts to engage all students in the discussion, but with only limited success.	Teacher successfully engages all students in the discussion.	Students themselves ensure that all voices are heard in the discussion.

and the number is typically larger for nontenured than for tenured teachers. Moreover, the requisite number of classroom observations generally refers to formal observations, those that last for a certain length of time (usually 30–40 minutes).

Are the Observations Announced or Unannounced? It's important to recognize how observed lessons are situated within all of teaching. Teachers work with students on average five or six hours per day, 180 days per year, for a total of about one thousand hours. The maximum time teachers can be observed for evaluation purposes is about four hours, and frequently far less. This time represents well under 1 percent of the total, in fact, under one-half of 1 percent. Therefore, the best that can be hoped for is that the teaching represents typical practice so an accurate assessment of practice may be made.

However, this outcome is extremely unlikely with announced observations. In most systems of teacher evaluation, evaluators establish a time with a teacher when a lesson observation would be convenient, which permits the teacher, of course, to fully prepare for the lesson. Such prepared lessons are often referred to as dog and pony shows, and they fool no one. Some evaluators argue that even with a highly prepared lesson, they are able to ascertain that a teacher is capable of planning and executing an excellent lesson. This may be true. Nonetheless, these considerations argue in favor of including at least some unannounced observations in an evaluation system. If all observations are announced, with the lesson well prepared and the students possibly coached as to how to perform well, an evaluator has no assurance that what is observed represents typical practice.

Are There Conferences Before and After the Observations? Clearly, if an observation is unannounced, there cannot be a conference prior to it. But for an announced observation, a preobservation (better called a planning) conference could be conducted. The principal advantage of a planning conference is that it permits a conversation about a teacher's intent during the lesson and provides evidence of a teacher's skill in planning and preparation (Domain One). This information enables an evaluator to ascertain whether teachers are clear about their desired learning outcomes, know the subjects they teach and the related pedagogy, have chosen materials and activities that are suitable to their students and to the discipline, and have a plan for assessing student understanding and incorporating formative assessment into their instruction. Some of these matters may be discussed following a lesson, although then they don't represent the teacher's plan but the teacher's reflective thinking about the planning.

Of course, the conversation prior to a lesson encompasses planning only for that single lesson and does not address a teacher's skill in long-range planning for a unit or for an entire quarter or year. These skills are different and include longer-range thinking about aims, sequence and variety of activities, and materials. Hence, a comprehensive system of teacher evaluation includes procedures to elicit a teacher's skill in long-range planning.

When designing an evaluation system to include classroom observations, it's also important to consider extended observations that may capture certain aspects of teaching that aren't accessible in a brief or single observation. At the elementary level, such observations might encompass an entire morning, and at the secondary level, the third-period class every day for a week.

Interviews and Conferences

During the observation cycle, in which an observation of practice is sandwiched between a planning (preobservation) conference and a reflection (postobservation) conference, the conferences themselves provide important evidence of a teacher's skill. The planning conference supplies an indication of the teacher's command of the subject, awareness of the students and their varying needs, clarity in formulating instructional outcomes and designing coherent instruction, and preparation for both summative and formative assessments of student learning.

In the reflecting (postobservation) conference, teachers demonstrate their skill in reflecting on their practice (Domain Four, item a, in the framework for teaching). This evidence is important for teacher evaluation, but perhaps more important, it helps the teacher engage in structured reflection following a lesson. Several intertwined activities during the postobservation conference contribute to teacher learning: self-assessment, reflection on practice, and professional conversation.

Some evaluators feel the need to cut out everything from their schedule that is not absolutely required and therefore conduct only a cursory postobservation conference—or they eliminate it altogether. This practice reflects a poor understanding of the value of such a conference to promote professional learning. During the conference, the teacher and the evaluator compare notes as to their impressions of the lesson. Though the evaluator's view must ultimately prevail in the event of disagreement, such differences of judgment are relatively rare, and in many situations it is the teacher who assesses the lesson the more harshly of the two. It is the act of reflection that contributes materially to the extent of the learning teachers take from the experience.

Examination of Artifacts

Virtually all systems to evaluate teacher performance include the observation of classroom practice. This is not surprising, since the essential work of teaching is engaging students in learning important content. However, interacting with students is not the only thing teachers do; one could observe all day every day in a classroom and never witness other important aspects of teaching, such as communicating with families or collaborating with peers. Thus, a comprehensive system of teacher evaluation must devise methods to capture evidence of all the work of teaching, including that which happens beyond the classroom walls.

Teachers demonstrate, at least indirectly, a few of these components of practice in the classroom, such as their knowledge of the subjects they teach. However, in general, if the backstage components of teaching are to be included in a teacher-evaluation system, evidence of them must be specifically elicited, typically through the examination of artifacts.

So what are these artifacts and how do they supply evidence? The answer to that question depends entirely on which aspects of practice teachers are trying to illustrate or for which they are providing evidence. For educators using a definition of teaching similar to the framework for teaching, the following collection would suffice:

- Unit plan, including student assessment
- Instructional artifact or assignment from the unit to demonstrate the teacher's skill in designing meaningful work for students
- Samples of student work, with teacher comments to illustrate the teacher's use of feedback to students
- Examples of record-keeping
- Examples of communication with families
- Evidence of contributions to the school and the profession
- Evidence of professional growth

Instruments for Teacher Evaluation

The instruments, or forms and directions, used in a system of teacher evaluation are an important aspect of the system. Some educators consider that these are the system, and they have been heard to say such things as, "We need to update our teacher-evaluation system; we need a new form." Indeed, they are not the same thing; the forms are simply the documents used by an evaluator while conducting observations (both formal and informal), examining artifacts, and completing an evaluation. The instruments also include the questions teachers should be prepared to discuss in a conversation both before and after an observation, and any written guidelines for teachers to use in assembling their artifacts.

While the instruments are not the whole of an evaluation system, they are a critically important component. After all, they serve to structure both what teachers and evaluators do in the course of the evaluation activities and how they discuss what has occurred. That is, they frame the conversation, which is the critical element of an evaluation system for promoting teachers' professional learning. Furthermore, the use of instruments in an evaluation system ensures consistency across a school or a district so that the evaluations are—and are perceived to be—fair.

There are a few important requirements for evaluation instruments:

Provide clarity. The principal requirement for instruments is that they be clear and unambiguous in what they ask of both teachers and evaluators. Such clarity contributes to the consistency of an evaluation system across different schools and among different evaluators within a single school.

Create efficiency. Many educators criticize an evaluation system that is perceived as too paper intensive. Instruments should ask teachers and administrators to consider the most important aspects of the lesson or of an artifact, such as a unit plan, and to answer questions about it, either briefly in writing or as a basis for conversation.

Promote reflection. Instruments should ask teachers to consider such questions as, "What are other ways I might have accomplished what I was intending to accomplish?" Such reflection makes an enormous contribution to teacher self-assessment and, when supported by an administrator, leads to thoughtful examination of practice and instructional improvement.

Elicit important evidence of practice. Instruments must elicit all the important elements of the definition of good teaching. Furthermore, if the rating teachers receive is a high-stakes affair, teachers must have ample opportunity to demonstrate their skills.

Personnel

Who are the evaluators? Are they only principals, or assistant principals and department chairs as well? What about district-level curriculum specialists? In some schools, particularly small elementary schools, site administrators are typically the only evaluators. But there are other options as well, depending on the resources available and the manner in which responsibilities have been apportioned. In some schools and districts, teachers play a role in teacher evaluation. This practice, typically called peer assistance and review, is controversial in some settings and is discussed in more detail in chapter 12 of this book. Ultimately, the decision is, of course, for individual districts and schools to determine; it is typically spelled out in a negotiated agreement.

Timelines

Districts must develop a clear timeline for key actions. When do observations happen? If an evaluation system has specified that there are a certain number of formal and/or informal observations and a collection of artifacts as part of an evaluation system, when do the observations occur and when are the artifacts discussed? When is the final evaluation report due and to whom?

In general, the activities undertaken for teacher evaluation should be scheduled in such a manner that they are possible within the other demands on teachers' and evaluators' time, while at the same time maximizing professional learning. This consideration suggests that performance evaluations should not occur at the same time as parent conferences or the due dates for report cards, as teachers are focused on meeting those deadlines. It is also important that the timeline allows sufficient opportunity for evaluation to be used to guide professional development and maximize teacher improvement.

Due Process

Finally, any system of teacher evaluation must respect principles of due process, in which teachers are made aware of any deficiencies found in their practice and are provided the opportunity to make a good-faith effort to improve. These provisions are typically spelled out in statute or in negotiated agreements.

CHALLENGES FOR EVALUATING TEACHER PERFORMANCE

Teacher evaluation holds a very important place in the OPE framework, since the results of evaluation contribute directly to a teacher's compensation and career progression. To ensure that the outcomes are both accurate and credible, districts must respond to a number of challenges.

Professional Development and Training

A viable system of teacher evaluation, particularly if it is to be used for high-stakes purposes, must include a provision for professional development and training for everyone concerned—both teachers and evaluators.

Evaluators must receive adequate training in the evaluation system so they are capable of making consistent judgments based on evidence of teaching. This is absolutely essential; if a system cannot guarantee this provision, it will be neither credible nor defensible. Evaluator training typically consists of several important elements: familiarity with the evaluative criteria, experience in identifying these aspects of practice in daily teaching and as reflected in a portfolio, skill in conducting conferences with teachers, and mastery of the use of the instruments and procedures. The principal outcome of evaluator training is consistency, insofar as evaluators can achieve inter-rater agreement. Only when such agreement can be ensured will teachers, and the public, have confidence that the system can yield a reliable assessment of teaching.

An issue that arises concerning evaluator training relates to whether they are required to demonstrate their skill before they are permitted to make high-stakes decisions about teachers' futures. In the most rigorous systems, evaluators are required to pass a proficiency test, which generally consists of a simulated evaluation on which they must demonstrate that they can arrive at the same judgment as the official correct decision. In some systems they must not only arrive at the same score, but do so for the right reasons; that is, evaluators must cite relevant evidence in making their judgments.

When possible, it's important for teachers to participate in evaluator training sessions, even if they are not to be conducting evaluations. This results in an increased confidence in the system and conveys that there are no secrets being shared only with evaluators. In general, anyone who participates in evaluator training finds it to be a rich professional experience, during which educators engage in in-depth conversations about teaching. In fact, many teachers report that their own teaching has improved as a result of participating in evaluator training, due to the examination of components of good teaching, identifying evidence of those components in practice, and discussing their findings with colleagues.

Even more important, open participation contributes to the general transparency of the entire system, and teachers and evaluators come to shared understandings about good practice. The resulting evaluation system, then, is not one in which evaluation is done by evaluators *to* teachers; instead, the two parties can together examine teaching as reflected in classroom teaching and artifacts and determine its strengths and areas for growth. Teachers must be well aware of the criteria for teaching that are to be used in the system; they should never have the impression that judgments are made about their practice without clarity regarding the basis on which those judgments are being made. This requires professional development and training in which teachers become familiar with the components of professional practice in use and can apply them to their own setting.

Initial training for both evaluators and teachers is essential, but so is the maintenance of high levels of skill. Many schools and districts, appreciating the need to train administrators in the accurate collection and analysis of evidence of teaching, invest heavily in the early years. However, as other initiatives come to the fore, it is tempting to ease up and to focus elsewhere. When this phenomenon is combined with turnover of both teachers and evaluators, the result can be a serious undermining of the accuracy of judgments and the consequent loss of confidence in the system by teachers and the public. Therefore, vigilance and frequent refresher trainings are important to the long-term viability of the system.

Standard-Setting

Standard-setting refers to the decision of how good is good enough to move from one level of a salary plan to another. Educators who have used a rubric, such as the framework for teaching, for high-stakes decisions find that they must establish a rule of thumb for demarcating different levels of teacher effectiveness. If, as in the OPE framework, a district designates teachers as novice, career, and advanced, the question becomes how to determine the move from one level to another. In making these decisions, districts must take the following criteria into account:

Time of year. A teacher's performance is more likely to reflect a high-level proficient or distinguished level at the end of the year than in the beginning. It can take several months to achieve smooth routines and to establish good rapport with students. Hence, if some teachers are observed toward the end of the school year, they would be more likely to perform well than would those observed at the beginning.

Experience in an assignment. When teachers have taught in a given assignment for a number of years, they develop considerable expertise in it. However, when teachers are moved to a different grade level or when they take on a new course, their performance is more tentative; they are, after all, doing virtually everything for the first time. Hence, their performance is likely to be stronger the longer they have held a given position.

Risk-taking. When teachers try new activities or when they use a different way of, for example, organizing group work, there is always the possibility that the new approach will not be fully successful. If teachers' ratings carry significant consequences, they may be less likely to try something new. This issue of risk-taking is part of a larger concern related to teachers' ability to "game" the system, particularly if the results are used for a high-stakes decision. It would be troubling if teachers, in their efforts to receive a strong performance evaluation, adopted attitudes and practices that were not in the best interest of the school as a whole. One aspect that will help with this dilemma is that to advance on the career ladder and the compensation scale in the OPE system, teachers must also achieve highly effective results with students, according to value-added analysis. Both measures must be in alignment, alleviating to some degree the danger of over-reliance on either one. Even with this safeguard, districts must think strategically about how to overcome this potential pitfall—whether through increased professional development, multiple observations, etc.

Weighting. Another issue that arises in connection with teacher evaluation concerns the weighting of the different components of practice. Are all the aspects of teaching equally important or are some more important than others? Assuming that one believes that some are more important than others, are the same aspects cited regardless of the students' age, the subject, whether the teacher is new to the profession, or whether it's the beginning or the end of the school year? There are no right answers to these questions, but in order to evaluate performance, it's essential to determine whether some components of teaching are absolutely critical or whether they all are of roughly equal importance.

Score-combining. A challenge inherent in teacher evaluation is to combine all of the aspects of performance into a single judgment of teacher effectiveness. Every observation of performance yields a preliminary judgment on at least some aspects of practice. Depending on the number of formal and informal observations and the number of artifacts examined, there may be literally hundreds of data points from which to formulate a single judgment, yes or no. Furthermore, such decisions are complicated by the question of whether excellent performance in one area can compensate for relatively poor performance elsewhere. Districts might consider creating a formula or algorithm to make such decisions; they plug in the results of the different observations and the formula spits out a decision, usually some sort of average score. Again, these questions have no right answers; they are a matter for professional judgment and they should be explored carefully, after consultation with all relevant parties.

Other options. There are, of course, other options for the evaluation of teacher performance in addition to the traditional methods of classroom observation and the examination of artifacts. Teachers can be evaluated on the extent to which they engage in action research or take on teacher-leadership projects. It's possible to envision a system in which traditional evaluation of teacher performance, based on the framework for teaching or another similar structure, is used to establish acceptable teacher performance. The framework can also serve as the basis for an analysis of practice and the formulation of a professional growth plan, where those are needed. But to be eligible for a high-level performance award, it's possible that teachers would be expected to engage in other professional activities, such as action research, or assume informal leadership responsibilities.

Recommendations and Next Steps

School districts that have created teacher-evaluation systems based on these guidelines have reported many benefits, primarily in the quality of professional conversations. Such an effort requires, of course, a considerable investment of time and energy, although such benefits extend far beyond the area of evaluation, infuse the entire school with an enhanced culture of professional inquiry, and contribute to significant professional development.

To implement such an approach, however, a school or district must take the following steps, which have been outlined in detail throughout this chapter:

- Decide on a means for defining good teaching.[5] This process should engage all stakeholders in the school: teachers, administrators, and officials of the teachers union.
- Engage in a process to develop the procedures and instruments to be used in the evaluation system.[6] These decisions include all operational details of the system, such as number of observations (announced/unannounced), conferences, choice of artifacts, instruments, personnel, timeline, etc.[7]
- Design and deliver professional development/training for both teachers and evaluators to ensure that both groups understand the elements of professional practice and that consistent judgments are based on evidence.[8]

CONCLUSION

The benefits of a well-designed evaluation system extend well beyond the imperative for ensuring high-quality teaching. As noted in this chapter, if the procedures and instruments are developed with the aim of promoting teacher learning, such a system can support continuous teacher self-assessment, reflection on practice, and professional conversation—all essential components of professional development. These benefits will accrue as long as the specific framework used is grounded in a solid research base and reflects important assumptions about teaching and learning held by the professional staff.

The combination of common language and professional conversation yields shared understanding about good teaching across an entire faculty and, most certainly, between teachers and administrators. Evaluations, then, are not simply a matter of the administrator's opinion or her or his personal view of good teaching. A coherent framework for teaching becomes the basis of shared understanding. Grounded in common language and values, subsequent conversations are richer and deeper and drive teachers to improve their practice.

CHAPTER FIVE

Administrator Evaluation

JOHN DEASY

Though research has demonstrated that quality principal leadership can significantly impact student achievement, the role of the principal is complex. Effective principals must use data to develop a vision for teaching and learning, foster a productive culture focused on high expectations, and manage and support their staff to achieve these outcomes.[1] Unfortunately, most principal evaluation systems lack frameworks tied to existing literature on effective school leadership.[2] Additionally, evaluation rubrics typically employ a binary approach—principals either have the skill or they don't. As a result, most principals receive positive evaluations, and few find that evaluations provide detailed information about how to improve their practice.[3]

Some school districts have begun to use more comprehensive mechanisms for evaluating administrators, such as the Administrator Portfolio Evaluation Process (APEP).[4] APEP modifies the Interstate School Leaders Licensure Consortium (ISLLC) leadership standards, which are based on empirical research about what works, and applies the concepts of a performance-based rubric discussed in the previous chapter. Administrators are evaluated by assessing how effectively they promote high standards for all students, use student-learning data to make decisions, and create an environment for their staff that focuses on student achievement and continuous professional development. While APEP can be used as a portion of the annual evaluation of school administrators, it also catalyzes school leaders' professional growth through self-assessment and reflection.

The APEP system, developed under the direction of John Deasy when he was superintendent of the Santa Monica-Malibu Unified School District in California, provides evaluation and self-reflection tools that support administrator growth, school improvement, and student achievement. Below, Deasy expounds upon these evaluation mechanisms and how they can be utilized to assess administrator quality and enhance school improvement efforts.

INTRODUCTION

Research on effective schools supports the conclusion that administrators critically impact teacher behavior and student learning.[5] While limited evidence exists of the direct effects of leadership on student learning, ample evidence demonstrates that school leaders exert considerable influence over developing and maintaining a school community committed to a shared vision that promotes student achievement.[6]

Accordingly, school-based administrative evaluation should reveal and reflect the quality of the individual administrator's leadership, as well as the impact of that leadership on school quality and student achievement. A comprehensive evaluation should include the following components:

- A reflective self-assessment.[7] The reflective component provides insight into administrators' thinking and allows them to assess the efficacy of their actions and the potential impact on results. Structured reflection on one's own practice during the evaluation process promotes personal and professional growth.[8]
- A standards-based, performance-driven formal external summative evaluation, which measures administrators' actions (or inputs).
- An assessment of student learning results, which evaluates one dimension of administrators' results (or outputs).

Districts should develop a comprehensive plan to nurture instructional leadership and support newly appointed administrators. The Administrator's Portfolio and Evaluation Process described here was developed for use in Santa Monica-Malibu (California) Unified School District.[9] The APEP provides a common tool and process that promotes administrator growth, school improvement, and student achievement. Initial implementation of the portfolio and the peer/evaluator support process convincingly demonstrated to administrators and central office staff that this type of reflection added important professional learning to the evaluation process.

This chapter will offer several key considerations for districts interested in implementing a new administrator evaluation system or modifying their own system:

- *Defining good performance.* This definition should set clear expectations for high-quality school leader performance.
- *Aligning with strategic plans.* Districts want to ensure that performance standards align with systemic and school strategic plans.
- *Developing procedures and instruments for use in the evaluation system.* These decisions include all operational details of the system, such as number of ob-

servations, whether observations are announced or unannounced, conferences, choice of artifacts, instruments, personnel, timeline, etc.

- *Designing professional development and creating peer learning communities.* These processes must ensure that school leaders understand the elements of professional practice and take ownership over their development.

The benefits of a well-designed administrator evaluation system extend beyond the imperative for monitoring administrator performance. If the tools and procedures are developed with the aim of promoting administrator growth, such a system can support continuous self-assessment, reflection on practice, and improved performance.

DEFINING GOOD PERFORMANCE

An administrator portfolio and evaluation system, which defines good performance, should include three components: (1) clear standards, (2) statements of knowledge/dispositions/behaviors, and (3) rubrics.

Clear Standards

Districts will need to begin by setting standards for high-quality administrator performance.[10] As with teacher evaluation, an administrator-evaluation system must rest on an agreed-upon definition of what constitutes good administrator leadership. This definition should be explicated through clear, concise standards that are both research and performance based, reflect a professional view of leadership, and delineate between levels of performance.

Districts will need to decide whether to adopt a new framework or alter a set of standards to reflect local circumstances and priorities. APEP was created by modifying the six standards for school leaders developed by the Interstate School Leaders Licensure Consortium to meet the distinct needs of our system (shown below). The first four standards used are identical to the ISLLC standards, while the final two standards were customized to respond to our district's need for school leaders who foster multicultural awareness and communicate effectively. Districts will need to define their own vision of high-quality school leadership:

- *Standard 1: Instructional Leadership.* A school administrator is an educational leader who promotes the success of all students by facilitating the development, articulation, implementation, and stewardship of a vision of learning that is shared and supported by the school community.
- *Standard 2: Assessment and Supervision.* A school administrator is an educational leader who promotes the success of all students by advocating, nurturing,

and sustaining a school culture and instructional program conducive to student learning and staff professional growth.

- *Standard 3: Management and Organizational Skills.* A school administrator is an educational leader who promotes the success of all students by ensuring management of the organization, operations, and resources for a safe, efficient, and effective learning environment.
- *Standard 4: Community-Parent Partnerships.* A school administrator is an educational leader who promotes the success of all students by collaborating with families and community members, responding to diverse community interests and needs, and mobilizing community resources.
- *Standard 5: Multicultural Awareness and Appreciation.* A school administrator is an educational leader who promotes the success of all students by insisting on respect for all members of the school community, acceptance of different points of view, a socially just community, fairness, and equity.
- *Standard 6: Effective Communication.* A school administrator is an educational leader who promotes the success of all students by clearly communicating, understanding, responding to, and influencing the larger political, social, economic, legal, and cultural context.

Once they have identified the leadership standards, districts must also describe what constitutes effective performance by creating (1) a set of statements regarding administrator knowledge, dispositions, and behaviors, and (2) rubrics that include varied levels of performance for key components of each standard.

Knowledge, Dispositions, and Behaviors

Knowledge, dispositions, and behaviors define clear performance expectations and ensure that both administrators and their evaluators share a common vision for what high-quality leadership looks like in practice. Figure 5.1 provides an example of the knowledge, dispositions, and behaviors for Standard 6: Effective Communication. Those statements with an asterisk (*) are from the ISLLC Standards for School Leaders document, while the remaining statements were customized by members of the school district community.

Rubrics

In addition to these statements, districts must construct rubrics for each standard by identifying key components and providing a set of observable behaviors for each strand. These rubrics must create levels of performance that represent the various levels of mastery of each component of a standard.

FIGURE 5.1
Excerpts of knowledge, dispositions, and behaviors associated with
Standard 6: Effective communication

Knowledge

The administrator has knowledge and understanding of

- the law as it relates to education and schooling*
- the political, social, cultural, and economic systems and processes that impact schools*
- models and strategies of change and conflict resolution as applied to the larger political, social, cultural, and economic contexts of schooling*
- effective communication with different audiences, verbally and non-verbally
- gender differences in communication styles
- conflict resolution training for self and staff

Dispositions

The administrator believes in, values, and is committed to

- education as a key to opportunity and social mobility*
- the importance of a continuing dialogue with other decision makers affecting education*
- maintaining poise and composure in stressful situations
- listening to parent and community concerns
- communicating with non-English-speaking students and parents
- remaining visible, available, and approachable to students, staff, and parents in the halls, gym, cafeteria, and other places throughout the day

Behaviors (referred to as "Performances" in the ISLLC document)

The administrator demonstrates effective communication by

- working with the governing board and district and local leaders to influence policies that benefit students and support the improvement of teaching and learning
- influencing and supporting public policies, which ensure the equitable distribution of resources and support for all subgroups of students
- ensuring that the school operates consistently within the parameters of federal, state and local laws, policies, regulations, and statutory requirements
- generating support for the school by two-way communication with key decision makers in the school community
- viewing oneself as a leader of a team and also as a member of a larger team
- opening the school to the public and welcoming and facilitating constructive conversations about how to improve student learning and achievement

Those statements with an asterisk (*) are from the ISLLC Standards for School Leaders document

---

Table 5.1 is a sample rubric for one of the key elements in Standard 6: Effective Communication. The entire rubric possesses the following essential qualities:

- *Key Elements.* Communication skills, interpersonal skills, communication with staff, student and parent communication, and communication/interaction with district
- *Distinct Levels of Performance.* Did not meet standard, met standard, or exceeded standard
- *Observable Behaviors.* Clearly defined for each element at each level of performance

The rubrics provide information about performance at a variety of levels and allow administrators to recognize gaps or strengths within a specific component.

TABLE 5.1
Rubric for Standard 6: Effective communication

	Does not meet standards	Meets standards	Exceeds standards
Communication skill	Is ineffective in communication and problem-solving with different audiences and insensitive to gender and cultural differences in communication styles.	Demonstrates effective communication and problem-solving skills with different audiences. Recognizes and demonstrates sensitivity to gender and cultural differences in communication styles.	Routinely demonstrates effective communication and problem-solving skills, demonstrates sensitivity to gender and cultural differences in communications styles, and recognizes communication barriers and devises strategies to overcome them.
	Does not maintain composure in stressful situations and acts or speaks tactlessly.	Maintains poise, composure, and tact in stressful situations.	Wins admiration for tact and for remaining gracious in stressful situations.
	Communicates in an insincere and/or disrespectful manner.	Is respectful and sincere in communications.	Is consistently respectful and sincere in communications.
	Oral and written communications are uneven, with frequent grammar and spelling errors.	Communicates using correct grammar and spelling.	Consistently demonstrates effective use of language in oral and written communications.

The standard of communication is broken down into discrete skills, which allows for a detailed examination of practice.

These rubrics are reviewed and used by administrators as part of their self-assessment, by fellow site administrators as part of the collaborative feedback and reflection sessions, and by the designated evaluator as part of the formal evaluation process.

Weighting, Score Combining, and Standard-Setting

Districts must decide how to weight and score certain components of practice to determine whether or not an administrator has met or exceeded standards. First, a district will need to determine whether some or all of the standards will be addressed in the portfolio each year. Next, they need to discuss whether some of the standards should be weighted more heavily than others. Finally, districts must clearly communicate the rationale for these decisions, as well as how the system will work, to all administrators participating in the process.

Districts will need to determine what constitutes acceptable and distinguished performance on the portfolio, which can be a challenging process. For example, should an administrator be allowed to receive a satisfactory assessment of the portfolio if one entry is judged "does not meet standard"? What about if two are judged unacceptable? On the other end of the performance spectrum, districts must determine what constitutes highly effective performance. Setting high standards or expectations for performance gives administrators targets to aim for, but should not be set so high that obtaining an above-expectations rating is impossible.

To address these issues, districts need to have thoughtful conversations about what combinations of performance across a range of portfolio entries will yield overall ratings of minimally satisfactory, satisfactory, or above expectations. Individual districts will undoubtedly approach the task of setting performance expectations differently, but we suggest convening an administrators union and management joint-planning committee to develop the first draft of the entire portfolio, including the rubrics and expectations regarding levels of performance.

Decisions about setting performance expectations should always attempt to balance the dual purpose of evaluation and professional growth. Our experience suggests that a system that emphasizes excellence over improvement will encourage administrators to highlight strengths and minimize weaknesses, reducing their focus on growth. Conversely, a system that prioritizes growth may inadvertently leave too much room for poor performance. A balance between the two is necessary if administrators are to be held to high standards while continually improving their practice in significant ways.

ALIGNMENT WITH STRATEGIC PLANS

After a district identifies standards, descriptions of practice, and rubrics that clearly define performance, it should verify that these standards align with system and school strategic plans. In the case of APEP, one of our strategic plan initiatives was to improve community engagement. As such, we needed to add specific items to our descriptions of practice and rubrics for communication beyond those included in the ISLLC framework. Other standards required little adaptation to match the goals set forth in our strategic plan.

At the school level, we ensured that the standards and descriptions of practice matched the goals set forth in school improvement plans. As with most school systems, the plans included specific school-based objectives, such as implementing a standards-based curriculum, assessing student learning, demonstrating accountability, and closing achievement gaps. Successful implementation of the school improvement plan requires high-quality administrative leadership.

Districts should align the requirements for the school-based improvement plan and the district's strategic plan to the standards that comprise the framework of the evaluation system (discussed above). This ensures that the portfolio-evaluation system not only supports personal administrator self-reflection but that this growth is reflected in organizational priorities. As will be discussed in a later section, data from the school-based improvement plan will be used to promote professional growth and assess administrator performance as part of the summative evaluation that considers portfolio entries, student growth data, and observations of practice.

PROCEDURES AND INSTRUMENTS

Districts need to develop procedures and instruments for all components of the formal evaluation process. To do so, it is essential to have at the start of this process some design principles related to portfolio construction. In our work with APEP, we began with a handful of nonnegotiable design principles:

- APEP is not viewed as a "show me everything you have accomplished" portfolio.
- APEP is used to demonstrate both growth and achievement (or excellence).
- Depth of reflection is sought over breadth of presentation.
- Attention to the selection of artifacts that are rich and multifaceted is paramount. Fewer artifacts with a rich reflection accompanying them are preferred to a handbook of artifacts with little to no reflective content included.

Districts should translate the principles they identify into simple instructions and instruments for administrators to use as they construct their portfolio and its individual entries:

School Administrator Self-Assessment Worksheet. Before beginning to create their portfolio, administrators should complete a self-assessment, where they rate their performance on the standards and key elements (discussed above) and cite evidence from past practice. The administrator and evaluator will use the results from the self-assessment to determine which of the standards will form the focus of the portfolio.

Directions for Portfolio Preparation. Districts need to make procedural decisions about whether the portfolio development process will be comprehensive or focused and then share the reasoning behind their decision with administrators. In the case of APEP, we opted for limiting the required number of standards to be addressed in a given year, consistent with our design principles described above. For example, our directions for portfolio entries read as follows:

> *The actual number of standards to be used as the basis of any evaluation will not exceed four (4). A maximum of five (5) artifacts (in total) will be used for the entire portfolio construction. One (1) of these artifacts must be a growth artifact and the remaining are to be achievement artifacts. The growth artifact should be chosen to document growth from a point of struggle, weakness, or failure in achieving a goal, completing a task or otherwise demonstrating mastery of a standard. Reflection on the growth artifact should be at least partly focused on the learning that has resulted from the struggle. The achievement artifacts are designed to demonstrate success in attaining proficiency or better in part or all of an individual standard. Part of the reflection on the achievement artifacts (and the growth artifact, if relevant) should be on how the artifact reflects growth on the selected standard. Also, reflection about how the artifact reflects growth on other standards that are related to the selected standards is also appropriate.*

Note that all four design principles are evident in these directions—administrators collect a small thoughtful sample of work, which demonstrates both growth and achievement, encourages integration across standards, and requires significant reflection on the part of the administrator.

After specifying how many standards will be addressed and what type of artifacts should be included, directions must convey the value of paying more attention to the quality of reflection and extension of learning rather than to the quantity of artifacts. We recommend that administrators use the "Natural Harvest" approach for choosing artifacts.[11] This methodology stresses the value of capturing many aspects of one's work through the inclusion of and reflection upon a few artifacts. The directions also reference Brown and Irby's *The Principal Portfolio,* which recommends three stages of construction for each portfolio entry:[12]

> *Stage 1.* Selecting relevant, carefully chosen documents or other artifacts that reflect attainment of or progress toward established criteria (in this case, one or more of the standards)

> *Stage 2.* Writing a reflection that describes, analyzes, and assesses the leadership experiences illustrated by the artifacts

> *Stage 3.* Preparing an action plan for future work based on assessment and analysis

In addition to the self-assessment and directions, reflective prompts should be created to ensure that all administrators and their evaluators have common expectations for what information is included in each reflection. In APEP, we used the reflection questions shown in figure 5.2.

Finally, forms must be created to guide the evaluator's review and assessment of the information in the portfolio entries. All instruments must be clear, concise, and designed to promote reflection.

Artifacts

The selection of artifacts included in the portfolio is dependent upon which aspects of practice administrators are trying to illustrate. For example, imagine that an administrator had decided to focus on improving communication with families as a growth goal. Any of the following artifacts would be suitable:

- A comparison of two samples of written communication to families highlighting changes between the two that illustrate improved practice
- A chain of linked information such as a PowerPoint presentation delivered to a PTSA meeting regarding student achievement, the feedback received from that presentation, and the subsequent PowerPoint presentation and feedback—all of which highlight changes the administrator made in response to feedback

FIGURE 5.2
Sample excerpts for reflection for administrators

---

(1) Describe the documents found in this section.

- Who was involved? What were the circumstances, concerns, issues?
- Where and when did the event or series of events occur?

(2) Analyze and appraise the action represented in the documentation.

- How were the activities related to the district strategic plan and/or school-based school improvement plan?
- Did the action(s) taken result in the intended outcomes?
- What impact did decisions or actions have on students, teachers, and/or community?
- How do the events or activities relate to leadership expectations?

(3) Describe the next steps and future direction to be taken based on the analysis.

- What effect did this have on the accomplishment of the strategic plan?
- How will the administrator build upon this action for future growth and improve practice?
- What plan for improving student learning can be developed from this data?

Source: Genevieve Brown and Beverly J. Irby. *The Principal Portfolio* (Thousand Oaks, CA: Corwin Press, 1997).

- Excerpts from an administrator's journal documenting Individual Education Program (IEP) meetings that describe successes and mistakes and include next steps
- Analysis of a plan for improved communication with a family with whom the administrator has had difficult interactions

The administrator's decision regarding which of these artifacts to select may also address other goals. In our case, the community was very concerned with the IEP process, so an administrator selecting this artifact would also be able to address this systemic goal. We also had a strong focus on using and explaining student achievement data to broad audiences, and the PowerPoint presentation to PTSA may serve that end as well.

Again, districts should reiterate to administrators that the goal in selecting artifacts and reflecting on their meaning is to provide an opportunity for in-depth assessment of the administrator's performance in a focused area. With APEP, our emphasis was to ensure that the majority of the effort administrators made on the evaluation portfolio was spent in reflection on a few artifacts rather than in superficial reflection on many.

Timeline and Personnel

Assuming the parameters have been established and the appropriate instruments created, districts should next develop a timeline for the cycle of administrator evaluation. It is imperative that this timeline be aligned with any local contractual deadlines that may impact employee status or renewal. The following recommended timeline and process is based on the APEP experience:

- *Summer leadership retreat.* District leadership should introduce and review the evaluation procedures with administrators.
- *Self-assessment completion.* Administrators should complete the self-assessment following the retreat, ideally by the third week of school.
- *Initial conference.* A conference should be held between the administrator and his or her designated evaluator to achieve two outcomes: select overall goals for the upcoming year and identify (at least provisionally) the standards that will be the focus of the administrator's portfolio and evaluation for that year.
- *Reflection period and final agreement.* Following this conference (two weeks later), the administrator and evaluator should communicate briefly to confirm and potentially adjust the selected standards. This extended period allows time for additional reflection.
- *Collection of evidence and formal conferences to chart progress.* For the remainder of the academic year, administrators and evaluators should set up a minimum of two additional formal conferences to chart progress during the evaluation cycle. This can also be accomplished through learning communities, discussed below.
- *Summative evaluation.* At the close of the year, the final portfolio and revised self-assessment should be submitted and reviewed with the evaluator. As discussed above, districts need to set guidelines around weighting the different pieces of evidence—including the portfolio, student achievement, and observational data—to determine the overall category of performance. If performance meets acceptable levels, the conference provides an opportunity for evaluators to assist administrators in setting goals for the next academic year and generating plans for achieving them over the summer months.
- *Remediation.* Depending on the parameters set by the district, if performance falls below acceptable standards, one of two options may be pursued. In the most severe cases, the administrator should be terminated or reassigned. In cases where administrators are not reassigned or terminated, evaluators must work with them to develop a comprehensive improvement plan to address the areas of weakness. This plan should include specific action steps, professional development, and follow-up to ensure that improvement is made during the next school year.

In most school systems, administrators and their evaluators are in a complex relationship. The evaluators are usually part of a central (or regional) office that is charged with providing information, direction, and support to those they also evaluate. As a result, it is recommended that additional support for the portfolio development process come through professional development in a learning community described next.

DESIGNING PROFESSIONAL DEVELOPMENT AND CREATING PEER LEARNING COMMUNITIES

An administrator-evaluation system, like a teacher-evaluation system, must serve two purposes—quality assurance and professional learning (see chapter 4). Although the portfolio is used as evidence in the summative evaluation process for administrators, one of its overarching goals is to encourage professional growth. It accomplishes this through an iterative process of self-assessment, focused artifact collection, reflective writing, and shared reflection with a small number of colleagues.

Districts should provide opportunities for sharing and receiving feedback through the creation of a professional learning community of administrators within the district. One way of accomplishing this outcome is to devote professional development time to this task within regularly scheduled administrator meetings and to create a monthly professional development calendar that emphasizes instructional leadership.

To build a principal's skill in artifact selection, districts should utilize these meetings to employ a process called consultancy, which is designed to improve either a product or practice.[13] A brief review of the modified consultancy protocol is described in table 5.2. This process is accomplished in self-selected triads of administrators, which gather for ninety minutes of uninterrupted time. Before the meeting, each administrator has selected one entry from his or her working portfolio to share with the group, including the artifact, description, reflections, and key questions. (Note: copies of this work are distributed ahead of time.) To build ownership, groups must self-govern their process.

In our experience, this protocol became invaluable to individuals as they prepared their portfolio for evaluation. Consultancy, at its best, helped the presenter think differently about the work, exposed ideas not previously considered, and revealed gaps in the presenter's thinking. Administrators also developed new reflective listening skills and built trust among colleagues. Instead of focusing on problems, conversations examined work that would result in improved teaching and learning in schools. We found that the process of reflecting on artifacts and then sharing them with peers required explicit modeling, sufficient time for sharing, and trust within the community of leaders.

TABLE 5.2
Consultancy protocol

Time	Activity	Description
3–5 minutes	Presentation of materials and posing of the central question.	Presenter provides short, concise information relevant to the entry and the question they will pose to the group.
2 minutes	Clarifying questions are asked to the presenter.	These questions address short factual issues needed for the group to move forward. *Example questions include:* Was this the first time you did…? How many people were involved…?
3–5 minutes	Probing questions are asked to the presenter.	These questions dig into the substance of the presentation and expose ideas that may not previously have been considered. These questions need not be answered, but instead are designed to push the presenter's thinking on the issue. *Examples question stems include:* Did you consider…? How did you come to this way of thinking…?
10 minutes	Consultancy takes place while presenter is silent and taking notes.	During this time, the presenter silently takes notes, while the remainder of the group has a conversation about the issue at hand. This structure forces presenters to reflect on what they are hearing, as opposed to becoming defensive.
5 minutes	Presenter reflects while group is silent.	The presenter synthesizes the group's discussion and shares any immediate next steps.
3 minutes	Group debriefs the process.	Together, the group debriefs how the process works and how it can be adjusted for future presenters.

CONCLUSION

School districts that have created administrator evaluation systems similar to APEP have reported many benefits, primarily in the quality of professional conversations. Such an effort will require an initial investment of time and resources, although benefits extend far beyond the area of evaluation and infuse the entire district with an enhanced culture of professional learning. As noted above, if the evaluation procedures and instruments are developed with the aim of promoting administrator growth, such a system can support continuous self-assessment, reflection on practice, and collaborative professional conversations.

Despite the benefits, there are some challenges and considerations districts should keep in mind when implementing an administrator portfolio-evaluation system:

- Many administrators find it difficult to set aside the time required to engage deeply in reflection. Our decision to share artifacts through peer consultancy provided the necessary structure to help administrators keep up with the work over the course of the year.
- Without a commitment to professional development, a new portfolio-evaluation system is unlikely to produce any real change in practice. An effective professional development plan provides systemic and integrated training. With APEP, we also saw the consultancy as a means to differentiate professional development, as triads examined a range of professional issues and provided opportunities for administrators to gain insight into appropriate next steps.
- Districts need to be prepared for the inherent, unintended consequences of the evaluation's design and implementation. For example, if the system allows for two growth standards and two achievement standards, do administrators or the community hear that as an acceptance of mediocrity? Or, if all standards must show excellence, is it then unsafe to explore areas for growth? Communication and clarity about system objectives can help ameliorate this potential problem.
- Portfolio construction can mean many things to many people. With APEP, the program was strengthened when we had samples of portfolio entries and reflections that guided the work of others.
- It is critical to integrate all components of an administrator's evaluation. As APEP was evolving, we saw that the program was more beneficial as the links between student achievement, professional practice, and external evaluation were clear, explicit, and aligned.

As school districts move to implement programs similar to APEP, they will certainly face their own unique challenges. We recommend that districts use the guidelines discussed in this chapter and the learning communities they establish to address concerns as they arise.

CHAPTER SIX

Compensation

MARC J. WALLACE JR.

The current emphasis on teacher quality, coupled with the increased educational demands of the new global economy have stimulated interest in performance-pay initiatives—in fact, according to recent estimates, at least one-third of all districts are currently primed to participate in such programs.[1] Despite this growing consensus that the teacher-compensation system should be reformed, well over 90 percent of the school districts today are still using a single-salary schedule to deliver pay raises to teachers and administrators. Two factors drive raises: (1) annual step increases (the "rows") and (2) acquisition of educational credentials (the "lanes"). Unfortunately, research demonstrates that neither factor (years beyond the first few or college courses beyond the bachelor's and mater's or educational credentials) has sufficient impact on student learning to be included in base salary.[2] Thus, the classic single-salary schedule sends an entitlement message. Instead, we should move to a system that encourages and rewards skill development and career progression related to improved student learning.[3]

Compensation reform should focus on the needs of current and future teachers. The goal with respect to the current teacher corps is to provide new incentives for developing more effective instructional skills and to keep more of our top performers from leaving their classrooms. Districts such as Houston, Texas, and Denver, Colorado and states such as Minnesota, have begun to experiment with approaches to pay that are tied to performance, many with the help of the federal Teacher Incentive Fund. Given the recent nature of these reforms, no conclusive evidence relates changes in compensation to improved teacher effectiveness. However, some preliminary research shows that when implemented as part of a comprehensive approach, these changes contribute to increased student achievement.[4]

The other goal of compensation reform should be to help schools succeed in recruiting a larger share of our best and brightest college graduates. In 1972, 30.3 percent of all professional women in America were teachers. By 2004, the proportion had fallen to 13.8 percent. In the intervening decades, the proportion of women becoming accountants, architects, auditors, dentists, engineers, lawyers, pharmacists, and physicians, among other professions, increased three- to sixfold.[5] To attract both women and men of talent will require a compensation system that pays highly effective teachers considerably more money, is based on performance rather than longevity, and makes it possible for them to reach the top of the salary schedule within seven to eight years rather than up to thirty.

In this chapter, Marc Wallace, founding partner of Teacher Excellence Through Compensation (TEC) and coauthor, with Allan Odden, of How to Create World Class Teacher Compensation, *draws on his experience to synthesize the key principles of an effective compensation system and to highlight how the OPE framework meets these essential criteria.[6]*

THE NEED FOR CHANGE

There is clear evidence that public education is in crisis, and an effective response will require massive changes in all systems, organizations, and methods in the field. Compensation (the way an organization delivers rewards) is no exception—it will have to change because the way organizations deliver compensation has three enormous effects on employees.[7] First, it sends important messages about what is important to the organization. Second, it can be used to signal that critical changes must occur in employee behavior for the organization to adapt and survive in a turbulent environment. Third, over the long term, the way we are paid shapes our reactions and behaviors as employees. That is, employees will learn and repeat those activities that are rewarded and will not adopt those that are not rewarded. Simply put, a change effort that ignores compensation will be sending all the wrong messages and reinforcing business as usual—a prescription for failure.

Odden and Wallace show that an effective compensation program is one that aligns with and supports an organization's mission, objectives, and strategy, much like in the private sector.[8] When the private sector radically changed pay systems in the last decades of the twentieth century, it did so for strategic reasons. Buffeted by pressures to dramatically increase performance, cut costs, and move new services and products more quickly into the marketplace, private companies shifted from paying employees for years of service to rewarding significant increases in the skills and knowledge required in the new economy. Similarly, they began to link pay increases and bonuses to the bottom-line performance of the organization, including growth in profits, reduced unit costs, and customer satisfaction. Pay shifted from being an entitlement to an incentive that must be earned through improved business performance.

There is no doubt that public education is being buffeted today by the same kinds of forces that have affected the private sector, so we can look to this experience to provide a clear road map for changing compensation in education.

Education's current practice of annual pay steps and raises associated with educational credentials is sending all the wrong messages. The traditional single-salary schedule made sense eighty years ago, when gender-based salary inequities needed to be corrected. In the turbulent twenty-first century, however, it sends a message of entitlement: "Get your master's degree and your salary will step up each year until you retire."

Sending the right message and rewarding the changes required by the educational strategies will demand changes in the way we deliver each element of teacher and administrator compensation:

- *Base salary.* The monthly or annual salary paid
- *Raises.* Progression in base salary over time
- *Variable pay.* Bonuses or incentives that are paid but do not roll into base salary

To alter the message we are sending about teacher compensation, these critical building blocks will have to change in the manner described in table 6.1.

TABLE 6.1
Messages about teacher compensation

Compensation element	From this message	To this message
Base-pay level	"This is what's been negotiated for you."	"This is the value of the personal skills, capacities, and accountability that you bring to the classroom."
Annual raises in base pay	"This represents one more year with the district."	"This rewards you for growth in your skills related to instruction (as assessed by observation protocols: see chapter 4) and your contribution to student learning (as assessed by a value-added model: see chapter 3)."
Variable pay	"Any bonuses are a privilege of membership."	"This is your reward for your individual contribution, as well as the group's contribution, to student learning gains."
Total cash compensation	"You are entitled to this simply because you are here."	"Here's what you and your colleagues have earned."

KEY PRINCIPLES FOR A STATE-OF-THE-ART
COMPENSATION STRATEGY

Making changes in teacher pay may initially be threatening to teachers and administrators. A compelling case can be made for change, but it requires that we make explicit what should be expected from pay systems and present clear, tangible evidence regarding the inability of current reward practices to achieve these results. To accomplish this goal, we need a strategy that shows how a better pay system will directly support the mission, objectives, and improvement strategies a district has set forth. Specifically, a good compensation strategy allows districts to (1) gain control over the process of compensation and direct it toward explicit programmatic goals (e.g., attracting talent, motivating peak performance); (2) raise its sights or expectations for compensation from being a cost to becoming an investment in performance; (3) provide a yardstick or standard for assessing the effectiveness of the district's current compensation strategy by diagnosing gaps and identifying areas where the compensation system needs to change; (4) create principles for identifying what an improved compensation program might look like; and (5) design architectural blueprints or principles for new compensation systems.

To achieve these purposes, a compensation strategy must have two components:

- *Objectives.* What districts want to accomplish with teacher compensation
- *Architecture.* A set of guiding principles, or a blueprint, for the design and operation of each building block of the total compensation package

Experience has yielded a model set of objectives and design principles that districts should embrace in their approach to compensation.

Model Set of Objectives for Teacher Compensation

Boost student learning and achievement. Contributing directly to improvements in student learning.

Support instructional improvement strategy. Contributing directly to the implementation and accomplishment of the school's and district's overall instructional improvement plan. Such a plan incorporates all initiatives intended to contribute to improved student learning and achievement.

Enhance attraction and retention. Contributing to recruiting and retaining sufficient numbers of effective and highly qualified teachers in all areas (especially hard-to-staff areas such as special education, math, and science) in all schools.

Expand teacher knowledge and skills. Enhancing the competencies, talents, motivation, and instructional expertise brought to and used in the classroom.

Improve teacher performance. Describing what a teacher accomplishes inside and outside of the classroom.

Create career path opportunity. Providing meaningful and rewarding opportunities for advancement in the teaching profession and education administration.

Provide for accountability. Contributing to a sense of ownership for student results and a commitment to perform in a manner that promotes student learning.

Increase communication. Sending an accurate message about district priorities.

Contain costs. Crafting affordable and predictable compensation programs that conform to the district's financial objectives.

Architecture for Teacher Compensation

Compensation architecture consists of a set of design principles that specify what compensation should look like and how it should operate in order to achieve the program's objectives. A design principle has three parts:

1. The message it sends about each compensation component
2. A description of how the component should work
3. A specification of how the compensation objective(s) is/are served by the component

Table 6.2 summarizes the recommended teacher compensation architecture.

So far, our compensation design principles have addressed monetary compensation, but an effective compensation system should also provide an opportunity for career advancement, as illustrated in table 6.3.

Districts should use this architecture to (1) assess the effectiveness of the district's current compensation system, (2) diagnose any deficiencies or gaps, (3) guide choices for changing the compensation system by making the compelling "business" case for change, and (4) provide the blueprints for a new compensation program.

OPE'S APPROACH TO PAY FOR PERFORMANCE

The desired educator compensation architecture calls for an entirely new system for paying teachers and administrators. OPE has designed an approach for districts that achieves the above compensation principles. It introduces pay for performance and eliminates automatic annual steps, pay for college courses beyond the bachelor's and master's degrees, and educational credentials as a basis for setting base pay. An educator's base salary level in the model is driven by moving up the career ladder

TABLE 6.2

Teacher compensation architecture

Teacher compensation component	Message	How it should work	Objectives served
Base-salary level: level of a teacher's salary	"Operating within the district's mission, this is fair and competitive pay for the skills and experience you bring to the district."	Teacher salaries at all levels are priced competitively with teacher pay in other districts and the external market.	1. Attraction and retention 2. Cost
Stipends: additional payments made	Circumstances, such as working in a hard-to-staff area or taking on temporary roles, are recognized by a stipend in addition to one's normal salary.	Stipends are established for hard-to-staff areas or for taking on specific roles. The stipend is paid only while the hard-to-staff assignment or other role is occupied.	1. Attraction and retention
Base-salary progression: salary raises or advancement over time	Salary raises are based on acquiring, using, and demonstrating knowledge and skills that increase instructional effectiveness, leading to improved student learning.	Salary raises are linked to career-level advancement, which requires growth in instructional skills and student learning gains.	1. Student learning and achievement 2. Support instructional improvement 3. Attraction and retention 4. Teacher knowledge and skills 5. Career path 6. Accountability
Variable pay: a payment that does not fold into base salary, and must be re-earned	"We want to work collectively and individually to accomplish ambitious/meaningful improvements in student learning and achievement."	Teachers and administrators are rewarded as a group and individually if they produce improvements in student learning and achievement.	1. Student learning and achievement 2. Support instructional improvement 3. Teacher performance 4. Communication 5. Accountability

based on two performance factors: (1) sustained achievement of the educator's students (using a value-added model; see chapter 3), and (2) growth in professional practice (using an observation framework; see chapter 4). Annual raises or steps are no longer automatic, but instead must be earned as a result of gains in student learning (using the value-added model; see figure 1.2 in chapter 1).

The OPE approach also introduces a variable-pay component. Teachers are eligible for annual incentive awards based on how their students perform (using

TABLE 6.3
Career advancement

Teacher compensation component	Message	How it should work	Objectives served
Career opportunity: the ability to increase the breadth and depth of skills and be rewarded for it.	"We encourage and provide the means for professional development to promote the continued growth of teachers in order to improve student performance."	Teachers periodically define their career paths and set and fulfill realistic professional goals toward that end. Such goals could include teacher leadership roles.	1. Attraction and retention 2. Teacher knowledge and skills 3. Teacher performance 4. Career path opportunity 5. Accountability

the value-added model) and how the entire school's or building's students perform (using the value-added model). Finally, educational credentials and national board certification are recognized by one-time, nonrecurring bonuses that do not fold into base salary. Table 6.4 provides a more detailed discussion of how base salary adjustments and variable pay work.

The Base Salary Model

OPE proposes the following salary schedule for teachers as a replacement for the traditional single-salary schedule. Table 6.5 is illustrative, as numbers will vary greatly by region.

TABLE 6.4
OPE approach to base salary and variable pay

Base Salary		Variable pay		
Base-salary level	Annual base-salary raise (steps)	Individual incentive award	Group incentive award	One-time bonus
Career Ladder Level (student learning gains and professional practice)	+ Annual student learning gains	+ Annual student learning gains (re-earned annually)	+ Annual student learning gains	+ MA/MS and PhD/EdD achievement, National Board Certification

TABLE 6.5
Sample base salary model

	Step within level	Salary
Distinguished	2	$93,473
	1	$90,313
Advanced	3	$78,533
	2	$75,877
	1	$73,311
Career	7	$61,093
	6	$59,027
	5	$57,031
	4	$55,102
	3	$53,239
	2	$51,438
	1	$49,699
Apprentice	3	$36,814
	2	$35,569
	1	$34,366

The OPE salary schedule incorporates several critical features that correspond with the principles discussed previously.

External Competitiveness. The initial starting salary is set at a competitive external market level, and the entire schedule is periodically adjusted upward to keep pace with movements in external labor markets and the starting salaries in other school districts.[9]

Bonuses for Educational Credentials. The new schedule eliminates educational credentials as the basis for pay raises, instead providing a one-time bonus for achieving National Board for Professional Teaching Standards (NBPTS) certification and educational degrees. The one-time bonuses need to be sizable enough to get educators' attention and reward the acquisition of these credentials, but individual districts may want to adjust these bonuses based on availability of funds. Such adjustments should maintain the relative size of the bonuses (e.g., more for NBPTS and the PhD/EdD than for the MS/MA).

Career Levels. New teachers begin as apprentices, making a salary that is set at a competitive external market level. A new teacher with no previous experience would need to spend a minimum of three years (the recommended length of time to get sound statistical measures of their instructional effectiveness) and a maximum of five years in order to move to the Career level. If a teacher doesn't meet the minimum requirements for the Career level, he or she will not receive a contract and will be dismissed.

As previously discussed, career-level increases are based on two factors. First, a teacher must grow in instructional practice as defined by performance rubrics and achieve ratings of effective (for Career) and highly effective (for Advanced and Distinguished) levels of student learning.

The career earnings progression can be accelerated or fast-tracked, thus allowing the district to compete powerfully for new talent. Teachers must spend a minimum of three years in the Apprentice category, two years in Career, and two years in Advanced before moving to the Distinguished level. In sum, because significant salary increases are associated with the promotion to each successive level, by their eighth year in the profession, teachers can be earning the highest salary paid in the district.

The OPE framework requires that all teachers achieve at least Career status to remain in the classroom and expects that subsets of teachers will reach Advanced and Distinguished levels. To move to the Distinguished rung of the career ladder, a teacher must (1) meet all the requirements for Advanced status—that is, be identified as highly effective through the empirical value-added analysis and rated in the highest category of the observation framework through a peer-review observation process—and (2) serve the district in one of several leadership capacities, such as mentor, coach, team leader, or content specialist. Local districts may choose to develop other criteria for the rank of Distinguished teacher, such as NBPTS, as long as the requirements for Advanced are satisfied.

Annual Steps. The new schedule maintains some annual steps within career-ladder levels, primarily to retain some of the feel of a traditional schedule so the transition is less threatening. Districts should place a greater number of steps for pay advancement within the Career level to recognize the fact that a majority of teachers will not go beyond this level. Although the steps are envisioned to be annual, OPE recommends that these steps be earned only if the teacher continues to meet the level's requirements. At the Career level, for example, a teacher must achieve an effective value-added estimate each year in order to qualify for the step.

To incentivize improved performance, the new schedule places the greatest weight on achieving career-ladder levels. Steps within levels should be more modest when compared to the raises between the Career, Advanced, and Distinguished levels.

The Variable Pay Model

In addition to the base salary program, the OPE approach calls for performance incentives or variable pay opportunities for teachers and administrators at the individual and group (building) level. The purpose of variable pay is to provide explicit rewards for continuous improvement in educational performance, especially student learning and achievement gains.

Variable pay for teachers in the OPE framework has two components: (1) individual incentive awards for achieving/exceeding student learning goals, and (2) group incentive awards rewarding all teachers in a building (or natural unit) for achieving/exceeding educational goals on a scorecard. These payments do not roll into base salary and must be earned anew each year.

Individual Teacher Incentives. Each teacher will be encouraged to achieve value-added learning goals for their students each year. If teachers are effective, they will receive a bonus; if they are highly effective, they will receive a larger bonus; and if they are ineffective, they will receive no bonus.

Group Incentives (Student-Based Performance Awards). In addition to individual incentives, all teachers in a building (or other natural unit) will be encouraged to work as a team to achieve a scorecard of critical educational measures. Each measure should be weighted by a percentage factor representing its relative importance. The most heavily weighted are the student achievement gains in reading, math, and language arts. Others such as school attendance, stakeholder engagement, human resource development, and use of resources focus on school measures that support educational achievement. They would be defined by portfolio elements that track progress on key indicators and projects.

The student-based performance award (SBPA) program is truly pay for performance because it rewards all the teachers and administrators in a building (or district) for student learning gains and performance on other key educational measures. Because the incentive payout does not roll into base salary, it must be earned each year through continuous improvement in performance.

Remediation

Although we recognize that it is practically impossible to demote people in terms of pay, when teachers or administrators stop performing at a given career-ladder level, OPE recommends that their pay be frozen and no steps or bonuses be awarded. Additionally, teachers who begin to perform at ineffective levels will be required to undergo a process of remediation (discussed in chapter 12). If the remediation program is completed successfully, the salary will be unfrozen and wages lost while in remediation will be restored.

IMPLEMENTATION

Over time, compensation costs fluctuate. They increase as teachers and administrators move up the schedule to higher levels of pay or if cost-of-living or market adjustments are made to the entire salary schedule. They decrease as teachers and administrators retire at relatively high salary levels and are replaced by teachers and administrators at lower pay levels, or as the number of teachers and administrators diminish through attrition or layoffs in times of declining enrollments.

A district implementing a new compensation system would need to employ the principles outlined here as a yardstick to assess deficiencies in its current program, determine any unique circumstances such as those described above, and adapt the base salary and variable pay components to meet district needs.

Cost of the New Salary Schedule

To accomplish this goal, districts must compare forecasted costs of their current salary schedules with those forecasted for the new approach. The major costs of teacher compensation are (1) base salary plus any stipends; (2) incentive payments earned under a variable pay program or one-time payments for NBPTS and educational credentials (MA/PhD); and (3) benefits (e.g., insurance, retirement contributions, and the like). Districts and unions will be able to negotiate the following costs:

- Base salary increases for jumps in level on the career ladder
- Steps within career-ladder levels
- Individual and group incentives
- Bonuses for NBPTS and educational credentials

To provide an example of how this process plays out in the OPE approach, we have used an actual school district's distribution of teachers across a traditional salary schedule to estimate the distribution in each of the five years of the forecast. We have set the following parameters for the analysis:

- The current schedule will remain in place if we do nothing for the next five years. The entire schedule will be adjusted for cost of living each year of the forecast by a factor of 3 percent. Teachers will move up a step each year with normal attrition through retirements and separations. Retiring teachers will be replaced by new people who will come in lower in the schedule.
- The teacher population will stay constant each year at a full-time-equivalent (FTE) count of 531.
- In order to estimate the percentage of all teachers at the Advanced and Distinguished levels, we used value-added data from Tennessee, where it is estimated that between 15 percent and 20 percent of teachers statewide perform at the level that OPE refers to as highly effective, although the percentage will

vary by grade and subject. Thus, for the sake of planning, we estimate the distribution at any one point in time, as shown below:

Teacher distribution

Career level	Percentage
Distinguished	5
Advanced	10
Career	55
Apprentice	30

- We estimate teacher earnings under the one-time bonuses for NBTS and education credentials as follows:

Teacher credentials

Credentials	Number	One Time Bonus
NBPTS	5	$7,500
MA/MS	53	$2,500
PhD/EdD	5	$5,000

- We estimate earnings under the teacher incentive system as follows:

Teacher incentive awards

Level	Rating	Bonus	Percent qualifying
Individual	Effective	5%	55
	Highly Effective	10%	15
Group	Effective	5%	55
	Highly Effective	10%	15

Given these assumptions, we modeled costs under two scenarios:

Scenario 1: No new money available. This assumes that the district is trying to change compensation practices without any additional funds. The OPE approach includes a grandfather clause that offers all current teachers the option of choosing to remain under the existing compensation system. All teachers who entered the profession after the OPE framework was in place would fall under the new compensation system, while veteran teachers selecting the grandfather option would be subject to the new evaluation system. As a result of no new money being available, under this scenario we were able to introduce only the OPE Career Ladder Salary Schedule and provide one-time bonuses to recognize educational credentials and NBPTS. Given the parameters we chose for the salary increases, there were not sufficient funds to provide annual performance incentives.

Scenario 2: New money available. In exchange for increased accountability, it is possible that a district would be able to secure additional funds from the pub-

TABLE 6.6
Summary of cost modeling for two scenarios

Cost	No new money	New money (17% increase in current compensation)
Significant base-salary increases for achieving OPE career ladder levels (Career, Advanced, Distinguished)	Apprentice to Career—30% Career to Advanced—20% Advanced to Distinguished—15%	Apprentice to Career—35% Career to Advanced—20% Advanced to Distinguished—15%
One-time bonuses for degree attainment (MS/MA/EdD/ PhD) and NBPTS certification	NBPTS—$7,500 PhD/EdD—$5,000 MA/MS—$2,500	NBPTS—$7,500 PhD/EdD—$5,000 MA/MS—$2,500
Maintenance of some annual steps with career ladder levels	Steps within the levels on the career ladder of 2.5%	Steps within the levels on the career ladder of 3.5%
Individual and group variable pay program	If the above parameters are maintained, then sufficient funds do not exist to cover an individual and group variable pay program. However, if the above numbers were adjusted, additional funds could become available.	Individual Awards • Effective (5%) • Highly effective (10%) Group/school awards • Effective (5%) • Highly effective (10%)

lic sector (either local, state, or federal governments). In the case modeled with the parameters listed above, the new money required to enhance career salary progression, performance incentives (individual and group), and one-time bonuses for NBPTS and educational credentials came out to be 17.09 percent over the five-year forecast. Given the parameters we chose, 7.25 percent was required for base salary enhancement, 9.12 percent for performance incentive bonuses, and 0.76 percent for NBPTS and educational credential bonuses. The costs for these two scenarios are described in table 6.6.

Guidelines

Districts should follow these steps to create their own cost forecast:

Step 1. Design a population database that contains the following information for each teacher and administrator: name, age, years of service in current position, years in teaching or administration, current base salary, step and lane placement in current salary schedule, stipends paid this year, and educational degrees.

Step 2. Determine the percentage distribution of teachers and administrators in the current salary schedule.

Step 3. Develop the current schedule in each of the five forecast years using this year's schedule as the base year (0). Districts may want to make across-the-board annual cost-of-living adjustments to the schedule. Use the percentage distribution developed in Step 2 to estimate the distribution of teachers and administrators in the schedule in each of the forecast years. Alternatively, districts may want to estimate these distributions at a more micro level, using specific information regarding retirements, replacements, attainment of educational credentials, etc.

Step 4. Adapt the OPE career-ladder schedule to specific circumstances. Estimate the percentage distribution across levels (Apprentice, Career, Advanced, and Distinguished) that would be expected in each year of the forecast, based on unique district factors. We recommend that absent specific circumstances, districts use the percentage estimates provided above since they are based on expert judgment.

Step 5. Estimate incentive program and stipend costs in each year of the forecast. Forecasting the cost of a variable pay program is a simpler task than that for base salary programs because there are fewer variables. Calculate the payout levels under various levels of target achievement. A liberal forecast might estimate that all schools achieve 100 percent or more of their targets, while a more conservative forecast would estimate considerably less than 100 percent. We recommend that the school district budget for the expected payout, but if actual achievement exceeds the forecast, the shortfall should be calculated as an index. Each teacher's payout would be adjusted downward by the index to fit the budget in a fair manner.

Step 6. Build a spreadsheet model to calculate and compare the total compensation cost of the current salary schedule with the total cost of the new schedule across all years of the forecast. Spreadsheet models are available at no cost at teachercomp.com.

Step 7. Adjust parameters in the forecast (e.g., across-the-board annual adjustments, steps within career-ladder levels, career-level adjustments, stipends, bonus levels) until an affordable result is found.

Step 8. Test the model against actual experience and revise.

CONCLUSION

Districts will face challenges when making the transition from current practices to new compensation systems. To ensure the success of pay initiatives, districts should adhere to the following implementation recommendations:

- Care and timing are critical. Most new pay programs fail not because of any inherent flaws in design but because of procedural and other errors during implementation.
- Effective implementation recognizes that the political dynamics involved in changing teacher pay are equally crucial to the mechanics and includes all critical stakeholder groups (school board, administrators, teachers, union, and community) in the process.
- Communication is critical. All channels (formal and informal) must be employed throughout the process to ensure that correct information is getting out, misinformation is eliminated, and feedback from stakeholders is incorporated.
- Information infrastructure is essential and almost always underestimated. Effective implementation requires that data regarding teacher and student performance are reliable, valid, and available on a timely and user-friendly basis.
- Piloting new teacher pay programs is essential. It allows unintended glitches to be ironed out before substantial damage is done. We recommend that new pay systems and all of their elements as discussed in this chapter be piloted for six to twelve months.
- Attention to process is critical. Successful change in pay systems recognizes the importance of attending to process at two junctures: (1) the piloting and testing of all program elements, and (2) the final transition from the old to the new system.
- Finally, long-term success requires that new programs be monitored with both formative and summative assessments throughout their life—not just after the first year. Continual assessment allows programs to grow and adapt to changing conditions.

Pay for performance is here to stay. The demands of the global economy will continue to drive policy that focuses on raising achievement, accelerating instructional improvement, promoting high-quality teaching, and reforming teacher pay. Because no single approach to pay for performance has yet emerged as the best, experimentation with different alternative salary structures, such as the OPE approach presented in this chapter, must characterize reform. States and districts should encourage researchers to study their innovations so that we can accumulate more knowledge and districts can begin to use this knowledge to design pay-for-performance systems based on strong evidence of what works and what doesn't.

Though it is relatively uncharted territory, changes in teacher and administrator pay provide an important opportunity for reforming American public education. Teachers will be able to advance in their careers more quickly while earning higher pay and status. School districts will be better equipped to attract and retain highly skilled teachers. And, most important, students will benefit from improved quality of instruction and an environment focused on student learning results.

CHAPTER SEVEN

Compensating Educators in the Absence of Value-Added Assessment

VIRGINIA ADAMS SIMON

If we provide teachers in tested subjects and grades with an opportunity to earn additional pay as part of new compensation systems, fairness suggests that we should provide other teachers and specialists with the same opportunity. Since individual awards are typically based on student performance on high-stakes exams, teachers and specialists outside of tested subjects are not usually eligible, sending the message that because their work is not assessed by state-mandated exams, it is somehow not as important. Two recent teacher task forces (the Center for Teacher Quality and the National Institute for Excellence in Teaching) have called for the inclusion of teachers of nontested subjects and grades as essential elements in any pay-for-performance model.[1] If a pay-for-performance system is going to be viewed as fair, then all educators, regardless of their specific assignment, must be eligible for additional pay.

Defenders of the single-salary schedule have often advanced the position that if all educators are not treated in the same way, the compensation system should not be changed. But this argument confuses equity with equality. Educators should be treated fairly, but not necessarily in identical fashion. Every member of a school team has an important role to play in increasing student achievement, and principles of fairness dictate that all staff who work with children be included in the benefits of a pay-for-performance system. Yet measuring a teacher's impact on student learning is a complex process in traditional academic areas, let alone in grades and subjects where annual testing does not exist and, consequently, value-added modeling cannot be applied.

In this chapter, Virginia Adams Simon, an education policy analyst at the University of California, Davis, and one of the original designers of Operation Public Education (OPE), provides districts with recommendations and options for how to include teachers in nontested subjects in pay-for-performance models by drawing on some key examples from other states and large districts. In doing so, she explores how to measure student learning in the absence of value-added and how to differentiate between highly effective, effective, and ineffective practice. Instead of offering one prototype or model, this chapter suggests several approaches that might be altered locally to match specific district conditions. To that end, the final section presents a set of principles and next steps to help guide the local creation of such a system.

Input for this chapter was gathered through a series of interviews with some of the teacher leaders from Denver who helped design the ProComp system for specialists, and half-day meetings conducted in Columbus, Ohio, with groups of educators. We are particularly indebted to Shirley Scott at the Denver Public Schools for her pioneering work with student growth objectives.

BACKGROUND

While the subject of differentiated compensation, pay-for-performance, and evaluation systems for educators continues to stir up considerable conflict, experiments in these approaches to measuring and rewarding teacher quality continue to gain momentum across the United States. Many states and large districts have adopted pay-for-performance models using value-added assessment or learning gains. The Teacher Incentive Fund under the Bush administration made it an even more popular approach for states to use to spur increased achievement. In some cases, states concentrate their investment on their lowest-performing districts, making pay for performance something used only in dire circumstances. It may be matched with state money and other types of investments in teacher quality in an effort to build capacity in the neediest districts. In others, pay for performance is offered to any district in the state that meets its growth objectives. The most common approach has been for the state to offer school- or district-based awards for those who meet or exceed their expected value-added growth. Districts are then left to determine how the awards should be paid out. Districts are also encouraged by their states to create their own incentive programs.

Most states and districts, however, avoid the difficulties of including staff for whom value-added measures are not available. In the OPE framework, roughly one-third of teachers can be evaluated using value-added data from the major subjects tested annually in grades 3–8. An additional one-third of teachers can be evaluated if they teach high school subjects for which there are end-of-course exams. The balance of school district employees fall into three categories:

1. K–2 teachers (i.e., kindergarten, first-, and second-grade teachers)
2. Noncore academic teachers (e.g., music, art, foreign languages, physical education, etc.)
3. Specialists (e.g., nurses, guidance counselors, librarians, social workers, etc.)

STATE AND DISTRICT APPROACHES: OPTIONS
FOR INCLUSION OR EXCLUSION

In few cases are these teachers included to the same extent as core classroom teachers. Current examples show us that the question of how to include these educators in pay-for-performance systems has been dealt with in a variety of ways. These decisions are, no doubt, a function of the policies of the teachers unions in question, but they will be important for districts to consider as they design their own approach.

The types of approaches found can be classified in six ways: (1) those that include K–2, noncore, and specialists in awards for attendance, retention, and professional development credits but not for classroom performance; (2) those that include them in individual performance awards but to a lesser degree; (3) those that include them in group awards only; (4) those that include K–2 but not noncore or specialists; (5) those that include them completely through group awards; and (6) those that include them completely in all aspects of the program.

Option 1: Attendance, Retention, and Professional Development

Guilford County, NC. Mission Possible is a district-based incentive program in Guilford County, North Carolina, that seeks to target the district's neediest schools and provide incentives to attract and retain high-growth teachers. There are two types of individual bonuses available in the program: performance bonuses, and recruitment and retention bonuses. All certified staff are eligible for recruitment and retention bonuses, which are tacked onto a teacher's salary each year if he or she receives a satisfactory performance review and attends 100 percent of mandated professional development activities, but only teachers in tested subjects are eligible for performance bonuses.

Option 2: Partial Inclusion in Individual Bonuses

Houston's ASPIRE (Accelerating Student Progress: Increasing Results & Expectations) Program. Houston offers a noteworthy example of partially including teachers in individual bonuses with its ASPIRE program, which organizes teachers into three categories—Core, Noncore Instructional, and Noninstructional Staff—and administers awards according to three strands:

- *Strand I: Campus Progress Awards.* A composite value-added score is calculated for all grades and subjects on the campus. If campus growth objectives are met, instructional staff may earn a $1,000 bonus, and noninstructional staff can earn $500.
- *Strand II: Teacher Progress Awards.* Value-added teacher-level scores are only available for teachers in grades 3–8 in core subjects. ASPIRE's solution is to

use a subject-area campus score for grades 9–12 as the determination of individual awards and a campuswide reading and math score for the K–2 teachers. In each scenario, teachers can earn up to $5,000, with the exception of the K–2 teachers, who can only earn $2,500.

- *Strand III: Campus Improvement and Achievement Awards.* Campus value-added scores are compared to similar schools across the state and campuses are viewed in light of the Texas Education Agency accountability ratings. Doing well on these measures can lead to another $300–$500 per instructional staff member.

All staff members, regardless of classification, are eligible for attendance bonuses. Houston has taken a "clean" approach in terms of value-added by not attempting to simulate value-added scores in areas where they are not available. Still problematic, however, is the fact that K–2 and noninstructional staff are not eligible for the same level of bonus, no matter how effective they are.

Option 3: Group Awards

Texas Educator Excellence Grant. Texas Governor Rick Perry issued an executive order initiating a $10 million statewide incentive plan in one hundred selected schools, which has since expanded to $100 million and eleven hundred schools. Schools that obtain grants receive payouts based on the achievement of school-wide growth objectives, and 75 percent of the plan's payout must go to teachers. Individual schools design their own criteria for these payouts, but the bonuses must be based partly on student performance gains and partly on other factors, such as serving in leadership roles or teaching at schools and in subjects that are hard to staff. All educators in the school are eligible for the group awards under this program.

Option 4: Inclusion of K–2

Charlotte-Mecklenburg, NC. The Charlotte-Mecklenburg School District's STAR Program (Successful Teacher Administrator Reward), which is now being folded into the LEAP initiative (Leadership for Educators' Advanced Performance), awards teachers up to $1,400 and principals up to $5,000 and ties in value-added growth at the classroom level for teachers and at the building level (along with annual yearly progress, or AYP, measurements) for principals. The program is only available to FOCUS schools, the state's lowest-performing schools. Charlotte-Mecklenburg has tackled the K–2 problem by using nonstandardized tests (such as the DIBELS) and their own calculations to determine growth or gain. Noncore teachers and specialists for whom there is no official testing program are not eligible for individual awards, but they are eligible for building-based awards when their building meets required growth targets.

Option 5: Full Inclusion Through Group Awards

Teacher Advancement Program (TAP). The TAP is a rapidly expanding national program first conceived by the Milken Family Foundation and now operating in fifteen states, fifty districts, and over two hundred schools across the country out of the National Institute for Excellence in Teaching. TAP's performance-based compensation model is grounded in the use of value-added assessment and a rigorous evaluation tool. Each school establishes an award pool, which determines the bonus amount that will be available to those who qualify. All staff members have multiple professional evaluations each year, which are scored using a rubric, and overall performance on the evaluation component is worth 50 percent of a teacher's performance score. The other 50 percent is measured by classroom and building-level value-added. Additionally, 30 percent of the classroom value-added score and 20 percent of the building score is used to determine the bonus for classroom teachers for whom value-added scores are available. The entire 50 percent of a noncore teacher's or specialist's bonus is based on the building level value-added score. As a result, all educators can earn the same amount.

Option 6: Full Inclusion in All Aspects

Denver's ProComp System. Denver's ProComp system is considered by many to be the most comprehensive pay-for-performance program in the country. It began in 1999 with an agreement between the Denver Classroom Teachers Association (DCTA) and the Denver Public Schools (DPS) to create a pay-for-performance pilot, which studied the effects of linking teaching, assessment of student growth, and teacher compensation. The ProComp system has four major components: market incentives, professional evaluation, knowledge and skills, and student growth objectives. All staff—whether teachers of tested subjects or grades, K–2, or specialists—are eligible. Because Denver is the only district that has attempted to fully include all educators in its pay-for-performance model using a student growth measure, we will spend the remainder of the chapter examining their process and discussing the challenges that districts undertaking an inclusive approach must be prepared to encounter.

STUDENT GROWTH OBJECTIVES

The Student Growth Objectives (SGOs) component of the ProComp system is by far the most comprehensive approach to linking student outcomes to educator compensation in the United States. Every teacher and student service professional (SSP) in the DPS system must set two annual goals for student growth, whether or not they have opted into the ProComp system. The rationale behind this approach is that the process of setting objectives sharpens a teacher's focus on what he or she wants students to learn and leads to better outcomes. Unlike more typical professional objective-setting requirements, DPS SGOs are not based on teachers' needs for professional growth but must be directly related to student growth. During the Pay-for-Performance Pilot, research by the Community Training and Assistance Center (CTAC) of Boston found that teachers who set the highest-quality objectives had students who made statistically significant gains in student achievement.[2]

Denver offers eight criteria for objectives and an extensive checklist to assist in the development of appropriate objectives. Objectives must be:

- job-based
- measurable
- focused on student performance
- based on learning content and teaching strategies
- discussed at least three times during the school year
- able to be adjusted during the school year
- unrelated to the specialist professional evaluation process
- recorded online

A checklist is published online for each type of teacher or professional and includes several indicators for each success factor. This list was developed during the pilot phase by the DPS design team and is informed by the CTAC evaluation study. Using student service professionals as an example, the seven factors are:

1. *Rationale.* Why that particular objective was chosen
2. *Population.* Which students the objective addresses
3. *Interval of Time.* Weeks, quarters, semesters, school year
4. *Assessment.* Measure used to show whether the objective was met (pre- and postdata)
5. *Expected Gain or Growth.* Based on the students' average baseline score
6. *Learning Content.* The academic skills, behavior, or attitudes teachers are trying to support, based on needs identified in the baseline data; includes realistic personal goal-setting and problem-solving strategies
7. *Strategies.* Teaching methods or interventions by service professionals to be used to achieve the objective; includes one-on-one contact, home visits, and referral to extracurricular activities

Specialists

Student services professionals write objectives addressing a department goal and another addressing a goal in the school improvement plan, a team goal, a districtwide goal, or a second department goal. See example 7.1.

K–2

K–2 and other elementary classroom teachers are expected to write one objective addressing student growth in reading and one in math. Typical assessments used by K–2 teachers are DRA2, SRI, Benchmarks, and Everyday Math. See example 7.2.

EXAMPLE 7.1
Elementary school librarian

Rationale: Supports reading content standard #5

Sample: Twenty-six fifth graders

Time frame: One school year

Assessment: Teacher Made Assessment

Baseline data: Twenty students scored a 6 or less; 6 students scored a 7 or better

Expected growth: 80% of the identified students will score at the proficient level using teacher-made rubric (7 out of 10 questions is considered proficient)

Learning content: Instruction using atlas, almanac, encyclopedia, Internet, thesaurus, and dictionary

Strategies: Whole-group instruction and individual practice; internet research, various methods of using reference materials in connection with research

---

EXAMPLE 7.2
First-grade literacy goal

Rationale: Supports the implementation of the literacy program

Sample: Twenty students

Time frame: One school year

Assessment: DRA

Baseline data: 70% at DRA level 3, 30% at DRA level A

Expected growth: 75% of students will advance three to five levels on the DRA

Learning content: Improve reading comprehension; develop good reading habits; increase word recognition

Strategies: Mini-lessons; shared, guided, and independent reading; reading con-ferences; skills sessions; high-frequency words; individual word study

---

EXAMPLE 7.3
Art teacher

Rationale: Supports department goals

Sample: Sixty-five students in Drawing and Painting

Time Frame: One semester

Assessment: Teacher-made exam

Baseline data: All students were 65% or below on the pretest

Expected growth: 80% of students will increase their grade score by 15 points or more

Learning content: The art elements—value, color, texture, form; the design principles—contrast, emphasis, pattern, rhythm; art vocabulary

Strategies: Study art vocabulary words and definitions; display visuals in art room that help illustrate each art vocabulary word, for example, art elements and design posters; discuss the elements and principles often as a class, with each individual art project; administer quizzes to check for student understanding; teacher and class also will play a game called ART BALL, where students are in two teams and take turns answering questions about art (vocabulary) to help students remember

---

Noncore Academic

Noncore academic teachers write objectives according to the subject they teach. For example, a physical education teacher or art teacher would write one objective focusing on student growth within the course content area and one objective focusing on a specific subgroup, or an objective focused on student growth within a specific unit of the content area. See example 7.3.

The assessments used to measure SGOs are perhaps the most creative aspect of Denver's program. Rather than believing that art or physical education can't be measured, or that what a librarian or guidance counselor does can't be quantified, they have attempted to measure growth in every area of the school. Colorado is not a value-added state but it has developed its own growth model, which provides an expected growth projection for individual teachers, schools, and districts. All subjects and grades (4–8 core subjects) tested by the state mandated assessments are analyzed using this methodology. These teachers are eligible for a 3 percent bonus if their growth scores exceed expectations. This is separate, however, from the process of setting SGOs. Each year these teachers must also set SGOs that are not related to the state tests.

CHALLENGES AND CONSIDERATIONS

Districts attempting to be as inclusive as Denver can expect to encounter a number of technical and philosophical concerns when deciding how to include teachers in nontested subjects in a pay-for-performance system. Table 7.1 summarizes the challenges raised during interviews with educators, which should be considered by any district attempting to include K–2, noncore, and specialist teachers in their pay-for-performance system.

The following sections will provide some considerations to keep in mind (based on the Denver experience) when approaching these challenges.

Equity versus Equality

Do districts value equity or equality in their compensation models? We may agree that all staff should be included in the pay-for-performance system and have the same opportunity to increase their pay if they perform their jobs well, but should everyone be eligible for the same dollar award? Denver's solution is to include everyone equally, but this has implications when the measures being used for some staff are seen as less "valid" than others. Places like Houston have avoided this dilemma by limiting individual bonuses to certain groups but still enabling those teachers to earn more through group awards.

Process and Communication

Districts must ensure significant buy-in across all stakeholder groups, from the teachers to the parents and taxpayers in the community. This goal can be accomplished through an inclusive and collaborative process from the beginning and ongoing evaluation, communication, and training. An opt-in feature allows teachers to feel free not to opt into the system until they are ready. As was done in Denver, information about the procedures and requirements can be delivered through a well-designed Web delivery system, and annual workshops should be held for new staff to introduce them to the program. Reinforcement and transparency are crucial.

Professional Development and Support

Intensive and ongoing professional development and coaching are required for staff to ensure more than just proper adherence to protocols. Training sessions must be designed to help educators embrace a student-centered and outcome-based approach to teaching. Working with staff whose students are not tested regularly and, as a result, do not typically view their work in measurable terms will be particularly challenging. Additionally, the administration must not only acknowledge the tremendous learning curve involved but also the significant time commitment expected of those who participate in professional development.

TABLE 7.1

Challenges to including K–2, non-core, and specialists in a pay-for-performance model

Challenge	Considerations/Options
Ensuring buy-in	• Establish a joint oversight committee and collaborative design teams that include teachers, union leaders, and administration to create a customized design. • Ensure transparency and communication through regular training, online systems, and mentoring. • Determine equality and equity standards for the system by deciding which staff should be eligible to access what level of reward through teacher vote. • Deputize representatives from the specialists, non-core, and K–2 staff groups to take the lead in designing and supervising the development of their evaluation and compensation differentiation system. • Allow veteran teachers to opt into the system. • Make sure "hardship" conditions are mitigated or accounted for in the system. • Invest time and money in continuous, high-quality professional development and coaching.
Rigor and expectations	• Look to national associations and organizations for standards. • Establish peer-review teams to develop quality controls and develop criteria for growth measures that will ensure proper rigor and create "tiers" for objectives. • Regularly evaluate the rigor of growth measures across buildings and provide feedback to principals and supervisors who appear not to be encouraging rigor.
Valid and reliable assessments	• Where no valid or reliable assessments are available, use group value-added scores only. • If using teacher-made tests, establish a joint committee on assessment quality to approve all assessments. • Encourage grade and content-area teams to use the same assessments. • Ensure unbiased scoring of locally developed assessments by using a team approach. • When possible, use vertically scaled tests aligned to what is being taught. • Utilize rubrics.
Sampling, sub-groups	• Include 100 percent of students in at least one growth objective, along with subgroup goals. • Divide class into quartiles of previous performance and determine separate growth objectives for each quartile, rather than using race or language status as a subgroup.
Differentiation of performance	• See considerations outlined in table 7.3.
Value-added vs. simple gain	• Avoid, where possible, the use of simple gain measures (pre and posttest only). Instead, attempt calculating expected growth for groups of students based on prior performance. • Educate participants to the difference between value-added and simple growth before voting to approve the design (see chapter 3 for additional information on value-added assessment).

Standards and Expectations

Standards for K–2, noncore, and specialists are sometimes difficult to pin down. In some cases they are available through their national organizations and through the state or school district standards. Without an external guide, expectations are also difficult to monitor. What one teacher thinks is a reasonable expectation might seem to be a stretch to another. Others are reluctant to set expectations altogether because they don't feel that one or two assessments can measure the whole child. One alternative would be to utilize a portfolio assessment that supplements standardized tests.

Quality Assessments

Most teachers have access to district-developed assessments or commercially available measurement tools that they can use to set growth targets. In their absence, teachers will need to develop their own assessments to measure progress and have them approved by an evaluation team. The teacher must then conduct pretests at the beginning of the year, make a calculation of expected growth, set objectives, and conduct a posttest to determine whether expected growth targets were met.

Quality control for choosing, developing, and scoring assessments should be incorporated into any plan that links student outcomes to pay. In the case of specialists who teach multiple grade levels, what assessment should they be using and who should administer and grade the assessment? As in the Charlotte-Mecklenburg example, while teacher-developed assessments are considered a valid measurement tool, they pose other problems when a teacher's salary is tied to students' performance on that assessment. To address this challenge, teachers could use a team approach to developing and grading assessments.

Population Size and Subgrouping

Another issue for districts to address is the way student populations should be determined for developing student growth objectives. For example, in a Denver teacher's classroom, a common objective might be that 75 percent or 80 percent of students score at a particular level, leaving 20 percent to 25 percent of the class out of the equation. Another population size issue is raised by those who only teach students in short increments—semesters or trimesters. In Denver, teachers who teach smaller groups of students for semester intervals are permitted to create shorter-term SGOs for their students. This means that a teacher has a choice between setting one objective for each semester or two objectives to span the entire school year.

Differentiating Performance

While performance rubrics can help us differentiate performance levels on the input side of the equation, how can this be reliably done with our three groups without value-added as our outcome? There are several approaches that districts can explore to differentiate performance and progress on the OPE career ladder (see figure 1.2 in chapter 1), based on the best fit for their population and needs: (1) focus on the number of goals that an educator achieves; (2) focus on the quality and rigor of the objectives and only advance those who meet the most challenging goals; (3) connect building or grade-level value-added scores to the SGOs of individuals not covered by value-added in a way similar to Houston's ASPIRE Program.

Option 1: Increasing Quantity of Goals. The simplest approach for differentiating SGOs is to increase the quantity of the goals achieved. For example, where value-added scores are not available, require that staff establish and meet two SGOs each year, as Denver does, in order to continue cost-of-living salary increases and maintain their position on the career ladder. To move up a rung on the career ladder, K–2, noncore, and specialist teachers might be asked to set three SGOs each year for three years in a row, and to achieve 100 percent of these goals over the three years. This process parallels the fact that value-added uses three-year running averages and rewards additional effort made by the educator. It does not, however, necessarily guarantee that excellence has been achieved, as there are no requirements for the rigor of the objectives.

Option 2: Using Quality and Rigor to Differentiate Performance. If the priority is rewarding outstanding performance, the quality of the objectives rather than the quantity must become the focus. Ensuring quality and rigor involves more work on the part of development teams to establish clear standards and definitions of what "high-quality" looks like, and more training for principals and supervisors to aid them in evaluating the quality and rigor of the objectives.

Districts could use a peer-review process to establish and maintain quality. Teams for each content area not covered by value-added might work to establish a rating system or rubrics for SGOs that places them into two tiers: A Tier One objective might be one that follows the approved guidelines but is not especially ambitious. A Tier Two objective would be an objective that was judged by peer reviewers to be ambitious, or a "stretch goal." Educators could be required to set different numbers of Tier One and Tier Two goals to advance on the career ladder.

Option 3: Using Group Level Value-Added With or Without SGOs. Districts interested in reinforcing the interdependency between K–2, noncore, and specialists and their colleagues might offer these educators the option of using the building- or grade-level value-added gain score in combination with two SGOs—or by it- self—to determine advancement on the career ladder. If the building exceeds ex- pectations and they meet the two SGOs and get advanced ratings on their evalua- tions, they are able to advance on the ladder. This is similar to the approach used by the TAP program. The risk, of course, is that individual educators might be highly effective but the team does not perform well, or the team might do well de- spite a particular teacher's ineffective performance. Furthermore, this approach is not as job-embedded as the SGO approach.

Simple Gains versus Value-Added

An important reality must be acknowledged when using growth or gain scores in areas not covered by value-added analysis: value-added analysis is a complex, robust statistical method that uses a student's performance history to calculate a projected trajectory of learning. The extent to which the student stays on or di- verts from this trajectory is attributed (in part) to the teacher effect. It is based on multiple years of data and requires that assessments are valid and reliable, vertically scaled, annually administered, aligned with the curriculum, and have sufficient "stretch" to adequately test the lowest and highest achievers in the class.

Given these criteria, value-added cannot be truly simulated in K–2, specialist, and noncore academic classrooms. Provisions can be made for expected growth and progress can be measured, and though these measures will show the real gains of the students in the classroom, they are not equivalent to the teacher effect cap- tured by value-added analysis. This does not mean that attempts should not be made to measure student learning in these disciplines, but rather that educators should be made aware of the differences between the methodologies.

IMPLEMENTATION GUIDELINES

Moving forward, districts should consider the information in this chapter to de- cide which option to pursue when compensating educators in subjects outside of those tested by value-added methodology. Table 7.2 provides a summary of the various approaches discussed, as well as their respective rationales.

Districts interested in pursuing an equitable approach, where all teachers and specialists are eligible for individual awards based on student outcomes, will need to plan how to differentiate student growth in the absence of value-added data. Table 7.3 describes the range of options discussed previously.

TABLE 7.2

Approaches to incorporating K–2, non-core and specialists in pay-for-performance plans

Option	Rationale	Examples
Attendance, Retention, or PD bonuses only.	Teachers who are not eligible for performance bonuses because of a lack of student achievement data should still be rewarded for their attendance, commitment, and fulfillment of professional development requirements.	Guilford County, NC www.gcsnc.com/ depts/mission_possible/ index.htm
Include them in individual bonuses but to a lesser degree.	Because value-added scores are not available to K–2, 9–12, non-core and non-instructional staff, these groups are eligible for individual bonuses based on composite group scores. These awards are lower than those made to teachers in the high-stakes testing areas. The rationale is presumably that these group composites cannot be reliably attached to an individual, so there is a lower payment to cover this margin of error.	Houston's ASPIRE Program www.houstonisd.org/aspire
Include them in group awards only.	This is a typical state approach, which awards bonuses to high-performing schools and districts, but leaves the assigning of individual bonuses to the locals. In most cases they are allocated based on the number of certified employees in a building.	Texas Educator Excellence Award www.tea.state.tx.us Florida Merit Award Program www.fldoe.org/justforteachers/ North Carolina-ABC Program http://abcs.ncpublicschools.org
Include K–2 but not non-core and specialists in individual bonuses.	There is no official testing program in place for non-core teachers and specialists, so there is no reliable measure for student growth that can be attributed to them. K–2 teachers can be handled with other types of reliable measures.	Charlotte-Mecklenburg, NC www.cms.k12.nc.us Chattanooga, TN www.pefchattanooga.org
Include them fully in the plan through group awards.	50% of the individual bonus calculation is based on professional evaluation, and the other 50% is based on the building's value-added score.	Teacher Advancement Program: National Program www.talentedteachers.org
Include them fully in all aspects of the plan.	While no official or standardized testing is available for these groups, student growth can be measured using locally developed tests or off-the-shelf tests approved by the district. This enables every professional to take part in the program.	Denver's ProComp Program http://Denverprocomp.org

TABLE 7.3

Options for differentiation of student growth in the absence of value-added

Option	Rationale	Pros	Cons	Example
Increase quantity of growth objectives to be achieved.	This requires additional effort and commitment that should be rewarded.	Students are receiving more intensive instruction.	Does not ensure that the objectives being established are rigorous.	For teachers to advance on the career ladder, they must meet three student growth objectives three years in a row instead of two in one year.
Increase the rigor of the growth objectives to be achieved.	The growth objectives should mirror as closely as possible the value-added measure of "exceeding" growth expectations.	This makes the system more similar to that of value-added staff and ensures that excellence is being achieved.	Even with a rigorous peer-review process in place, it is still not a perfect match to value-added measures. Some areas may get closer to others depending on the assessments being used, but significant capacity is also required to differentiate and evaluate the objectives.	Two tiers of growth objectives are designed by peer review to delineate "stretch" growth versus expected growth. In order to advance on the career ladder, a teacher opts to set one high-tier or stretch goal in addition to her two expected growth goals.
Associate with a group value-added score in addition to a teacher's individual growth objectives or instead of them.	Using value-added to measure, at least in part, what a teacher's contribution might be gets us a little closer to equity with other staff.	Provides a statistically valid measure.	The group that a teacher is assigned to may do well when the teacher did not, or the group may not do well when the teacher did.	To advance on the career ladder, educators must not only meet their own growth objectives, but must be willing to be judged by a grade level or subject composite value-added score.

Regardless of the option chosen, all districts will need to design a comprehensive communication and implementation plan based on the following general principles:

- Seek proper buy-in and collaboration from all stakeholders.
- Insist on transparency.
- Develop thorough communication, professional development, and coaching programs for the system.
- Let those who will be held accountable take the lead in designing and supervising the development of the system.
- Address or mitigate hardship factors before they become a source of resistance.
- Ensure scoring honesty and inter-rater reliability through a team scoring approach.
- Allow multiple measures to determine student growth, not just one test.
- Don't reinvent the wheel. Start with current models from other districts that are working and refine them to meet local needs and conditions.
- Understand the difference between value-added and simple gains and make sure others do as well.
- Match evaluators and supervisors based on content area expertise whenever possible and provide professional development to fill in gaps for out-of-field evaluators.
- Determine desired outcomes up front and evaluate constantly.

The task is not simple. The road may be a long one. But, using the work that has already been done by pioneers in Denver, Houston, TAP, and others, districts have some examples to guide them.[3] It has not been the intent of this chapter to provide a one-size-fits-all solution to the important question of how to equitably or equally include K–2, noncore teachers, and specialists in pay-for-performance systems. The main objective has been to ground readers in the important issues to be considered. It is our hope that districts interested in implementing pay-for-performance plans sincerely consider the options presented and reward the hard work of all educators laboring in our schools.

PART III

Support for Educators

CHAPTER EIGHT

Integrated Assessment—Summative, Formative, and Assessment for Learning

MARGARET JORGENSEN

CLAIRE ROBERTSON-KRAFT

THEODORE HERSHBERG

Where once there were different standards required for success following high school, depending on whether one chose military service, higher education, or the world of work, there is now a convergence around a common set of requisite skills and knowledge. Unfortunately, even when students graduate meeting academic proficiency on state and district assessments, they typically fall far short of the level now required for success.[1] States and districts need to adopt both higher standards and much improved summative assessments that address a broader range of cognitive skills and content. This need suggests that America would be well served by a national system of high-quality standards and assessments.

Even though most current assessments are imperfect proxies for the needed skills, research has shown that use of formative assessment can give rise to unprecedented gains in student achievement and that these results are especially pronounced for low achievers.[2] Not only does quality assessment provide teachers with valuable information about their students' progress so they can adjust their classroom instruction, but if used appropriately, it can also empower students to take ownership over their own learning process.

To achieve these ends, districts need to create or acquire an integrated assessment system that is designed to increase—not merely monitor—student achievement. If teachers are held accountable for student learning results, districts should provide them with access throughout the school year to meaningful data that can be used strategically to drive their practice. These data must come from tests that are closely aligned to content standards, are reliable, and have sufficient stretch to allow students to show growth in what they know and can do. Additionally, assessment must not be viewed as a one-time process that occurs at the end of the year. Instead, an integrated assessment system needs to link high-quality summative exams that emphasize higher-order thinking skills with formative assessments throughout the school year. Furthermore, these assessments must yield usable data that provide teachers with information to improve the quality of their classroom instruction. In this chapter, Margaret Jorgensen, former senior vice president of Harcourt Educational Measurement, Claire Robertson-Kraft, associate director of Operation Public Education (OPE), and Theodore Hershberg, OPE's director, discuss how districts can design an assessment system that meets these criteria. This chapter draws heavily on the work of Richard Stiggins and his colleagues at the Assessment Training Institute.

INTRODUCTION

Assessment critics have argued that the current emphasis on accountability associated with high-stakes testing has led schools to limit curriculum, teachers to employ drill-and-kill instructional practices, and students to feel increased anxiety around performance. However, despite their shortcomings, when used strategically, current assessments provide districts with the opportunity to track the growth of individual students and identify areas for improvement.

The answer is not to abandon standardized testing. If districts want their students to graduate with the skills and knowledge required by the twenty-first-century global economy, they must press their states to adopt high-quality summative exams. The current movement toward rigorous internationally benchmarked national standards is welcomed and encouraging.[3] In the meantime, districts should develop or purchase assessments that help students develop critical thinking skills and change the way assessments are used to promote high-quality teaching and learning. They should begin by analyzing their current assessment practices to determine what holds educators back from more effectively using assessment to drive instruction. Then, they should implement practices that align with the following principles of an integrated system.[4]

PRINCIPLES OF AN INTEGRATED ASSESSMENT SYSTEM

Clear and Meaningful Standards for Student Learning

To develop an accurate vision for student learning, educators must have a clear understanding of the standards students are expected to master at each grade level and in each subject area. Though every district has likely already developed some set of expectations, these standards often represent discrete knowledge and skills or are too broad, and as a result, they are unnecessarily difficult for teachers to translate into daily lesson objectives. Additionally, the level of specificity varies state by state, as does the sheer quantity of the enumerated expectations for what should be taught at each grade level. In many cases, the scope and breadth of state content standards make it virtually impossible for teachers to be effective.[5] Perhaps most problematic is the fact that content standards are not prioritized in terms of significance.

When designing an integrated assessment system, districts should first determine common outcomes for student learning. The end result must be a set of standards that represent the knowledge and skills students should be taught at various levels of the system. Districts need to ensure that this content possesses several distinct characteristics:

- *Assesses truly important standards.* It is recommended that districts limit the number of standards per content level and grade level by identifying the key critical curricular aims.[6] Superintendents should rely on their curriculum and instructional staff leaders to identify and design systems that focus on these aims.
- *Provides teacher-palatable descriptions.* If educators are to help students meet standards, they must be able to interpret and apply them to instructional practice. To accelerate this process, districts should develop clear and succinct descriptions of each standard that highlight the knowledge and skills students will need to master.
- *Aligns across the grade levels.* To promote continuity across the system, district curriculum and instructional staff should ensure that these standards are aligned across all grade levels.

Multiple Purposes and Users

Assessment results must meet the needs of multiple users at various points in time. While summative assessments document yearlong achievement, ongoing assessments provide information on where students are along the path to mastery. Though each of these types of assessment results serves an important purpose, they will vary in use by different constituencies—teachers, students, policy makers, etc. Consequently, to build an effective assessment system, districts must consider who the decision makers are and what kind of assessment information will best meet their needs.

Summative Assessments. Summative assessments tell the user how each student performs on end-of-year content standards and should be characterized by higher-order thinking and problem-solving skills. Districts must administer summative assessments that are instructionally sensitive—that is, they reflect the actual thinking required by the objective and mirror the way it should be taught. The fundamental characteristic of such content is whether students who receive effective instruction are more likely to perform well on the exam.

On summative assessments used for accountability purposes, there are often significant social and political pressures to have a combination of multiple-choice items (prized for their efficiency of measurement) and open-ended items (prized for their demonstration of what students can produce without the advantage of having all option choices provided). There is also the persistent belief that open-ended items are much more likely to measure critical thinking skills. And while this debate on the pros and cons of different item types will not likely end soon, it is worth noting that the difference between low- and high-quality items for summative assessment is not whether they are multiple choice or open ended but whether they require students to engage in and reason through the targeted content.

To ensure high-quality multiple-choice summative assessment items, it is critical that well-accepted best practice techniques for writing and selecting operational items be followed: the stems must be clear, there must be one and only one correct answer, and the incorrect answers should be equally attractive and appear to be plausible, correct answers to students who do not have mastery of the skill being tested.

Formative Assessments. Districts should complement these summative assessments by creating or procuring high-quality formative assessments, which reflect student learning along the progression to mastery of a particular skill. While summative tests are intended to capture the impact of a course or a year's worth of learning, formative tests should be used throughout the year to verify student progress toward achieving these broader content standards. Students will not master a complex standard all at once but will begin by acquiring basic knowledge and skills and continue to progress until they are interacting with the content at a more rigorous level. Ongoing assessment should reflect this progression of skill development and provide specific information about students' misunderstandings.

Current debate in the field centers on the appropriate use of the term *formative assessment.* Some experts contend that formative assessment is a process used by teachers during instruction to adjust ongoing teaching and exists solely between them and their students—if a test publisher is involved, it is not formative assessment. For our purposes, the definition of formative assessment need not be this restrictive. Formative assessment can also be understood as systematic group-based assessment throughout the course of the year that can provide specific information about what students are or are not learning and where learning has broken down. Multiple types of formative assessment are necessary components of an integrated assessment system.

> *Benchmark assessments.* Benchmark tests should mirror the summative tests in content, format, and reporting and, as a result, accurately reflect student mastery and progress toward end-of-year targets. They should be given at sev-

eral points during the fall and spring to provide teachers with knowledge about how their students are doing in meeting the standards that will be measured on the summative exams. Benchmark assessments offer the following additional benefits:

- By exposing students to the format of the end-of-year test, benchmark assessments considerably reduce student anxiety on formal state tests.
- They provide valuable information as to whether material covered earlier in the year was retained or whether re-teaching is necessary.
- Because data on benchmark assessments can be aggregated at the school level, they can serve as the foundation for professional collaboration around classroom best practices.

Feedback assessments. Feedback assessments, in contrast, do not mirror the summative exams. They should be designed to provide teachers with a greater degree of information on how their students are doing across a broad range of indicators. To create these assessments, districts should begin breaking down the local standards into discrete knowledge and skills that will build over the course of the year. Districts should also develop suggested pedagogical interventions that will accompany these formative assessment results. For example, if a student misses a specific question, educators should be provided with insight as to what might be causing the misunderstanding and recommended instructional strategies for working with that particular student. In sum, feedback assessments reveal where the student is on the scaffolding leading up to mastery of a standard, provide educators with key information about what should come next in the learning process, and suggest appropriate strategies and resources for intervention.

Assessments for learning. The Assessment Training Institute has created a framework that synthesizes research-based recommendations for engaging students through assessment *for* learning best practices. Assessments *for* learning happen throughout the learning process to provide teachers with invaluable information about student needs, which they can use immediately to inform instructional practice and engage students. This process acknowledges the critical importance of the daily instructional decisions made by students and their teachers. Not only do students become consumers of assessment information by using evidence of their own progress to set and monitor goals, but continuous descriptive feedback also nourishes their belief that with hard work, success is possible. Currently, assessments *of* learning are the priority in most districts. If all students are going to be motivated to meet rigorous standards, districts must expand this purpose "to ensure that our classroom assessment practices maximize, not just measure, our students' achievement."[7]

These assessment *for* learning practices, elaborated in the book *Classroom Assessment for Student Learning: Doing It Right—Using It Well,* are organized around three fundamental requirements.[8] All students must know (1) where they are going, (2) where they are now, and (3) how to close the gap between the two. Educators can move students through this progression by employing the following strategies:

- *Provide a clear and understandable vision of the learning target.*
- *Use examples and models of strong and weak work.*
- *Offer regular descriptive feedback.*
- *Teach students to self-assess and set goals.*
- *Design lessons to focus on one aspect of quality at a time.*
- *Teach students focused revision.*
- *Engage students in self-reflection and let them keep track of and share their learning.*

It is critical to understand the fundamental differences in the kinds of information provided by these various assessments. Table 8.1 illustrates how different assessments can meet the needs of multiple users.

All parts of the system contribute to effective schooling. If assessment is not working effectively in the classroom, instructional support or policy levels of assessment cannot pick up the slack. If inaccurate decisions are being made during the learning process, benchmark or summative assessments cannot overcome the consequences for the learner. The essential question becomes how to ensure that all users are provided with the student achievement information they need in a clear and timely manner.

Effective Communication Systems

User-Friendly Language. Once assessments have been built, districts must develop systems that link information directly and automatically to instruction, and all constituencies—parents, students, teachers, principals—must understand how to use the data to maximize student achievement. To accomplish this, the information that is reported must be presented in an intuitive manner that mirrors the language educators use every day. If measurement terms such as *proficient* or *standard error* are required, they must be explained in a simple and straightforward manner with examples that are familiar to the relevant audiences.

Language must also be descriptive, not merely evaluative, so that students are clear on their strengths and next steps, and can be informed frequently about their progress and areas for improvement. Parents must understand what specific skills their children are lacking and what interventions are appropriate to employ at home. Accomplishing these goals will mean creating effective communications systems that are user-friendly and tailored to the needs of these various audiences.[9]

TABLE 8.1
Types and uses of assessments

Type of assessment	General purposes	Specific users/uses
Summative assessments	• Provide information about student mastery of achievement targets (typically on end-of-year exams). • Categorize students by levels of proficiency (often for promotion, graduation, grading decisions). • Evaluate the effectiveness of instructional programs and strategies.	*Students:* Understand how they are doing in relation to other classmates and if they hit the desired target. *Teachers:* Evaluate student proficiency on year-long content, determine which students should be retained and who is in need of special services. *Parents:* Determine if their child is where he/she needs to be and if the school is meeting his/her specific needs. *Principals:* Evaluate if instruction is producing desired results (and in which classrooms/for which types of students) and allocate resources based on need. *Superintendents:* Evaluate where instruction is producing desired results (which buildings/programs are working) and allocate resources based on need. *State policymakers:* Evaluate which programs/districts are producing desired results and allocate resources based on need.
Benchmark assessments	• Provide a snapshot of whole-class and individual mastery on end-of-year achievement targets. • Monitor growth in proficiency over time. • Prioritize standards for re-teaching, in both whole-class and small-group settings. • Help students (and their parents) understand how on track they are to mastering the required grade-level/subject-area content.	The users/needs are the same as those listed above. The difference is that benchmark assessments provide information during the course of the year, so data from these assessments can be used to make evaluations on a more frequent basis.
Feedback assessments	• Help teachers determine individual students' strengths and weaknesses on specific outcomes, as well as where learning is breaking down. • Provide teachers with information about how to target specific student misunderstandings.	*Students:* Understand which learning targets they are struggling with. *Teachers:* Diagnose individual student need to adjust instructional practices (grouping decisions, lesson explanations, focus skills, etc.). *Parents:* Understand what targeted skills can be reinforced at home.

continued

TABLE 8.1
Types and uses of assessments, *continued*

Type of assessment	General purposes	Specific users/uses
Assessments for learning	• Help teachers diagnose student need in the moment, so they can immediately adjust their instruction. • Provide students with key insights, so they can monitor their own growth and take ownership over the learning process.	*Students:* Understand how they are progressing over time and what they should do next to accelerate their learning. *Teachers:* Diagnose individual student need to adjust instructional practices in the moment (pacing, student conferencing, etc.).

Source: Drawn in part from Stephen Chappuis, Richard J. Stiggins, Judith Arter, and Jan Chappuis, *Assessment FOR Learning: An Action Guide for School Leaders.* (Portland, OR: Educational Testing Service, 2005), 22–24, 59–60; Rick Stiggins, Judith Arter, Jan Chappuis, and Steve Chappuis, *Classroom Assessment for Student Learning* (Portland, OR: Educational Testing Service, 2006), 35–36.

Clear Display. Districts should take advantage of software programs to create effective information-management systems that display information clearly. As an example, the Wyoming Department of Education created a simple "stoplight" report that quickly indicates how a student or group of students are doing on specific content standards. If the student has a green mark, he or she has demonstrated proficiency on that specific content standard. If the mark is yellow, additional work may be required. If the mark is red, intervention is necessary. A stoplight report for classrooms, schools, and districts employs the same logic.

Recommended Interventions. An effective communication system should not only display information in an understandable manner but must also suggest appropriate student interventions and teacher actions. To accomplish this, districts could index instructional content and recommended lessons and strategies by individual standards. As an example, the asTTle program in New Zealand distributes tests and instructional materials on a CD-ROM and recommends interventions and resources based on student assessment results. (For more information, see www.tki.org.nz/r/asttle/index_e.php.)

High-Quality Professional Development

To realize the value of an integrated assessment system, educators must be provided the professional development necessary to internalize the standards their students are to master; understand the principles of sound assessment practice; use data to inform practice; and become proficient in specific instructional strategies that will help engage their students in the learning process. Unfortunately, many teachers and school administrators have not been given the opportunity to use data to assess student learning, as neither preservice nor in-service teacher training programs typically include this kind of professional development.

Districts implementing an integrated assessment system must understand that by itself, assessment cannot increase student achievement, and we cannot circumvent the need to develop deeper assessment expertise among our teacher corps.[10] Changing the culture of assessment in schools will not be easy, as building assessment competence requires that educators rethink foundational aspects of their teaching practice. Consequently, districts must provide the professional development needed for faculties to understand the principles of sound assessment practice and design steps for creating a productive learning environment that maximizes the use of these assessments. To accomplish these goals, high-quality professional development must consider the appropriate content and the ideal dissemination method:

Content. Teachers must master the following skills:[11]

- designing tests and test items that align with achievement targets
- sampling and scoring work to provide an accurate picture of student learning
- interpreting and using assessment results to alter instruction (student groupings, curriculum pacing, etc.)
- identifying and clarifying learning goals in a student-friendly manner
- providing timely and understandable feedback that accelerates student improvement
- involving students in the learning process through self- and peer evaluation

Method. Districts will need to take the following steps to determine the ideal strategy for professional development:

Identifying and understanding the needs of the professional development participants. Districts should administer needs assessments to verify the current state of faculty understanding and practices in relation to what is known about best practices in assessment. The discrepancies identified then become the focus of professional development.[12]

Choosing delivery strategies. Given the specific content, evidence of effectiveness, and available resources, districts must select the intervention most likely to have the desired impact, for example, workshops, learning communities and study groups, conferences, in-class modeling and coaching, coteaching and reviewing data, or online study.

CHALLENGES AND CONSIDERATIONS

Designing Accurate Assessments

As discussed above, districts must begin improving assessments by prioritizing the appropriate content and aligning questions with these standards. Designing appropriate summative and benchmark assessments that meet this high bar will be a major challenge for districts. To ensure the validity and reliability of the designed assessments, specific measurement, content, and psychometric requirements—as detailed at www.nciea.org and www.cresst.org—must be met. These requirements outline how assessment developers can (1) create an acceptable level of precision, (2) protect against bias, and (3) ensure that test content remains fresh from year to year. Since item and test development are skills that require training and consistent feedback and review, districts within a state could attempt to join efforts and either build or buy benchmark tests that are aligned to their state standards.

Ensuring Rigor

In 1987, Lauren Resnick wrote, "We teach what we test. We don't teach what we don't test. And we had better test it the way we want it taught."[13] Resnick's plea was that the work that students were expected to do on tests would become the model for how teachers taught that content. If tests included writing, teachers would teach writing. If tests included only low-level skills, that is what teachers would teach.

To ensure that all students can compete in the global marketplace, districts must develop or access more rigorous assessments that require complex cognitive skills and deeper content expertise than is now included on state achievement tests. As these tests become the standard for achievement, teachers will transform their instruction to help students master more demanding knowledge and skills.

Minimizing Cost

Testing is, ultimately, an economic activity. Given this reality, we must find ways to have tests that measure complex cognitive behaviors and that are aligned to critical content standards but that are within a district's budget. Examples from recent state tests reveal that appropriately constructed multiple-choice questions can in fact assess higher-order thinking skills, but these items must reflect the actual thinking required by the objective and mirror the way that it should be taught. Additionally, rather than having all of the answer choices be similar in cognitive complexity, incorrect choices must be crafted to capture specific student misunderstanding.

The costs of building assessments that are valid, reliable, and appropriately aligned to state content standards are substantial. To minimize the burden, districts should work collaboratively to demand that states and test publishers create this quality of assessment. Customer consolidation will make it clear to testing companies that only credible products will survive in the market.

Shifting Classroom Practice

To help educators understand that assessment is a valuable tool for improving student achievement, districts will need to transform the culture of assessment in their schools. In the past, assessments have been used primarily for accountability purposes, and now we are calling for a balanced system of both summative and formative assessments used to evaluate effectiveness and drive school improvement efforts. Instead of focusing solely on the adults, this integrated assessment system recognizes the importance of communicating information to all assessment users, including students. All educators will need ongoing support and time to make the necessary alterations in classroom practice.[14]

IMPLEMENTATION GUIDELINES

This section provides districts with guidelines for addressing these challenges and developing excellence in assessment practice. It is important to note that though districts may choose to modify their approach depending on their initial status, capacity, and budget, the same general guidelines apply.

Diagnose current assessment practices. The Assessment Training Institute has developed recommendations for districts that are compiling an inventory of all current assessments. This analysis should reveal whose needs are being met and which standards are being assessed. The Institute suggests that districts analyze current assessments based on the following characteristics:[15]

- amount of time required for administering the test
- students tested
- specific achievement targets
- specific state or district standards assessed through those test items
- specific assessment method used
- how the results will be reported
- intended users of results and decisions made based on those results
- procedures for communicating the results to relevant users

Create an assessment and reporting schedule. There is a fine line between frequent enough testing to ensure that learning gaps are quickly identified and therefore addressed and a drill-and-kill mentality. We recommend testing critical content standards on a monthly basis throughout the year, which means that districts' formative assessment systems will need to create eight or nine appropriate tests per grade and content area. These tests must be quickly scored, and the data should be made accessible to teachers within days, not weeks, and certainly not months. When data is readily available, assessment systems allow teachers to meet the learning needs of each student.

Design a sustainable structure. Creating a new culture of assessment will take time and investment, making both sustainability and capacity-building essential considerations. Data-driven instruction is not going to be at the forefront of teachers' minds unless it is a requirement from the administration and an expectation from peers and parents. Building principals, superintendents, and curriculum and instruction leaders within a district all need to focus on these data. With continuous review and discussion of how to improve learning based on evidence, teachers (and students) will eventually become advocates of data-driven instruction. But mastering the professional development content discussed above will require significant changes in current teacher practice that are developed over time. From the teacher's point of view, a lack of time to engage in high-quality assessment practices is likely to be viewed as a significant obstacle. As such, release time must be provided so that educators can engage with their colleagues as members of learning communities, creating the opportunity for enhanced student achievement and professional growth.[16]

CONCLUSION

An integrated assessment system should serve as the foundation for comprehensive school reform efforts. Without this system, districts cannot know if students are on track to attain the level of achievement they need to succeed in the global economy, or if teachers are effective in supporting individual students' learning needs. In the current system, assessment has mainly been used for evaluation purposes and as the basis for making high-stakes accountability decisions. If all students are going to be motivated to meet rigorous standards, we must expand this purpose to ensure that our assessment practices also enhance students' achievement.

CHAPTER NINE

Value-Added as a Classroom Diagnostic

JOEL GIFFIN

THEODORE HERSHBERG

CLAIRE ROBERTSON-KRAFT

In providing educators with unique data collected at the classroom level, value-added assessment can transform the quality of instruction. Patterns emerge from these data that allow teachers for the first time in their careers to learn which students were the focus of their instruction (previously low, average, or high achieving) and what the impact of their instruction was (how effective it was in providing students with expected growth from where they began the year). Value-added data helps teachers to differentiate instruction, understand the growth trajectories of their students, and develop appropriate intervention strategies.

Value-added reports can also serve as the basis for strategic school improvement decisions. Accompanied by high-quality training discussed in the following chapter, school leaders will have the requisite data and skill set to make strategic decisions about student groupings, curricula, and professional development, and teachers can form learning communities to engage in informed discussions about how to improve their instructional practices. Even when not part of an evaluation and compensation system, value-added can be used by administrators to ensure that struggling students are matched with stronger teachers to help them make up lost ground.

In this chapter, Theodore Hershberg and Claire Robertson-Kraft provide districts with information about value-added reports, generated by the EVAAS SAS Institute, Inc., and how they can be used to evaluate the effectiveness of instruction. Then, Joel Giffin, a recently retired middle school principal with thirty-three years' tenure and now an educational consultant, explains the innovative model he developed using value-added data to make Maryville Middle School the most successful school in Tennessee in accelerating student progress. Though value-added was just one part of his strategic approach, it was instrumental to the school's success. It is hard to argue with the remarkable results of his methods: a ten-year average of 144 percent of the national norm growth in math, science, reading, language arts, and social studies.

REFLECTIVE REPORTING

Value-added data can transform the quality of instruction by providing educational entities with measures of their influence on student academic progress at three levels: teacher, school, and district. Reporting from these analyses engages educators in school improvement in two distinct ways—reflectively, by quantifying the effects of previous policies and practices, and proactively, by providing a reliable metric of students' likelihood of reaching important academic performance levels in the future. Equipped with this information, teachers, principals, administrators, and school board leaders can assess the extent to which schools and classroom teachers are effective in raising performance and make strategic decisions to increase student achievement.

District and School Reports

As discussed in chapter 3, districts must create systems that display value-added results in user-friendly ways so that information can drive school improvement efforts. To provide an accurate assessment of student progress, it is essential that district reporting systems provide results by student subgroup, in addition to district and school averages. For example, in figure 9.1, value-added scores report the performance of five levels of achievement, ranging from the lowest-performing to the

FIGURE 9.1
Fourth-grade math

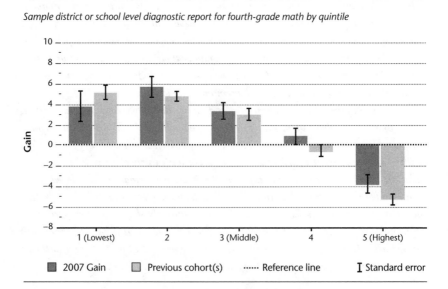

Sample district or school level diagnostic report for fourth-grade math by quintile

highest-performing students. These results illustrate which groups of students made greater than expected gains and which made less than adequate progress in relation to the state average growth (represented by the horizontal reference line at zero) on the fourth-grade math test given in Tennessee, the Tennessee Comprehensive Assessment Program, or TCAP. Data from the previous cohort of students are also included, so that districts and schools can compare this year's students with the previous cohort's performance. The standard error represents the measure of uncertainty around the score.

The results in figure 9.1 demonstrate that although students entering fourth grade at lower-achieving levels are meeting the growth standard, the higher-achieving students in level five have made insufficient progress in the current year. The light-gray bar indicates that comparably prepared fourth graders in previous years have also made insufficient progress. If data had not been broken down by subgroup, then district and school officials may have incorrectly assumed that all students were making the expected gain.

Teacher Reports

Reporting systems should also produce analyses similar to the ones above for individual teachers so that they can assess the progress rates that groups of students— low, average, or above average in achievement—have made relative to what was expected. The report shown in figure 9.2 is structured the same way as was discussed above, with three instead of five levels of achievement.

In this specific example, Teacher 2 at ABC Elementary School is highly effective in fifth-grade math. Note that Teacher 2's gain is decidedly greater than the growth standard, taking into account 2.0 standard errors associated with that teacher's estimate. In the bar chart at the bottom of the teacher's report, observe that this highly effective teacher has made reasonable progress with students at different achievement levels in the class, though the lowest- and highest-achieving students have made the most progress.

Student Projections

Since the goal of the K–12 educational system is for students to leave twelfth grade prepared to meet real-world demands, a system of student projections can offer districts a longitudinal view to assess the distance to that goal. In other words, these projections can predict the likelihood that each student will reach a variety of academic milestones, thus enabling policy makers to better assess the resources required to meet expectations and allowing educators to design appropriate interventions—personal education plans, or PEPs—for individual students.[1] This proactive use of more reliable information at the individual student level increases the likelihood that all students will benefit from schooling.

FIGURE 9.2
Teacher value-added report for 2007 sample district

School: ABC Elementary School
Teacher: Teacher 2
Subject: Math grade 5

Year	Teacher NCE gain	Std error of gain	Growth standard	Teacher comparison
2007	2.8	1.2	0.0	Above

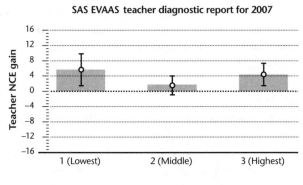

SAS EVAAS teacher diagnostic report for 2007

Source: SAS EVAAS®

Several sets of projections can be made from these data. The first set is designed to determine the likelihood that students will meet minimal proficiencies in future years; for example, whether a student will pass the eighth-grade algebra exam if he or she continues along the same trajectory. With this knowledge, educators can identify populations of students who are going to require entirely different curricular and instructional strategies. The second set determines which students are on track to meeting high school graduation requirements. These data can be especially useful for policy makers who are interested in decreasing the dropout rate by employing targeted early intervention strategies. The third set of projections determines whether students are on track for meeting requirements for higher education institutions, and the final set predicts the likelihood of success in specific college majors. In each of these instances, the results allow educators to determine appropriate intervention strategies for maximizing students' achievement.

INTERPRETING VALUE-ADDED DATA

These value-added reports make it possible for educators to have information that enables them to establish two critical determinants of effective practice. The first identifies the focus of their practice: the students—previously low, average, or high achieving—who have been the target, either purposefully or inadvertently, of their teaching. The second describes the impact of their practice: how successful they have been—ineffective, effective, or highly effective—in providing their student populations as a whole, as well as those in each achievement group, with appropriate academic progress commensurate with their past rate of growth.

Using this information, teachers, principals, district administrators, and school board members can learn whether previously low, average, or high achievers are making the most progress, and the extent to which individual schools and classroom teachers are effective in raising student performance.

Instructional Focus

Using the early data collected from Tennessee in the development of the Tennessee Value-Added Assessment System (TVAAS), Dr. William Sanders identified three distinct progress patterns whose names reflect the shape of the slopes in the descriptive charts. These patterns can be found in any classroom, school, or district, but they occur disproportionately in the circumstances described below.

The shed pattern (see figure 9.3) may be observed in schools or classrooms in low-income communities, where the incidence of precocious students tends to fall consistently over time. Teachers in these schools, faced with many low-performing children, focus on the bottom of the student distribution so that previously low achievers score high gains from where they began the school year, while previously average and high achievers get low gains. Sustaining this focus of instruction in elementary school results in few high-achieving children by middle school. The problem is not the attention to students in the bottom of the distribution, but rather the absence of attention to average and above-average achieving students.

The reverse shed pattern (see figure 9.4), found disproportionately in high-income districts, reveals the opposite. Here teachers appear to respond to the central concern of their communities by concentrating on their highest performers. As a result, previously low and average achievers get low gains, while previously high-achievers get high gains.

The final pattern is the tent (see figure 9.5). In these classrooms, teachers are concerned with the average performer. By focusing on the middle of the distribution, both previously low and high achievers get low gains, while the previously average achievers get high gains. This pattern typically indicates a scenario with a narrowly defined interpretation of the curricular window for a grade and subject,

FIGURE 9.3
Shed pattern: instructional focus on previously low achievers

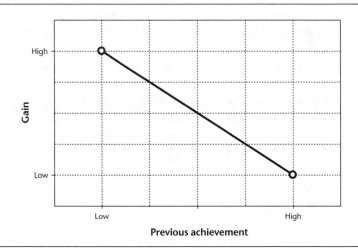

FIGURE 9.4
Reverse shed pattern: instructional focus on previously high achievers

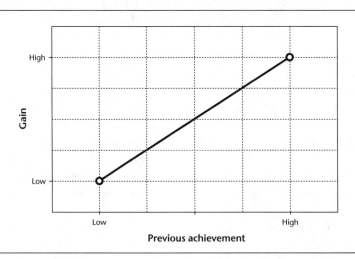

FIGURE 9.5
Tent pattern: instructional focus on previously average achievers

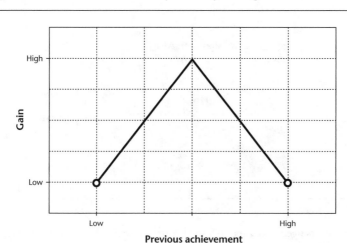

and with little or no evidence of differentiated instruction according to the specific academic needs of the students attending the class.

Instructional Impact

To describe the impact of instruction on student learning, value-added assessment provides estimates of schooling influence by districts, schools, and teachers for a given grade or subject. A three-year average of these estimates provides a more conservative metric than one year's worth of data for use in accountability or school improvement plans.

These instructional results can be characterized as follows (see figure 9.6): highly effective—students are "stretched" so that their performance significantly exceeds their records of past achievement; effective—students make appropriate growth from where they began the year; and ineffective—students' performance consistently and significantly falls below the level of achievement they demonstrated in past years.

When the data from these patterns are combined, educators can see simultaneously the focus and impact of their instruction. In evaluating the combined patterns, educators must always keep in mind students' achievement levels before deciding whether the growth or value-added patterns are satisfactory or whether they

FIGURE 9.6
Value-added: three instructional results

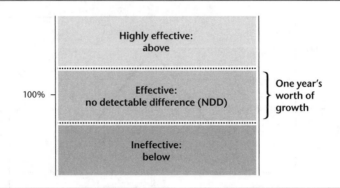

need to be changed. Teaching in a shed pattern (see figure 9.7), for example, means one thing if the instruction is effective for all groups of students and quite another if the instruction for all groups is ineffective.

For example, a shed pattern where students at all achievement levels have made appropriate progress but the lower-achieving students have been significantly accelerated in their progress would be a desired pattern for schools facing

FIGURE 9.7
Instructional focus and impact

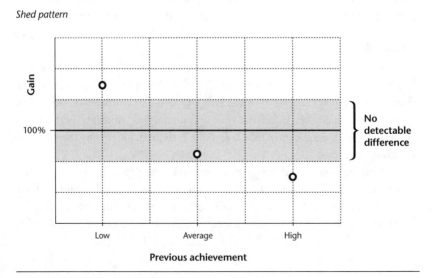

the federal requirements of No Child Left Behind (NCLB). But in defining adequate yearly progress (AYP) only in terms of achievement rather than growth, NCLB created what many call a "perverse incentive" for educators: focus like a laser beam on one group of students to the exclusion of all others—those close to but below proficiency. Schools could choose to ignore students far below proficiency and those whose scores already exceed proficiency, the argument goes, because the prime directive in federal law is for schools to hit their annual AYP targets.[2] Teaching in these patterns long predates NCLB, and AYP might simply illuminate the fact that the gains made by those who start just below proficiency are coming at the expense of those who start the year above it or far below it. In either instance, higher-achieving students in the most challenging schools continue to have less opportunity for academic progress.[3]

USING VALUE-ADDED DATA

Value-added assessment by itself does not improve student achievement. But if educators are committed to analyzing the valuable data it provides and use what they learn to guide instruction and professional development, and if administrators create an environment that encourages these activities, more students will be able to achieve at higher levels. Value-added assessment can catalyze high-quality instruction in many ways.

First, it provides unique assessments of effectiveness for districts, schools, and classrooms. The reports discussed above allow educators to reflect on what has and hasn't worked and design appropriate interventions to improve student learning opportunities. This information has additional benefits at the policy level. As an example, upon receiving student projections, one principal realized that even though over one hundred students were projected to be on the trajectory for success in eighth-grade algebra upon the completion of sixth grade, the school only had twenty-one seats for this class. This is one example of poor resource allocation and capacity at the school level. Superintendents could use these student projections to estimate the number of seats required in classrooms for students with various academic levels, enabling them to deploy resources accordingly and ensure that all students reach their maximum educational potential.

Regardless of entering achievement, all students must be engaged in learning that targets their specific academic needs, and policy makers need a realistic understanding of the funding and resources required to make this type of educational programming possible. For schools serving more academically at-risk students, the primary use of resources would be to improve instructional strategies for lower-achieving students. However, for students at these schools who have already achieved proficiency, the focus should remain on ensuring that they are in a position to meet graduation requirements and be competitive in their desired college majors. Teachers, curricular specialists, and service providers can develop educational opportunities and curricula that specifically target each student's present academic performance and future academic aspirations.

Second, appropriate use of value-added assessment can end the isolation of teachers by bringing them together to collectively discuss their student-progress patterns. Learning communities form as teachers explore ways to change student growth patterns in desired directions and meet regularly with their colleagues to discuss what they have learned. In these ways, the potential diagnostic value of these patterns of focus and impact can be realized if the data are used by teachers to improve instruction.

As discussed in chapter 10, teachers must be trained to effectively utilize these data. Imagine a session at which all six of a school's fifth-grade teachers convene to discuss the efficacy of their math instruction. Everyone present has a copy of each other's value-added patterns, and whoever serves as the instructional leader begins by asking, for example, the highly effective teachers—those most successful with previously low-, average-, or high-achieving students—to explain their pedagogical strategies. The chances that math instruction will improve in that school have just been raised significantly. Value-added data, in short, can serve as the foundation on which to build a learning community.

Another illustration of the diagnostic utility of value-added is provided in the experience of a high school English department chairman (see figure 9.8). He ex-

FIGURE 9.8
Example: high school english department

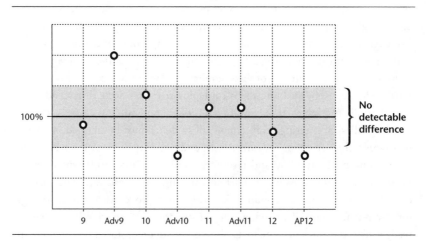

amined the performance of eight teachers in grades nine through twelve who taught either a regular English class or an advanced class. In five of the eight classrooms, students were making appropriate progress from where they began the year. But, in the ninth-grade advanced classroom, previously high-achieving students were being stretched academically, and in the tenth-grade advanced classroom, they were losing ground.

Since the teachers in the advanced ninth- and tenth-grade classrooms were assigned because the chairman believed them both to be excellent instructors, he found the results puzzling. This example is presented with caution. The easy explanation is that there was something wrong with the tenth-grade teacher's classroom instruction. That turns out, however, not to be the case. The real problem was that the tenth-grade instructor did not communicate with his colleague teaching ninth grade and hence didn't know that these students were performing at exceptionally high levels. As a result, he spent a good part of the fall term reviewing what these students had already mastered, thus depriving them of the growth to which they were entitled.

Effective educational practice, in other words, must also extend to behaviors outside rather than simply inside classrooms. It reinforces the importance of course articulation, monitoring the content of courses across grade levels to avoid repetition and to ensure that the pace of learning is sustained. This is especially consequential between lower and middle school and middle and high school, where students often experience suppressed progress rates as compared to students in the same grades and subjects who do not move from one building to another.

Third, school leaders as well as teachers will have the requisite data to drive decisions about curricula and professional development. States now have the opportunity to provide appropriate datasets to undertake analyses that will yield critically valuable results about what does and does not work. Experiments can be constructed that hold constant the achievement levels of students and the value-added effectiveness of teachers to determine which, among competing curricula modules or professional development interventions, are making measurable differences in students' academic progress.

Finally, value-added analysis can have a positive impact on the morale of teachers working in low-income, high-minority, or working-class school districts if they do a good job in providing their students with appropriate academic progress each year. Districts that historically have ranked low in standings based on achievement tests can compete for the first time on a level playing field with schools in wealthier communities, because their rank will be determined by value-added results rather than by absolute test scores that are highly influenced by family income.

A CASE STUDY: MARYVILLE MIDDLE SCHOOL

Value-added data served as the foundation of a comprehensive school renewal model at Maryville Middle School, which also included integrating technology into the core curriculum, engaging students through interdisciplinary projects, and instituting a schoolwide discipline program. The remarkable impact of this model on student progress is demonstrated in table 9.1.

In this section, we focus on the role value-added reporting played in the larger model. It was used to access information about the progress of all students—previously high, medium, and low achieving—and enabled the administration to take the following steps:

- *Create strategic placements for students and teachers.* Plans were developed for all students based on their specific learning profile. Teachers were then matched strategically to classes based on their respective strengths with different subgroups of students.
- *Train staff to be data-driven instructional decision makers.* Staff meetings were used to train staff on interpreting and utilizing data to guide instructional decisions.
- *Design meaningful academic intervention.* Value-added data helped to identify low-performing students, who were provided extra support during the school day through the development of academic intervention classes.

Create Strategic Placements for Students and Teachers

Student Groupings. Value-added data help educators form strategic groupings, allowing each student to reach his or her maximum learning potential. Districts and

TABLE 9.1
Maryville Middle School's TVAAS student gains

Subjects grades 6, 7, 8	National benchmark norm (percentage)	Maryville scores ten-year average 1993–2002 (percentage)
Math	100	156.0
Reading	100	135.6
Language arts	100	183.6
Social studies	100	107.5
Science	100	137.0
School average	100	144.0

schools should base grouping decisions on available resources and student need, and grouping decisions must be grounded in what is best for individual students. Maryville Middle School employed the following three grouping strategies (refer to table 9.2).

Educators at Maryville Middle School used prior achievement data to identify the appropriate placement for every student in each subject. These placements were based on academic achievement, not behavior or level of effort, and both the principal and parents were required to review and sign off on student placements. Once individual student plans had been created, this information was aggregated to determine the number of students who needed each subject by grade and level and used to determine the number of sections that would be required for each level of the course.

Homogenous groupings of this nature offered some clear advantages. In a typical classroom of twenty-five students at Maryville Middle School, half of the students are on grade level and the remaining students are scattered across a wide range of instructional levels. When provided with a choice of teaching a class like this or one of thirty-five students grouped homogenously by achievement, teachers invariably selected the latter because it significantly reduced the burden of differentiating instruction. This decision, in turn, gave the principal the capacity to create small classes for the students most in need.

TABLE 9.2
Grouping strategies

Type of student grouping	Description	Impact on teaching and learning
Heterogeneous	Includes students from the same grade with various levels of academic achievement.	Despite being the most common form of grouping in K–12 education today, the wide range of ability makes it extremely difficult, if not impossible, for teachers to effectively meet all students' needs. Despite these shortcomings, sometimes heterogeneous groupings are beneficial because students can learn from their peers.
Homogeneous	Includes students from the same grade level with similar levels of academic achievement.	Because students are most likely to succeed when they are in sync with their curriculum, this type of grouping leads to targeted learning and a reduction in the incidence of behavior problems.
Multi-grade	Includes students from different grade levels with similar curriculum and instructional needs.	Multigrade grouping uses research-based instruction and technology to serve students who demonstrated a need for additional support and remediation.

Matching Teacher Strengths to Student Needs. To match teacher strength with student needs, individual teachers plotted the scores of their students from the current year against the previous year. By arraying diagnostic value-added data, teachers could determine their relative effectiveness with low-, middle-, or high-performing students in each subject and grade and reflect on strengths and areas for improvement. Teachers were subsequently assigned groups of students based on their effectiveness with each group.

These groupings maximized both student and teacher potential. With the use of value-added data, teachers were placed with the students they could best serve, resulting in instruction of the highest possible caliber. Lower student-teacher ratios in lower-ability classes allowed for individualized instruction and extra support for students who needed it most. Because students were in sync with their curriculum, behavioral problems decreased and motivation increased substantially.

Once a placement was made, additional staff meetings were held on an as-needed basis to monitor student progress and evaluate whether the current placement was in the student's best interest. Since the appropriate placement of each student is critical, students could be moved from one group to another at any time, ensuring that the system was always designed to maximize student potential.

This assignment process does not always work seamlessly, but the guiding principle is clear: principals should use value-added data to make assignment decisions by matching teacher strength to student need. Operating in this way dramatically increases student learning while simultaneously boosting teacher morale.

Train Staff to Be Data-Driven Instructional Decision Makers

Through a collaborative process, the administration, departmental teams, and interdisciplinary teams thoroughly analyzed value-added data. Meetings, held annually and on an ongoing basis as needed, were designed to train staff on how best to interpret and use data to inform instructional practice.

Interpreting Data. The staff learned to slice data by student subgroup and identify trends in performance. Once teachers identified subgroup progress and gaps, the team discussed what might be leading to these results: Why were certain subgroups excelling? What was holding the groups of students with lower growth rates back? Did they lack motivation? Understanding? By grounding the conversation in data, the focus remained on the ultimate goal: raising academic achievement for all students.

Using Data to Inform Instructional Practice. After the initial data analysis was completed, teachers began to reflect on which of their actions contributed to student outcomes. The focus was on celebrating success as well as exploring areas for improvement. Specifically, teams would discuss how to sustain and modify instructional choices and curricular/grouping decisions that would maximize student achievement.

Teachers must be provided with ownership over the process of data analysis. If provided with this type of active role, as discussed above, they are more likely to be invested in the outcome. To build buy-in, it is important to always acknowledge and reward teachers' areas of strengths first. Doing so increases the likelihood that educators will be willing to engage in a meaningful discussion around instructional improvement. For the use of value-added data to be successful, districts must invest resources in high-quality value-added training for administrators and teachers (as discussed in chapter 10).

Design Meaningful Academic Intervention

Some students are significantly behind, and the instructional program simply does not provide enough time for them to catch up. To compound the problem, their low level of achievement often results in feelings of learned helplessness. Value-added data can help to identify these students so that educators can design appropriate academic intervention.

At Maryville Middle School, all students identified as requiring additional support were placed into an extra intervention class. With an additional full-time intervention teacher, these classes could remain small (seven or eight students). Because struggling students do not often get the necessary support either in or outside of school, intervention classes were designed so that students could receive assistance from the school's most effective classroom teachers within the school hours.

CONCLUSION

If used appropriately, the reporting discussed in this chapter has the potential to catalyze critical changes in the school system. However, if educators don't transform their behavior in response to the metric, no change will occur. Though not a panacea, value-added provides an unprecedented, rich opportunity to improve classroom instruction.

CHAPTER TEN

Value-Added Training

JAMES W. MAHONEY

MICHAEL THOMAS

JACQUELYN ASBURY

Value-added assessment by itself does not improve student achievement. However, if educators are committed to analyzing the valuable data it provides and using what they learn to guide instruction and professional development, and if administrators create an environment that encourages these activities, more students will be able to achieve at higher levels. To derive the full benefit of the value-added system, teachers and administrators must be provided the extensive professional development necessary to make strategic use of the metric.

Battelle for Kids (BFK), based in Columbus, Ohio, has developed the capacity to support districtwide value-added training. BFK currently trains educators in over one hundred school districts in Ohio through Project SOAR. All 612 Ohio school districts now receive value-added reports in grades four through eight in reading and math. BFK is also currently partnering with the Houston Independent School District (HISD) to provide strategic consulting and deliver professional development and communications and technical support to implement ASPIRE, HISD's educational-improvement model, including the use of value-added for school improvement and in their differentiated-compensation program.

BFK resources make value-added analysis both understandable and inspiring to its users. Their professional development modules provide theoretical background to the development of the metric; outline concrete resources for building educator's knowledge, skills, and attitudes about value-added analysis; and develop strategies for navigating, interpreting, and utilizing value-added reports as the basis of school improvement efforts. In this chapter, James Mahoney, a former school superintendent and executive director of BFK, Michael Thomas, BFK's senior director of innovative solutions, and education consultant Jacquelyn Asbury discuss strategies for implementing value-added training.

INTRODUCTION

Professional development is the impetus for change in teacher practices and student growth. Without professional development focused on value-added data, teachers will quickly view it negatively as a tool used solely to judge teacher quality—not as an instrument for improvement. To prevent this outcome, districts must invest in professional development systems that engage educators in making value-added understandable, useful, and routine. This chapter addresses these three developmental dimensions—meaning, usage, and behavioral change—in a sequential manner. However, they are in fact integrated and happen simultaneously. Typically, the predominant focus of training and support shifts with the passage of time. Early work tends to focus more on definition and meaning, while subsequent work tends to focus more on usage and behavioral change. Each dimension grows out of the work of the others.

MAKING VALUE-ADDED INFORMATION UNDERSTANDABLE

The first step in the training process is to help educators understand what progress measures are, how they differ from the achievement measures with which they are familiar, and how to read value-added reports.

Before training begins, it is important for superintendents to set the stage and evaluate the readiness of their administrative and teaching staff to accept the concept of using a progress metric that can positively impact classroom and school improvement. District leadership must take the time to emphasize the difference between achievement and progress and the importance of measuring both:

- Achievement measures are about place. They provide point-in-time snapshots of where students are, relative to the larger standards-based system.
- Progress, or a value-added metric, is about rate. It provides information on how efficiently and effectively students are moving or progressing in a standards-based environment.

Creating this climate for change can occur by demonstrating to staff members the importance of analyzing and using data to improve teaching and learning and emphasizing that progress data are new pieces of information that let them know the effect they are having on their students. Superintendents must be willing to commit time, attention, and support to their school personnel to help them acquire a positive attitude about using the value-added metric.

One of the most useful aspects of the value-added methodology is that it provides searchable value-added reports at multiple levels of a school system, including the district, building, and classroom levels. However, new users find this feature one of the most intimidating aspects of the system. Professional development efforts must stress that not everyone needs to know everything about how the metric is calculated. By directing educators' attention to the segments of value-added reports most relevant to them, each user is provided different but meaningful starting points to inform their individual learning plans.

Superintendents

Superintendents and other district leaders need to be familiar with district-level and school comparison reports. With these reports, systemic issues can be diagnosed and solutions can be discussed. This information can also be used to monitor the district from an accountability perspective. If the district has subgroups not making adequate yearly progress (AYP) or schools not meeting state requirements, for instance, value-added information can provide strong clues about where the real problems may reside.

Principals

Principals need to understand their schools' value-added scores at the macro and micro levels. They must know how their schools are performing relative to other schools within the district. The district and building-level reports allow principals to understand the strengths and weaknesses within their own school by grade level, subject area, and classroom. Principals also benefit from seeing the district summary report for all buildings so that they can seek help or extend services to other schools within their district, based on the information revealed in their value-added reports.

Teachers

Teachers need information specific to the grade level(s) and subject area(s) they teach. They need to know who is benefiting most and who is benefiting least from their instruction. With this knowledge, teachers have a better idea of curricular areas that need attention and practices that should be modified or repeated.

MAKING VALUE-ADDED INFORMATION USEFUL

Providing informative, accurate content to teachers, principals, and central office personnel is only the first step in supporting informed use of value-added information. The next step is to help educators understand how the metric can be used. It takes more than talk about usage to make it a reality. Currently, value-added analysis can be used for school improvement, for accountability, and to differentiate educator compensation. These uses are interrelated, but some may interfere with each other if not presented appropriately.

Using Value-Added Analysis for School Improvement

Value-added should be used as a vehicle for in-process diagnostic feedback. Achievement measures have been around for a long time, but these data sources provide scant conclusive evidence of the quality of a particular program or set of instructional strategies. Achievement data tell educators where students are relative to state achievement targets, but they provide only a snapshot of student performance and not an evaluation of the instructional program. Here lies the problem with using achievement measures to assess program quality: Student achievement levels may be less indicative of program quality and more indicative of each group of students' prior achievement levels, which are best predicted by family income. Value-added analysis overcomes this liability by measuring all students' growth relative to their prior growth and achievement levels. The teacher and school effects or "mean student gains" that are produced through value-added analysis are a much more accurate measure of the effectiveness of teaching practices and curricular programs.

The challenge for a superintendent is that his or her staff is unfamiliar with this kind of information and how to use it. To make this important use of value-added real, teachers and principals need to understand how to interpret value-added information and use it to leverage change in schools. Educators at all levels must believe in the metric's viability. They must have the training, resources, and support necessary to use value-added information to inform teaching practices. School leaders should guide their teams through the process of examining their value-added and achievement information to uncover instructional strengths and weaknesses; exploring the root causes of both strengths and weaknesses; and setting grade- or departmental-level goals based on the analysis.

This three-phase process is illustrated in figure 10.1.

To fully engage in this process, educators need to take part in collaboration and group discussion by:

1. Working through a common dataset within a professional learning community (PLC) environment. The PLC is an effective and collaborative team structure that allows teachers to dialogue about teaching and learning and to examine their instructional practices. It provides an opportunity for professional development whereby teachers learn from each other in a nonthreatening, student-focused setting.
2. Exploring the same process with their own data, typically data from a single grade level or department within a school.

Using Value-Added Analysis for Accountability

Accountability may not be a glamorous use of value-added, but it is a use that garners attention. The last thing a superintendent wants to see is a story in the

FIGURE 10.1
Battelle for Kids focus

Battelle *for* Kids · Focus
A Data-Based, Goal-Setting Process for Educators

Enabling Conditions

Clearly articulated vision of continuous improvement
at the district and school levels.

District policies and frameworks support continuous improvement mindset.

Districts and schools focus on the use of data for continuous improvement.

All educators understand both progress and achievement measures.

Principals are expected to be instructional leaders.

Collaborative planning and learning time
is built into the schedule.

What results are we producing?

Level One Analysis **1**

Value-Added Data   Achievement Data

FILTER ONE   RELATIVE STRENGTHS AND WEAKNESSES

Why are we getting these results?

Level Two Analysis **2**

Instructional Practices?
Curriculum? School Processes?
Subject-Area Expertise?
Time-on-Task?
Standards Alignment?
Assessment Practices?

FILTER TWO   CAUSALITY MAP

How do we improve?

Level Three Analysis **3**

Curriculum Planning
Lesson Design
Differentiation
Instructional Strategies
Curriculum Mapping
Assessment Training
Short-Cycle Assessments

FILTER THREE

FOCUSED
STRATEGIES

Strength-Based Goal
Deficit-Based Goal
Action Plan
CCIP Planning
Differentiated Professional Development
Collaborative Improvement

Source: Copyright © 2008 Battelle for Kids.

newspaper proclaiming that the local schools' students are producing lower than expected gains. Use of value-added analysis for accountability makes it an instrument of summative evaluation. It is a way to make judgments about the extent to which districts and schools are doing what state statutes oblige them to do.

Training for these purposes must emphasize trust. When value-added analysis becomes part of a state's accountability system, practitioners must perceive the data as both reliable and valid. Most educators don't mind being evaluated; they simply want to be evaluated fairly. The only way to build this kind of trust is through effective professional development and solid leadership at the district and building levels. Superintendents can confront the issue of trust through consistent and candid communication about using value-added analysis for school improvement.

Using Value-Added Analysis to Inform Differentiated-Compensation Programs

Districts may also use value-added analysis as criteria to inform differentiated-compensation programs. This use of value-added analysis is still in its infancy and, in many circles, controversial. In most cases, teachers who produce exemplary gains are provided additional compensation; teachers who produce less than optimal results are provided remediation to improve their skills.

Superintendents need to be aware of at least two critical training implications of this use of value-added analysis. First, when educators' compensation is tied to value-added analysis, it tends to overshadow other possible uses—at least in the short term. Initially, educators are likely not to pay much attention to the school improvement uses of the metric. They first need to be convinced that the compensation program is valid, reliable and fair.

Our experience suggests that if educators receive professional development that provides a rationale for change and if social networks are meaningfully engaged to support the work, then a simultaneous inclusion of rewards and sanctions can be effective. It is critical, however, that rewards and sanctions are adopted as only one component of a more comprehensive school improvement process. Otherwise, rewards and sanctions are likely to prove counterproductive.

Additional training and reporting are required when value-added is tied to differentiated compensation. For example, differentiated compensation requires teacher-level value-added reporting in grade levels in which the testing regimen makes that possible. Classroom-level value-added reporting assumes that teachers can be accurately linked to the students they teach. Districts must have systems in place that account for students moving across school systems, shared instruction, and students leaving the classroom.

In some cases, school systems keep track of all this in their data systems, but in most cases they do not. In response to this issue, Battelle for Kids developed an instructional verification and linkage system that allows principals and teachers to go online in a secure location and (1) build, amend, and verify their classroom rosters; (2) account for students who move in and out of the classroom during the school year; and (3) account for students whose instruction is shared across multiple teachers.

Without this roster-verification process, classroom-level value-added reporting seems less valid to teachers, and without classroom-level reporting, most compensation models fall apart. Superintendents and districts must give careful consideration to this issue. A verification system can be designed and implemented, but it requires technical expertise, infrastructure, and time. A challenge commensurate with a verification and linking system is the additional training required to teach principals and teachers to use the system in a limited number of training days. For most districts, if more training is required for some aspects of the system, it means less training in other aspects.

MAKING VALUE-ADDED ROUTINE

Conventional wisdom says that if people understand the purpose of a tool, how it works, and when and where to use it, the tool will be used. However, experience suggests that this is not necessarily the case, as adults are often slow to adopt new technologies and new routines, especially if those technologies upset or interfere with existing practices.

The following cautions are especially important to consider when talking about routine use of value-added analysis:

- The concepts of measuring student progress and data-based school improvement are new ideas to most educators. These ideas have not, as a rule, been taught in preservice or graduate programs or been around long enough to be a staple of yearly professional development activities.
- Value-added analysis is produced through sophisticated statistical processes. Some individuals will find value-added naturally appealing, while others will come to appreciate value-added analysis when they see how the numbers can inform their practice.
- Value-added measures are typically produced once a year. Teaching educators about the metric when information is available and fresh is one thing. Asking them to remember how to use this information a year later when it is available again is quite another.
- Value-added measures cut close to the bone. More than any other educational metric, value-added analysis provides direct and objective feedback on the efficacy of educators' work. Value-added analysis, especially at the classroom level, provides a mirror into which many are reluctant to look.

How can practitioners move toward routine use of value-added information? The traditional answer in most schools is professional development. The primary purpose of professional development is behavioral change. For educators, this means more effective practice that produces higher levels of student achievement. If professional development does not lead to this end, it is largely a waste of time and money.

High-quality professional development that leads to altered behavior must develop educators' abilities as well as their values. In the recent book *Influencer: The Power to Change Anything,* the authors contend, "When it comes to altering behavior, you need to help others answer only two questions. First: Is it worth it? (If not, why waste the effort?) And second: Can they do this thing? (If not, why try?)"[1]

On the surface, these sound like simple questions. In practice, they are complex, powerful, and at the heart of why change-oriented professional development is so difficult. In many ways, the problems associated with professional development are the same problems plaguing the teaching profession as a whole. Good professional development, like good teaching, used to be about delivering a good performance. But, like the practice of teaching, professional development is no longer just about performance. It is about results.

Real, lasting behavioral change only happens when the right information, processes, and supports are put in place to make behavioral change "worth it" and "doable." At the individual level, these questions address issues of personal motivation and ability. An important goal of value-added professional development must be to enlist educators in a quest for academic growth. Educators must choose to use the value-added metric to assess their work. Educators must also understand the damage that will occur if they are unsuccessful at their craft.

However, motivation is not sufficient. Professional development must include significant amounts of skill development and practice time. Educators must spend time personally navigating the value-added system, interpreting value-added reports, and designing goals based on their information, and they must receive direct feedback on these efforts. In practice, effective use of value-added information must be acknowledged and praised. Ineffective practice must be sanctioned.

Considerable time must be spent building a rationale for why student progress should be measured, why teachers' work is so important, and why a continuous-improvement mindset is central to what it means to be a teacher.

These messages cannot be glossed over. They must be stressed in multiple ways and at every professional development interface available to educators so that they can decide if the work we are asking of them is "worth it." Multiple opportunities and venues must be provided for educators to develop the skills they need to navigate, interpret, and use value-added information. Experience shows that these kinds of activities can never be done enough.

CHALLENGES AND CONSIDERATIONS

Value-added analysis and the school improvement processes associated with this information are new to most educators. Educators need time, resources, and support to be able to use this information to improve practice—especially because value-added information is not typically accessed on a daily basis. The following factors are critical to this effort.

Social Networks

Superintendents should enlist social networks to help build educators' value-added knowledge. We recommend that superintendents (1) leverage the relationships that exist within schools to help build support; (2) recognize the importance of educators' daily interactions and develop learning communities to encourage professional growth and collaboration; and (3) empower professional developers to harness and gain access to social networks.

Formal and Informal School Leaders

Formal and informal school leaders are two primary vehicles through which to gain access to and positively influence staff members. Formal leaders can help identify these informal leaders and ensure their inclusion in all trainings. While informal leaders may initially be resistant to a value-added initiative, ultimately they are the ones who can plug into existing networks to support it and carry forth important messages. Equally important to engaging district and school leadership is engaging social networks by reaching out to teacher associations, administrative associations, key legislators, and business leaders and encouraging them to be part of a solution.

Capacity

The following elements must be in place to ensure that districts have the appropriate capacity to make value-added training effective:

- School schedules are put together in ways that allow educators to get together to talk about their practice, such as providing common planning time.
- Planning tools are adopted to help educators efficiently and effectively use value-added analysis to inform teaching practices.
- Administrators have time to support planning processes and monitor implementation.
- PLCs offer a viable structure for ongoing professional development to occur.
- Early release or professional development days are part of the district calendar.

- District leadership is committed to implementing value-added for school improvement.
- Union leadership is involved in the discussions about value-added and the implications surrounding its use.

These elements address the amount of and way in which time and other resources are brought to bear on the use of value-added information. It is one thing to understand something well enough to make effective use of it. It is quite another to have the time and institutional support to make this use likely. If a district's leadership is thoughtful about the structures adopted, the probability that value-added analysis will be used efficiently and effectively is greatly multiplied.

Support Staff

Recognizing that the effort to inform, prepare, and train district personnel will be immense, each district should select at least two individuals to become district value-added specialists (DVAS)—personnel identified to be trained in accessing, interpreting, and using reports so that they can, in turn, train and support others. DVAS should serve as districts' in-house experts on the use of value-added analysis.

Principals and teachers require value-added support during specific time frames. This support is most relevant when information becomes available. Otherwise, their ability to make effective use of the information is delayed each year as they relearn what they need to know to use their value-added reports. As such, DVAS training should occur in the late spring or during the summer and should address the following topics:

- Expectations and role clarification
- The concept of value-added analysis
- How to identify and interpret various value-added reports
- How value-added measures can be integrated into the school improvement process
- How grade-level teams can analyze value-added information to make instructional decisions

Resources

Understanding and Using Value-Added Analysis: A Toolkit for School Leaders. Districts should provide resources to school leaders to help their staff members learn to use value-added information for school improvement. An example is Battelle for Kids' *Understanding and Using Value-Added Analysis: A Toolkit for School Leaders,* which contains an array of resources for multimodal learning, including instructional videos, user manuals, PowerPoint presentations, and sample school improvement plans.[2]

LEARN—Online Value-Added Course Suite. Because value-added information is new and the methodology used to develop it is sophisticated, it is important to find ways to provide professional development to help teachers learn to understand and use this information. One effective way to support this effort is to provide online professional development—offering anytime and anyplace learning. Battelle for Kids created the LEARN Network (http://portal.battelleforkids.org/Ohio/Learn-Info/OnlineLearning.html), which is comprised of one-hour online courses that address learning concepts ranging from explaining the distinction between progress and achievement to suggesting guidelines to help principals get their schools ready to use value-added analysis. The LEARN Network's current twenty-eight courses address the following major concepts: Do I Understand Value-Added Concepts? Am I Able to Access, Navigate, and Interpret Value-Added Reports? Am I Ready to Start Using the Value-Added Metric? These courses help educators recognize how value-added information can be used to improve teaching and learning. Each course includes a pretest, posttest, and "knowledge-and-application" activities to stretch users' knowledge beyond the confines of the course. A survey component is embedded to obtain feedback from users. The network also includes an easy-to-manage administration tool that allows network administrators to oversee, rather than conduct, the training. DVAS and principals can monitor and facilitate learning as well.

IMPLEMENTATION GUIDELINES

To effectively implement value-added training, districts need to take the following steps:

1. *Engage formal and informal leadership in a discussion about the uses of value-added information.* In doing so, districts will need to consider the advantages and limitations of value-added analysis, determine how value-added data will be used, assign responsibility for overseeing implementation, and construct a compelling vision for change.
2. *Plan for using value-added information for school improvement.*
    - *Develop and provide training for the leadership team.* Build the leadership team's understanding of value-added analysis, its intended uses, advantages, and limitations.
    - *Set goals and a timeline for implementation.* Determine who will be involved in districtwide implementation and assign appropriate roles and responsibilities.

- *Develop a structural plan.* Develop and adapt structures, such as PLCs, to maximize opportunity for collaboration.
- *Develop a communications plan.* Use and expand current communication mechanisms to ensure stakeholder investment and successful implementation.
- *Develop a training plan.* Select a core team of trainers and develop a general training structure and calendar.

3. *Organize the core training team.* Prepare a core team of trainers to explain value-added concepts in educator-friendly language, define the intended uses of value-added information, and differentiate training to meet various users' needs.

4. *Train principals and teachers.* Decide who needs to know what, design a value-added rollout plan for each school, offer professional development that involves sufficient practice time and multiple opportunities and venues for educators to build their skills.

5. *Monitor and refine implementation strategies as needed.* Monitor the execution of the school rollout plans and provide additional support where necessary.

CLOSING THOUGHTS

Value-added analysis has enormous potential to transform the way educators engage in their practice, when educators

- understand the need to measure and ensure that *all* students make at least one year's worth of progress for a year's worth of school;
- can access, navigate, and accurately interpret their value-added reports to inform various aspects of school improvement, including personalized learning paths for educators and personalized instruction for students;
- know how to use value-added information for various uses, such as accountability and compensation, where applicable;
- align social and structural dimensions of their organization to cultivate commitment and gain support for these uses.

If we fall short in addressing these dimensions, use of value-added analysis can become another forgotten, ancillary aspect of educational practice. In contrast, if thoughtfully addressed, value-added analysis can be one of the most powerful and enlightening tools to help educators accelerate progress and maximize opportunity for all the students they serve.

CHAPTER ELEVEN

Mentoring and New Teacher Induction

ELLEN MOIR

PATRICIA MARTIN

Thirty-three percent of new teachers leave the profession within the first three years of their careers, and that number is nearly a third higher in high-need urban areas.[1] *Learning their trade by trial and error, new teachers rarely take part in a meaningful internship program, leading to feelings of isolation and ineffectiveness. This result is an indictment of the inadequate sink-or-swim or survival-of-the-fittest induction processes that many school districts have in place for new teachers.*

Research on effective mentorship programs shows that new teachers who have strong mentors are more likely to stay in the classroom and become effective teachers.[2] *The model constructed by the New Teacher Center (NTC), which calls for multiyear mentoring of new teachers, during which a specifically trained and highly effective classroom teacher works as a mentor, is an example of one such comprehensive program.*

The New Teacher Center, based in Santa Cruz, California, has been synonymous with high-quality mentor-based teacher induction since its inception in 1998. The NTC, a national resource for practice, research, and policy on induction, has developed a model to help new teachers maintain a strategic focus on student learning and classroom instruction with the guidance of highly trained and supported mentors. The NTC also works with principals and content coaches to create environments that support the professional learning and ongoing development of teachers. More than 125 districts in California use the NTC formative-assessment system, and districts in forty states and four countries use NTC professional development and/or materials in their induction programs. In this chapter, Ellen Moir, executive director of NTC, and Patricia Martin, a development associate with NTC, discuss how districts can design and implement successful mentorship programs.

INTRODUCTION

A high-quality new teacher induction program has many components—one-on-one mentoring, participation in professional learning communities, and ongoing professional development that is specially designed for beginning teachers. New teacher induction, moreover, is a subset of the district's overall program to maximize the potential of human capital in the system. A high-quality mentoring and induction program can serve as a model for the district's overall vision and ongoing commitment to excellence in teaching and learning, a vision that includes a career pipeline to leadership.

The approach taken by Operation Public Education (OPE), like NTC's, exemplifies the aim of quality education for all students. The framework includes an array of important components, of which mentoring of new (and experienced) teachers is central. When the OPE framework is deployed in a formal pilot, teacher induction and mentoring, in conjunction with a strong evaluation process, will be critical to its success.

WHY INVEST IN MENTORING NEW TEACHERS?

The nation needs to prepare and retain approximately 125,000 new teachers every year, yet new teachers continue to be greeted in most states by sink-or-swim induction. This neglect of new teacher development contributes to national teacher attrition rates that average nearly 50 percent over five years.[3] Because new teachers disproportionately work with poor and minority students, the national failure to offer these teachers effective professional induction can mean that struggling students are assigned a succession of inexperienced teachers. This pattern widens the achievement gap between advantaged and disadvantaged students, and guarantees the career-ending discouragement of many talented and enthusiastic novices who will never realize their desire to make a difference in the lives of children.

Rapid turnover of teachers also has a dollar cost, and district administrators have come to realize that it is a high one. The National Commission on Teaching and America's Future (NCTAF) estimated in their 2007 research report, "The High Cost of Teacher Turnover," that teacher turnover costs the nation $7.3 billion each year. NTC's own research demonstrates that the process of hiring a single new teacher can cost a district well in excess of $15,000.[4]

Large urban school districts with the lowest rates of new teacher retention pay a "turnover tax" in the tens of millions of dollars annually. Dollars spent on teacher turnover are dollars that could be used to support instruction, paying for books, aides, computers, and other much needed educational materials. The neediest schools, those most likely to see a preponderance of new teachers, cannot afford their current rates of teacher turnover. As all districts become more aware of these cost trade-offs, the need for an overall design for maximizing human capital becomes apparent. A program aimed at developing and retaining excellent teachers is fundamental to this design.

THE THREEFOLD BENEFITS OF HIGH-QUALITY INDUCTION

Benefit #1: Improving Student Learning

High-quality induction by trained mentors can raise the quality of a new teacher's instructional practice. A research study conducted by NTC suggests that a comprehensive new teacher mentoring program, continued over the first two years of a teacher's career, results in comparatively higher student achievement gains. Figure 11.1 demonstrates the higher reading gains on the Stanford Achievement Test (SAT9) for the students of teachers in one district (District C), who had the benefit of two years of intensive mentoring based on the NTC model, compared with teachers in other districts that offered intensive mentoring for only the first year. The study employed a quasi-experimental design (that is, no random selection or assignment), but poverty, student achievement levels, and minority status were entered into the statistical model.

Further analysis of the performance of the new teachers from District C is encouraging. Researchers compared the reading scores of 271 new teachers in this

FIGURE 11.1
Intensive induction results in greater student learning gains

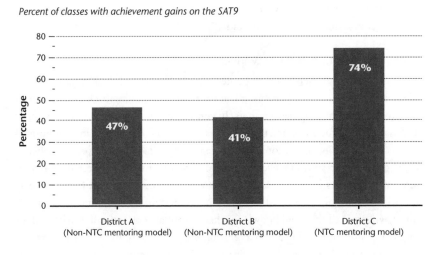

Percent of classes with achievement gains on the SAT9

Notes:
• All three districts have a 1:15 mentor-novice ratio for Year 1 teachers
• For Year 2 Teachers, District A has a buddy system, District B has 1:35 ratio, District C maintains 1:15 ratio.

Source:
Stephen Fletcher, Michael Strong and Anthony Villar. *Percent of Classes with Achievement Gains: Data for New Teachers in Three California Districts.* (Santa Cruz, CA: University of California, Santa Cruz, 2008).

district over five years, all of whom had the benefit of two years of intensive mentoring in the NTC model. Despite the fact that the new teachers were more likely to be assigned to underachieving classes, 68 percent of the new teachers' classes showed reading gains that were above the district's average gain.

Benefit #2: Reducing Teacher Turnover

School systems—rural, urban, and suburban—are facing the dual pressures of statewide testing and the inevitable wave of boomer-teacher retirements, factors that contribute to a struggle to attract and retain large numbers of the highest-caliber new teachers. Under these pressures, districts are more inclined than ever to invest in a program that ensures that good candidates become excellent teachers and that, with the support of a thoughtful tenure process, those excellent teachers choose to stay in the profession.

Figure 11.2 illustrates the successful teacher retention experienced by all districts served by the Santa Cruz, California, New Teacher Project, employing the NTC model for teacher induction, compared with the national teacher retention average. Eighty-eight percent of teachers in that county were still teaching there six years after they began their teaching careers; this compares strikingly with the national retention average after six years of only 56 percent. In another example, the Chicago New Teacher Center's intensive mentoring program has more than tripled the percentage of new teachers who intend to continue teaching in their current schools on Chicago's South Side.

Benefit #3: Creating Teacher Leaders

The outstanding teachers who are trained as mentors expand their capabilities and their value to the district, benefiting from the mentor training itself and also from the process of mentoring new teachers. In constantly guiding teachers' development and assessing instructional practice, mentors expand their capacities in communication, administration, and in conscious awareness of the factors that come together to make good teachers into excellent teachers. When mentors complete their typical term of three years in that role, many return to the classroom, but large numbers move into leadership roles in administration or curriculum development. The mentors, having gained skills and knowledge that can enhance the overall district goals of improving student learning and maximizing the potential of its teacher leaders, become an invaluable resource for the district and the profession at large.

PRINCIPLES OF HIGH-QUALITY TEACHER INDUCTION

High-quality teacher induction and mentoring has many facets. As districts examine their current induction models with the goal of moving to a higher-quality

FIGURE 11.2
Percentage of teacher retention over six years

Comparing rates of retention of teachers participating in NTC-model induction with national average retention

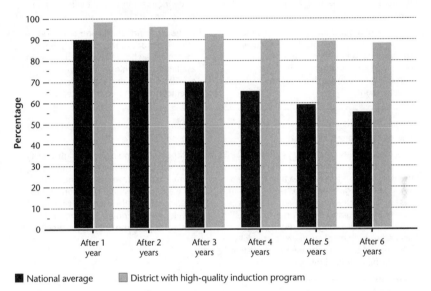

■ National average   ▨ District with high-quality induction program

Sources: Richard M. Ingersoll. "The Teacher Shortage: A Case of Wrong Diagnosis and Wrong Prescription." *NASSP Bulletin* 86, no. 631 (2002): 16; California Commission on Teacher Credentialing. *Annual Report* 2002. (Sacramento, CA: California Commission on Teacher Credentialing, 2002); Michael Strong and Linda St. John. *A Study of Teacher Retention: The Effects of Mentoring for Beginning Teachers.* (Santa Cruz, CA: University of California, Santa Cruz, 2001).

and more comprehensive version, it will be useful to consider the key principles of the mentoring model described in table 11.1.

Rigorous Mentor Selection

Before a district begins to recruit mentors from their staff, it is important to agree on the qualifications that are appropriate for the position. Sample mentor selection criteria, developed by the New Teacher Center, are shown in figure 11.3.

Assertive recruitment efforts are necessary to ensure a pool of strong mentor candidates. Many of the district's best educators may not become aware of the new position if traditional, often passive, methods for publicizing position openings are relied on (e.g., postings on physical or electronic bulletin boards). Districts should employ more effective recruiting methods: multiple presentations at school sites, regular announcements at educator/leadership meetings, personal invitations to

TABLE 11.1

High quality mentoring and induction practices

Moving toward . . .	Moving away from . .
Rigorous mentor selection based on qualities of an effective mentor	*Choosing mentors without criteria or an explicit process*
Qualities of a good mentor may include evidence of outstanding teaching practice, strong intra- and interpersonal skills, experience with adult learners, respect for peers, current knowledge of professional development.	Without strong criteria and a rigorous selection process, there is a risk that mentors may be chosen based more on availability or seniority than on their qualifications to engage in meaningful interactions with beginning teachers.
Ongoing professional development and support for mentors	*Insufficient professional development and support for mentors*
Effective teachers don't always know what it is about their teaching that is effective. Many mentors are also surprised to find that translating knowledge to students is not the same as translating knowledge to adults. High-quality and ongoing development, as well as a professional learning community, are needed to help mentors develop the skills to identify and translate the elements of effective teaching to beginning teachers.	Without initial and ongoing high-quality professional development to support them, mentors miss out on the guidance and professional community they need regarding the complex practice of developing beginning teachers and strategizing for the challenges they face.
Sanctioned time for mentor-teacher interactions	*Meetings happen occasionally or "whenever the mentor and teacher are available"*
Mentors need sanctioned time to focus on beginning teacher development. Mentors and beginning teachers should have 1.25–2.5 hours per week to allow for the most rigorous mentoring activities. That time should be protected by teachers and administrators.	Often both parties are so busy that meeting time gets relegated down the list of priorities. The short fragments of time that may be found are typically insufficient for fostering real relationships and growth.
Intensive and specific guidance moving teaching practice forward	*Nonspecific, emotional, or logistical support alone*
Focusing on professional teaching standards and the appropriate content-area standards allows for instructional growth to help teachers know concretely how to improve. Example: "Let's look at your assessment data and talk about what strategies will help you address the concern you had about reaching your struggling English-language learner students."	Emotional support is important, but alone it is not sufficient to improve teacher practice. Without specific instructional feedback, mentoring cannot impact student learning. Example: "You're doing a great job, Jane. Keep it up!"

Moving toward . . .	Moving away from . .
Professional teaching standards and data-driven conversations	*Informal and non-evidenced-based feedback*
Just as in student learning, beginning teacher learning should be data driven and standards based. To be effective, feedback to beginning teachers must be grounded in evidence about their practice, including information gathered through classroom observations and student work. Use of professional teaching standards, documentation of mentoring conversations, and data collection on various components of classroom practice ensures a solid structure for focusing on continuous instructional growth.	The rigor of the program may be compromised when interactions are too often based on informal conversations and opinions not drawn from evidence. Without a structure and focus on real-time data derived from beginning teacher practice, interactions may not result in improved teaching practice.
Ongoing beginning teacher professional development	*Professional development not specifically tailored to the needs of beginning teachers*
Beginning teachers benefit from a professional learning community that is guided by professional teaching standards and the appropriate content-area standards, and is focused on teacher development, problem-solving, and mutual support. Opportunities such as regularly scheduled seminars and online learning communities provide a context for rich networking, professional dialogue, and reflection, as well as ways to combat isolation.	Novices are in a unique developmental phase that cannot be addressed by "one-size-fits-all" workshops. Professional development disconnected from teacher needs is irrelevant at best, and in many situations only serves to overwhelm beginning teachers.
Clear roles and responsibilities for principals	*Lack of development for/communication with principals*
Administrators play a critical role in setting the stage for beginning teacher and mentor success, creating time for induction, and establishing a positive culture for teacher development in their buildings and in the system. Professional development for principals and ongoing communication with them about the needs of new teachers and the nature of the program ensures that they understand their role in fully supporting induction.	Without clearly articulated strategies to support beginning teachers and protect induction activity time, principals may inadvertently undermine the prospects of beginning teacher success (e.g., assigning beginning teachers the most challenging classes, assigning additional responsibilities, or not anticipating their needs for basic resources).
Collaboration with all stakeholders	*Isolated programming and lack of alignment*
Strong communication and collaboration among stakeholders, including administration, school boards, union/association leadership, and professional partners creates a culture of commitment and ensures that the program will succeed and complement the district's overall strategy for maximizing human capital.	Without strong partnerships and alignment, instructional initiatives can be undermined. Beginning teachers may receive mixed messages from varying support providers and feel overwhelmed, confused, and frustrated by all the different layers of information coming at them.

FIGURE 11.3
NTC mentor-selection criteria

---

1. Recognition as exemplary classroom teacher and professional role model
2. Current or former classroom teacher with at least 5 years successful experience
3. Effective interpersonal skills
4. Experience working with linguistically and ethnically diverse students
5. Demonstrated commitment to personal professional growth and learning
6. Willingness to participate in professional preparation to acquire the knowledge and skills needed to be effective
7. Willingness to engage in formative assessment process, including non-evaluative, reflective conversations with beginning teachers about formative assessment evidence
8. Willingness to work collaboratively and share instructional ideas and materials with beginning teachers
9. Knowledge of beginning teacher development
10. Strong literacy and numeracy skills in elementary grades
11. Strong subject-matter competence and knowledge of literacy and English-language development in secondary grades

---

highly respected educators, flyers in mailboxes, articles in newsletters, coverage in local media, requests for districtwide nominations, union-sponsored outreach, personal networks, and so on.

The mentor-recruitment process requires the cooperation of district principals. If they do not perceive the mentoring program as ultimately building capacity for their own schools as well as the district, principals could view mentor recruitment as a raid on their top teaching staff. Therefore, communication with principals about the need and benefits of recommending their most-talented teachers will be vital.

Mentor Professional Development

An effective induction program has many components, but the mentor's ability to help new teachers accelerate their learning is most critical to the overall quality of the program. A district's teacher-induction program is only as good as the quality of the mentors. While selecting the best candidates to be mentors is the first part of the equation, to maximize the effectiveness of the mentors, districts must develop an intensive training program and system for ongoing professional development.

To design a thoughtful professional development plan for mentors, districts must consider the specific context and any unique circumstances that mentors and new teachers will face. By clarifying these circumstances at the outset, it is more likely that the professional development can be aligned with the needs and expectations of the district. These needs will vary not just by the nature of the district, for example, suburban or rural, but also by the nature of the teaching assignments and unique student population.

Effective mentoring programs should follow a sequenced, standards-based curriculum and use formative-assessment tools throughout the process. NTC's own program of professional development for mentors includes either mentor academies or a series of trainings that present daylong or longer sessions on the following topics:

- Foundations in mentoring
- Coaching and observation strategies
- Mentoring for powerful teaching: using student work to guide instruction
- Coaching in complex situations
- Designing and presenting professional development for beginning teachers
- Mentoring for equity
- Mentoring for differentiating instruction
- Mentoring for academic literacy across content areas
- Mentoring for teaching English-language learners
- Creating and facilitating meetings that promote mentor development
- The site administrator's role in supporting beginning teachers[5]

It is important to note that districts will inevitably find areas that require additional (or reduced) emphasis in order to meet their particular needs. As districts contemplate the extent and content of their mentor professional development, they should do so with the realization that high-quality mentor trainers will need to act as role models for new mentors. For that reason, mentor trainers should be taken from the ranks of respected and successful mentors. It is important to provide new mentors with opportunities to hear and practice mentoring language, to observe and analyze mentoring behaviors, to be surrounded by the language of professional practice, and to experience adult learning communities that mentors can then replicate with their mentees and school colleagues. Until a district has built a cadre of experienced mentors, they might send their new mentor candidates to the training sessions of other districts with established mentor professional development programs or to NTC's own mentor academy.

Mentor-Teacher Interactions

New teachers don't need one-size-fits-all professional development sessions; they need on-the-job help from mentors who can analyze their practice constructively and offer specific suggestions. Trained instructional mentors for beginning teachers bring a vision of outstanding teaching to the novice practitioner, and they have learned to articulate this vision in terms of best practices framed by professional teaching standards of the district and/or state. Excellent mentors understand not just the goals as defined by these standards, but the progression that teachers must move through on their way to achieving instructional excellence. Mentoring calls for sensitive communication because not all teachers will progress at the same rate or enhance all their skills with equal speed. Like good teachers, mentors need to differentiate their support, depending on the needs of the teacher, whether new or experienced. However unique each school district and each new teacher's progress, intensive mentoring-based new teacher induction programs will have important features in common:

Sanctioned Time for Mentoring and a Multiyear Commitment. Mentors should be released entirely or part-time from their teaching duties to work with each new teacher in their districts for at least one and one-half to two and one-half hours per week over the course of two years. This is probably the biggest leap that a district considering establishing a high-quality teacher-induction program must make. Though districts will need to consider the budgetary implications of replacing the mentors in their classrooms, they must also keep in mind that they are making a long-term investment in teacher quality. Taking fine teachers away from the classroom to be mentors will ensure that even more fine teachers will be teaching the district's students in the future. As mentors complete their several years in that role, the district profits further by having helped to create its next generation of teacher leaders.

Intensive and Specific Mentoring Guidelines. Each teacher-mentor combination is unique, but the course of inquiry into teaching practices should follow a guided structure. During the conversation, the mentor should begin by inviting the new teacher to share classroom successes and challenges. Collaboratively, the mentor and new teacher should next identify the focus of the current meeting. Throughout the conversation, the mentor must remain sensitive to the needs of the new teacher while ultimately prioritizing the needs of the teacher's students. The interactions between mentors and beginning teachers should be grounded in an inquiry approach to teaching and learning. Rather than pointing out deficiencies or providing a myriad of resources and suggestions, mentors facilitate and guide conversations that involve continual analysis of what students are learning.

Mentorship must offer much more than a sympathetic ear; it should provide individually tailored support and assistance focused on accelerating the development of the new teacher's emerging classroom practice. In high-quality new teacher induction, the mentor and new teacher engage in an ongoing collaborative inquiry into the new teacher's practice that is shaped and guided by standards and an expectation of professional growth over time. Over the course of the two years of new teacher induction, mentors and new teachers work on engaging, assessing, and meeting the needs of all students. They work on topics such as classroom management, lesson planning, differentiated instruction, and effective practices for working with English-language learners. The primary goal that directs the mentor-teacher interaction should always be improving instruction in order to accelerate the learning of all students. Another important goal is ensuring the new teachers' constructive participation in learning communities, including their grade level or department teams, their schools, and their districts.

Teaching Standards and Formative Assessment. The valuable time invested in mentoring new teachers should be structured by a set of protocols and tools that define the anticipated growth in teaching practice and professional behavior. Recognizing that new teachers' skills evolve as they mature in their practice, NTC has created a continuum of teacher development.[6] This continuum describes five stages of professional development, from beginner to innovator, and is organized around six professional teaching standards: (1) engaging and supporting all students in learning; (2) creating and maintaining an effective environment for student learning; (3) understanding and organizing subject matter for student learning; (4) planning instruction and designing learning experiences for all students; (5) assessing student learning; and (6) developing as a professional educator. The continuum helps define that maturation and can serve as a guide for working with new teachers.

Districts must also ensure that mentor-teacher discussions are grounded in state and district standards and research-based instructional practice. In the NTC program, this progression is framed by a formal formative-assessment system, which is designed to help mentors and new teachers use assessment data to accelerate development. Districts should consider modifying existing tools or developing their own set of tools in the following areas:

- Creating collaborative assessment logs
- Exploring school and community resources
- Assembling a class profile
- Setting professional goals
- Analyzing student work
- Planning lessons
- Observing classroom sessions
- Communicating with parents

These tools will help mentors identify new teachers' progress and challenges, as well as students' academic needs.[7]

Data-Driven Mentoring Conversations. Together, the mentor and new teacher should collect and analyze data, assess student learning against instructional standards, and tailor lesson plans to improve instructional effectiveness in a cyclical process of teaching, data collection, analysis, reflection, and refinement. Mentors select formative-assessment tools that will strengthen and enhance the process. For example, if a mentor and new teacher were using a formative-assessment tool geared to analyzing student work, they would sort selected student work into categories relative to the standards-based grade-level expectations for the work, noting any performance patterns that may emerge. This process would then allow them to clarify the performance of each group and their attendant instructional needs. Lastly, the mentor and new teacher would generate differentiated strategies for reaching each group and summarize next steps. This type of conversation, based on actual student materials and data, allows the mentor to provide strategic support as well as specific suggestions without assuming a judgmental posture. The data gleaned from the analysis of student work permit the teacher and the mentor to maintain the focus on improving instruction to meet students' needs.

Modeling Self-Assessment and Lifelong Learning. From their mentors, teachers learn to assess their own practice using the same rich formative-assessment process that should play out in their classrooms as they collect and analyze multiple sources of student data to inform day-to-day instruction. Furthermore, by engaging in this process of collaborative continuous improvement in their first years in the profession, new teachers are learning professional habits of mind that can influence their career-long approach to teaching. Mentors model a professional stance for the entire district, emphasizing career-long learning and continuous improvement as essential attitudes for top-notch teachers.

Ongoing Professional Development

In addition to one-on-one mentoring, districts should develop new teacher induction programs that offer ongoing professional development tailored to beginning teachers. Ideally, new teachers should come together monthly for a seminar series designed specifically to meet their curricular and instructional needs. Beginning teachers should be given an opportunity to choose from a menu of appropriate topics and network with similarly directed peers. School districts wishing to maximize the growth of their new teachers will want to offer specialized professional development opportunities for new teachers and encourage their participation in the larger learning community, rather than lumping them into general sessions that may not meet their specific needs. Above all, new teacher professional development should be perceived and structured as part of the district's program of lifelong learning, and be designed to target educators in all stages of their careers.

MAKING IT HAPPEN: CHALLENGES AND CONSIDERATIONS

Stakeholder Commitment

Whenever funding and staff restructuring is involved, proponents of high-quality induction confront the challenge of seeking many levels of approvals and buy-in (see figure 11.4). Almost without exception, all those involved want high-quality teachers and instruction, but it can be complicated to bring stakeholders to mutual agreement on the centrality of teacher induction to the improvement of teaching and learning. The buy-in process works best when all of the stakeholder groups are represented from the beginning and when new teacher induction is seen by all as part of a districtwide design to build human capacity at every level.

The Principal's Crucial Role

While all the stakeholders are important, principals are critical to the day-to-day success of the program. High-quality new teacher induction programs require the

FIGURE 11.4
Key players in the induction process

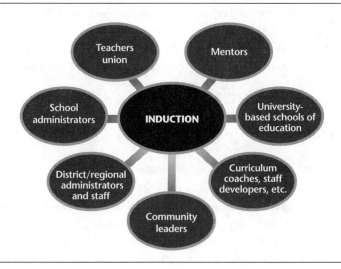

supportive and informed cooperation of the principal or administrator of the school. Mentors and novices alike benefit when the principal fully understands and values the work of the mentor and sets induction experiences as a high priority. Strong principals also realize that new teachers require more than just a high-quality mentor; they need to become fully integrated into the culture and social fabric of the school and develop a thorough understanding of the students and the community. Principals can help mentors by assigning a carefully selected on-site colleague to assist in orienting the new teacher to school policies and practices. In addition, principals can reassess policies that might discriminate against new colleagues—from class assignments, to the location of the new teacher's classroom, to access to materials, to the equitable allocation of resources, classroom furnishings, and, even parking spaces.

Principals who are convinced that the induction and mentoring program pays off in teacher excellence and student achievement in their schools will become supporters of the program. Mentors play an important part in supporting the principal in this process; part of professional development for mentors promotes building partnerships with principals. Principals and mentors become powerful allies, striving together for the success of all beginning teachers and their students, but with distinct roles and using different but aligned approaches.

To demonstrate the district's commitment to the mentoring program and to cultivate the principals' role in support of new teacher induction, districts should ensure the following:

- Outstanding candidates are selected to be principals, and they themselves provide models of lifelong learning and professional development.
- Principals become familiar with the mentoring program and new teacher development through professional development sessions.
- Mentors provide presentations on the progress of the mentoring program and teacher induction at principals' meetings, allowing for principals' input and discussion of the supportive role of principals.
- Mentors meet with principals on a regular basis to check specific goals principals have for new teachers and to encourage principals in their support of new teachers.

Principals and Mentor-Teacher Confidentiality

Mentors in the NTC model advance the school's mission and the principal's instructional agenda without divulging confidential or evaluative information about the individual teacher's progress. In the interest of building a trusting mentor-new teacher relationship, it is understood that mentors do not share their evaluations with principals. In some parts of the country, however, where peer assistance and review models are in place, the mentor-teacher relationship may not be confidential. This issue is less sensitive under such circumstances because it is built into the district culture, and because it is not the principal alone, but a peer-review board made up of fellow teachers and administrators, that makes decisions about a new teacher's future.

Finding Funds for Teacher Induction: A Program That Pays for Itself

Funding is often the initial obstacle in induction program implementation. However, research shows that intensive mentoring creates major financial savings over a number of years by reducing the costs inherent in teacher attrition. Nonetheless, up-front costs to pay for release time for mentors and extensive professional development can be an initial hurdle. When planning a teacher-induction program, districts need to consider a number of elements in addition to the main cost of release time for mentors—professional development for mentors and new teachers, administrative costs (including at least a part-time program director), materials and printing, and possible room and food costs.

Anthony Villar and Michael Strong analyzed the costs and benefits of NTC's comprehensive induction program in one district.[8] When costs and benefits were computed over five years (costs are incurred only in the first two years, but benefits continue to accrue), the researchers were able to provide the net present value of the program to each interested constituent. The program produced an overall return on investment at the societal level of $1.66 for each dollar spent.[9]

While more than thirty states currently mandate teacher induction, in most cases the required induction is loosely defined and unfunded. It is not surprising that many districts have responded with the lowest-cost program. Only a few states provide significant financial support for district induction programs. Many systems solicit state and/or federal Department of Education grants to support induction programs. Some districts have used Title II dollars; others have combined their own funds with foundation grants to support high-quality teacher-induction programs. In soliciting funding from any source, districts are well served by thoroughly documenting their teacher attrition rates over time and using research-based methods to assess the financial costs of teacher turnover and the benefits associated with teacher-induction programs.

Ensuring Appropriate Ratios

Districts must assess how many new teachers they expect annually—a number that should actually decrease over time as the quality induction program lowers the attrition rate—and then calculate the number of mentors that will be needed at an estimated maximum teacher-to-mentor ratio of 15:1. To ensure that adequate ratios can be maintained, recruitment of mentor candidates needs to be very active and multidimensional, beginning in the spring or earlier, if possible.

Incorporating Mentoring into a Broader Strategy

An induction program that supports new teachers will be most successful when it is part of a districtwide human capital approach. Regardless of where the program administration resides, the district's plan must first address recruitment—getting the best teachers hired—and then development, ensuring that every teacher and administrator has the professional learning and feedback to keep them on the path toward excellence. The district's plan for maximizing its professional capacity also needs a strong tenure component combined with a teacher-evaluation process that is congruent with the outcomes for teacher development across the district. This commitment to career-long learning and development must be flexible enough to enhance all the stages of an educator's career. Equally important is the development of outstanding principals in every school. Their development needs to be explicit and aligned with the district's plan for building capacity throughout the system.

CONCLUSION

A high-quality new teacher induction experience has the potential to permanently expand instructional capacity by improving teacher practice and teacher retention simultaneously, a win-win for students and educators. The results of a mentor-centered teacher-induction program are incalculably valuable: effective, committed teachers who contribute to a stable community of learners and increased student achievement. It is a system that pays for itself over time by cutting teacher attrition dramatically and, more important, providing immeasurable returns in student growth and teacher leadership.

CHAPTER TWELVE

Peer Assistance and Review and Mandatory Remediation

JOHN GROSSMAN
CLAIRE ROBERTSON-KRAFT

Studies reveal that although teachers increase their effectiveness in the first few years in the classroom, on average the trajectory of improvement ends after three, five, or ten years, depending on the study.[1] This phenomenon is due in part to the fact that school systems rarely provide sufficient support for ongoing teacher development, and the support they do offer tends to come in the form of one-time professional development sessions that usually do not take into account specific school contexts or teachers' needs. To further complicate the problem, evaluation processes seldom provide the kind of feedback teachers need to grow professionally or the quality assurance necessary to ensure that ineffective teachers who fail to make acceptable progress are removed from the classroom.

In peer assistance and review (PAR), teachers assume responsibility for the observation of their colleagues through a districtwide peer-review process—a system pioneered in Toledo, Ohio, and used in Columbus, Ohio, for over twenty-five years. PAR provides a formula for teacher professional development and an evaluation system that identifies, remediates, and, if necessary, dismisses those who show little aptitude for the classroom. Peer review makes it statistically more likely that the evaluator is familiar with the subject matter being taught— after all, there are far more teachers than administrators—and by giving the observation responsibility to teachers, it makes it clear that evaluation is designed not as a "gotcha" system, but as one with a goal of helping teachers improve their instructional effectiveness.

John Grossman, formerly president of the Columbus Education Association for twenty-six years, wrote the first draft of this chapter, which outlines the issues that must be given careful consideration in the design and implementation of a PAR program. Following his death, the essay was abridged and revised for inclusion in this volume by Claire Robertson-Kraft.

BENEFITS

Evaluation systems should serve a dual purpose—to improve teaching and to ensure that only competent teachers are in classrooms. Too often, evaluation systems fail to achieve these purposes and do not maintain an approach to evaluation that builds confidence and emphasizes learning as a career-long development process. Successful evaluation systems must align evaluation with professional development by merging support and assistance. They should be supportive and continue to develop the professionalism of teachers and staff throughout their careers. The process of peer assistance and review accomplishes these purposes and leads to several important benefits.

Higher Levels of New Teacher Retention

Research shows that a third of new teachers leave the profession in the first three years, and that this number is significantly higher in urban areas.[2] Strong mentoring programs, such as the one discussed in chapter 11 and programs like PAR, have a significant impact on new teacher retention. For example, in Columbus, 80 percent of new teachers remain in the classroom after five years, compared to a national average of only 50 percent.[3]

Accurate Evaluation

As discussed in chapter 4, current systems of teacher evaluation often do not achieve their goals to improve practice and ensure instructional quality. An evaluation is typically conducted by an administrator, who may or may not be familiar with the content and only observes the teacher on a few occasions. In PAR programs, because teachers conduct the evaluations, it is statistically more likely that the observer will be knowledgeable about the content area and be able to provide constructive assistance. Additionally, multiple observations ensure that teachers have sufficient time to improve before their final evaluation, transforming teacher evaluation into a process aimed at promoting high-quality instruction.

Creation of Professional Learning Communities

Teaching should be viewed as a collaborative process focused on improving student learning. PAR programs transform the school system into a real professional learning community by increasing dialogue around common research-based expectations.

Dismissal of Ineffective Teachers

Research shows that students who have had two consecutive teachers who are identified by value-added models as ineffective never attain the level of accomplishment they could have reached had they had better instruction. However, the difficulty of winning a dismissal in due process hearings has led to the widespread belief that it is not worth the time, money, or aggravation to fire a teacher, so only a handful of teachers are dismissed for instructional ineffectiveness.[4] In PAR programs, ineffective teachers are dismissed at a much higher rate than when evaluations are conducted solely by the administration. For example, in the five years prior to the implementation of the PAR program in Toledo, Ohio, only one new teacher was terminated.[5] Since the implementation of the program, 10 percent of beginning teachers in Toledo are not asked back for a second year, and in Columbus, 20 percent of teachers who go through the program leave the school system.[6] Removing teachers who fail to improve their instructional effectiveness helps ensure that students receive high-quality instruction.

KEY PRINCIPLES IN A PAR PROGRAM

While various peer assistance and review programs differ somewhat in design, they possess several essential characteristics. When developing a PAR process, districts should take into account how each of these principles will inform the design of their program.

Support for Teachers at Critical Junctures

The need for quality professional development is not confined to new teachers, and, as such, districts must provide adequate support to meet the needs of all teachers interested in improving their craft. When capacity is limited, districts should focus investment on critical career junctures—entry and support for struggling educators—by establishing, at a minimum, an intern and intervention program. If additional resources are available, Operation Public Education (OPE) strongly recommends that support be provided for teachers throughout their career.

Intern Program for New Teachers. It is vital that all new teachers get off to a strong start if they are going to make education their careers. As such, intern programs should be mandatory for all teachers newly hired by a district, including those individuals who may have had years of experience in other school systems and current staff within the district returning to the classroom after working in nonteaching capacities for five years or more. By increasing teacher success and confidence, the intern program works to stabilize the teaching force and break the vicious cycle of teacher turnover. Each intern will be assigned a consulting teacher—often referred to as a mentor—by the PAR program. Though these consulting teachers serve a supportive role, they also prepare the final evaluative appraisal, recommending whether or not the intern should receive a teaching contract for the upcoming school year.

When setting up intern programs, districts should keep the following considerations in mind (see chapter 11 for a more detailed discussion):

- *Ensuring sufficient ongoing support.* Each consulting teacher should devote considerable time to carrying out classroom observations and conferencing with each intern. Though forty-five minutes is the recommended minimum observation period, the number and length of classroom visits will vary based on individual needs. That said, a good guideline is a minimum of twenty classroom observations and a minimum of ten conferences per year.
- *Limiting the ratio of consulting teachers to new teachers.* It is recommended that this ratio be minimized to ensure adequate support, ideally fifteen to one or lower.

Intervention Program for Struggling Teachers. Experienced teachers who are having difficulty must be able to find assistance and solid support within the school system, and it is important that districts create a culture where teachers referred for assistance are not categorized as unsuccessful teachers who must be removed from the profession. Instead, experienced teachers should be valued as professionals who require constructive support to increase their effectiveness.

Intervention programs should be designed to harness all available resources within the school system to help experienced teachers who are having difficulties in their performance or their professional classroom duties. Each intervention case should be assigned a consulting teacher to meet with over the course of the year. At the close of the year, consulting teachers will recommend whether the individual should return to the classroom or if administrative action should be taken. If dismissal is the desired result, all records of the intervention must be available as documentation of what transpired over the course of the year, so that no teacher leaving the intervention program can doubt that the maximum assistance has been made available.

When designing an intervention program, districts should keep the following considerations in mind:

- *Ensuring sufficient ongoing support.* It is recommended that intervention cases receive double the support of new teacher cases—in other words, forty observations and twenty conferences over the course of the year.
- *Maintaining a feasible consulting teacher to struggling teacher ratio.* Because intervention cases require additional support, struggling teachers should be considered as though they were two teachers, and the ratio of consulting teachers to teachers should be adjusted accordingly.

- *Designing a clear referral process.* Districts will need to develop a clear procedure for determining how struggling teachers enter the program by incorporating some or all of the following processes:

  Self-referral. The teacher simply writes a letter to the president of the local union and is automatically admitted into the program.

  Recommendation made by teachers or school councils. Peers or school councils could recommend colleagues based on a set of predetermined criteria. To ensure a fair process, districts should set up individual school councils to help make these decisions.

  Recommendation made by the building administrator. The building or unit principal may start the process of referral by recommending someone he or she believes could benefit from the program. This recommendation should be based on clear evaluative criteria.

  Student learning results. Teachers whose students continue to perform at an ineffective level according to value-added data could be required to enter the system.

In the Operation Public Education framework, two signals indicate that a teacher is a candidate for the intervention program: (1) unsatisfactory ratings on observations made using the observation frameworks discussed in chapter 4, and (2) a value-added or student growth objective score indicating ineffective instruction, as discussed in chapter 3 and chapter 7. Although self-referral and student learning results would lead teachers to be automatically enrolled in the process, districts will need to develop a process of checks and balances for identifying teachers through subjective means (refer to the example from the Columbus school district as shown in figure 12.1). Once the referral process is completed, teachers must be required to enter the program and receive assistance.

All Other Teachers. Some districts have begun experimenting with peer assistance and review programs that apply to all teachers. These could be made available for teachers making a move in grade level (such as going from a fifth-grade classroom to a first-grade classroom), shifting curricular areas (such as moving from math to science classes), or simply for teachers interested in accelerating their professional growth. OPE recommends that peer review be expanded to teachers at all stages of their careers for the same reasons that peer review addresses among new and struggling teachers: the greater likelihood of receiving fair treatment, and that those with subject-matter experience will conduct the evaluation.

FIGURE 12.1
PAR intervention referral process

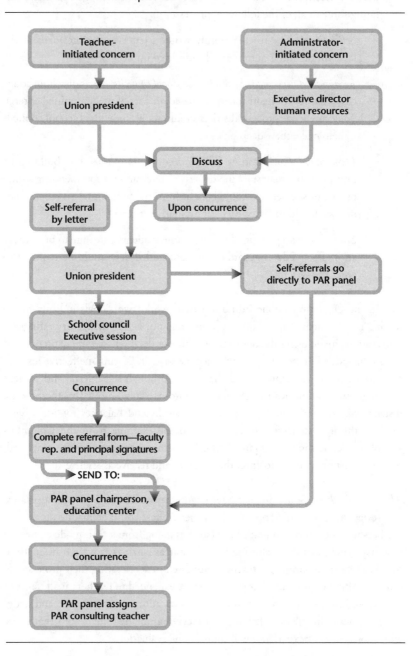

Furthermore, because moving up the OPE career ladder to higher pay requires enhanced classroom performance, all teachers will have an extra incentive to improve their practice. As a result, additional support should not be confined to new and struggling teachers; it needs to be made available to all teachers interested in building new knowledge and skills. As an example, for every three hundred students (in many states the size of a typical lower school), districts would deploy one full-time coach, recruited from the ranks of highly effective teachers. The coach's role should parallel the consulting teacher's role, including classroom observation and feedback. Since coaches usually have not worked this way in the past, districts must develop a program that will build trust with veteran teachers and principals to ease the transition.

Effective Consulting Teachers

Promoting high-quality practice means providing all teachers—new, struggling, and those just looking to improve—with the support they need to be successful in the classroom. To accomplish this, districts must carefully select full-time mentors, evaluators, and coaches, typically referred to in PAR programs as consulting teachers. Consulting teachers are responsible for observing teachers and meeting with them throughout the year, putting together a series of professional development courses and, ultimately, assessing peer performance and making the tough recommendation regarding future employment. The success of the program depends, in large part, on the efficacy of these teachers.

Clear Criteria for Selection. Given their essential role, districts should keep the following considerations in mind when developing selection criteria:

- *Look for a balance between teaching and communication skills.* Criteria should incorporate the following skills: outstanding classroom teaching ability, effective written and oral communication skills, and interpersonal skills. Though highly effective teaching should be a crucial requirement, effective consulting teachers must also be skilled in communication and relationship building.
- *Experience must be fresh.* Consulting teachers should be chosen from the ranks of classroom teachers. To make certain that their experience remains fresh, districts should institute a maximum term of service (recommended three years), after which consulting teachers will return to the classroom. This timeline will ensure that they remain attuned to the needs of teachers.
- *Keep a pool of teachers available.* Instead of having consulting teachers apply for a specific opening, districts should accept applications on a rolling basis and fill slots as necessary. This process will ensure that grade-level and subject-area needs can be met, and that a constant supply of consulting teachers is available.

Ongoing Training and Support. Consulting teachers need to develop strong relationships with the teachers they serve and must utilize conversation skills and formative-assessment tools to promote teacher development and student learning (see chapter 11 for more detail). When the coaching of experienced teachers is mandated due to unsatisfactory evaluations, consulting teachers will need specialized professional development to supplement their skills. With both new teachers and experienced teachers who request coaching, the consulting teacher is bringing welcome support. However, in mandatory coaching, the consulting teacher may meet outright or implied resistance from struggling teachers. All consulting teachers require training in designing and implementing action plans and evaluating progress that can be communicated to supervisors. But working with teachers who may not welcome efforts may be considerably more wearing than mentoring new teachers. All consulting teachers, but especially those engaged in mandated coaching, will benefit greatly by receiving ongoing support through regularly scheduled meetings with a lead consulting teacher and a community of consulting teachers doing similar work.

Because consulting teachers must develop a clear vision for effective teaching, as well as knowledge of coaching, mentoring, and evaluation best practices, districts should prioritize professional development and training. When doing so, they should keep the following considerations in mind:

- *Frequency.* Consulting teacher professional development should be held frequently, ideally at least once every two weeks.
- *Developing partnerships to ensure quality.* If possible, districts should attempt to establish relationships with local colleges to maximize the effectiveness of these trainings. In Columbus, a successful partnership has been developed with The Ohio State University.
- *Comprehensive training.* Consulting teachers should be trained in employing effective observation techniques, understanding stages of new teacher development, providing feedback, structuring conversations, and assessing performance against evaluation standards.
- *Various types of assistance.* Consulting teachers must have access to a variety of resources to help improve their teachers' instruction. These types of assistance include, but are not limited to, observation, high-quality contacts, professional reading, workshops, videotaping, and lesson planning.
- *Sufficient time.* Because immediate feedback through an observation cycle is a critical component of teacher improvement, consulting teachers must be provided with sufficient time to be in classrooms. To limit costs, districts may be tempted to cut corners in this area, but it is absolutely essential that the

consulting to new teacher ratio be minimized so that classroom time and feedback can be maximized.

- *Flexibility to differentiate support for veteran teachers.* Consulting teachers typically work easily with veteran teachers who are eager for additional support. However, differences may surface in scheduling meetings. New teachers should participate in frequent—ideally weekly—structured observations and conversations with their consulting teachers. Experienced teachers who have volunteered for coaching may benefit from a more loosely structured schedule. Often, experienced teachers prefer to meet with a consulting teacher and then work on implementation for a couple of weeks before meeting again to reflect on progress and identify continuing next steps.

Joint Governance

Shared decision making and joint governance are essential to the success of any PAR program. Districts must create a union-management panel, with teachers chosen by the union and administrators by the district, to take on the following responsibilities:

- Manage and determine the operation of PAR
- Select and evaluate the consulting teachers
- Oversee the training program and in-service of the consulting teachers
- Approve all rules and forms used by the program
- Vote to include a teacher entering through intervention
- Assign teachers to consulting teachers and balance the case loads
- Review all status reports and evaluations submitted by consulting teachers
- Set up a yearlong schedule for the program
- Prepare and approve all concluding summaries from the intervention program
- Approve all recommendations to the superintendent to terminate a teacher
- Review and approve the professional development program for the interns
- Maintain an office and resource library that supports the program
- Establish board of review procedures that make sense and provide for appeal
- Periodically review consulting teachers' work to ensure enforcement of performance standards

When designing its panel, a district should strive to maintain a balance of teachers and administrators. Many districts instituting PAR programs have opted for a five–four split: five teachers and four administrators. The chair of the panel typically rotates annually between the union president and the executive director of human resources. The commitment of top leadership demonstrates the value placed on this program. Designing the PAR panel so that the majority of members are teachers is more than symbolic, as it is vital that peers control the program and feel strongly invested in it. In Columbus, the panel is composed of four teachers and three administrators. In addition to the union president, there is a teacher from the elementary level, a teacher from the secondary level, and a teacher from special education/special programs on the panel. On the administrative side, a building-level administrator as well as representatives from the central office fill the remaining seats. To produce a positive synergy and encourage collaboration, it is recommended that all decisions require at least a two-thirds majority.

Fair Process for Evaluation and Dismissal

While the primary goal of the PAR program is to develop teachers' effectiveness, the program also ensures that incompetent teachers are removed from the classroom. This feature addresses a major shortcoming in the current public education system—namely, the widespread conventional wisdom that it is too time consuming and costly to undertake the dismissal process because of the legal and technical barriers that operate to protect teachers who should not be in classrooms. Districts should take the following steps to ensure that this process operates fairly and provides teachers with sufficient opportunity to improve instructional practice:

Develop clear and accepted standards of practice. Districts should develop clear expectations for teacher performance, which will likely include a common vision for high-quality instructional practice and a means for measuring student progress. Teachers must be invested in meeting these expectations of performance while enrolled in the program. For more detail on how to establish these evaluation standards and rubrics, please refer to chapters 3, 4, and 7.

Determine adequate levels of improvement. Districts will need to set standards for what qualifies as adequate improvement and provide sufficient feedback over the course of the year, so that teachers know where they stand in relation to these standards. This communication will ensure that those enrolled in the program are working purposefully toward a meaningful outcome.

Design a process for dismissing teachers. If adequate improvement does not occur, sufficient documentation must be kept to justify tough decisions that may result in termination. In the OPE framework, tenure remains an important protection against political and other abuses, but it cannot protect a teacher whose instructional practice is deemed ineffective by the PAR panel. Evaluation, in short, trumps tenure.

OPE recommends the following process for evaluation, support, and, if necessary, dismissal (see figure 12.2). As mentioned previously, the standards of practice in the OPE framework are based equally on teacher actions (observation) and student learning results. This means that two signals can indicate that a teacher is in need of additional support: (1) unsatisfactory ratings in observation using a framework for teaching (discussed in chapter 4) and (2) a value-added score indicating ineffective instruction (discussed in chapter 3) or ineffective student progress in specialist disciplines (discussed in chapter 7).

FIGURE 12.2
Remediation process

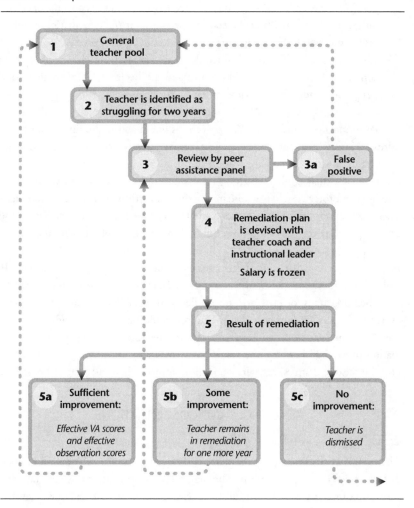

Two consecutive years with a signal from either one of these indicators, or both in the same year, would bring the case before the PAR panel, which should consist of balanced leadership. If the PAR panel determines that extenuating circumstances cannot explain the problem (no "false positive," to use the medical analogy), the teacher will undergo a year of remediation, resulting in one of three outcomes:

1. *Successful remediation.* If the teacher performs at the effective level, then the salary, which was frozen during the year, is not only unfrozen, but lost wages are restored.
2. *Some improvement.* The teacher's coach and PAR panel agree that one more year—the most allowed—can be provided to the teacher to continue her or his improvement efforts. If at the end of a second year the remediation program proves successful, the salary is unfrozen and wages are restored.
3. *No improvement.* The panel concludes that—either through lack of effort or lack of ability—the teacher did not make the necessary improvement, and the process ends with a recommendation for dismissal.

Personnel decisions in the PAR process, as noted above, should require a two-thirds majority. In this scenario, teachers cannot be outvoted, and at least one administrator must vote with them for a decision. However, no vote can protect a teacher when their student learning results continue to be ineffective. In short, nothing can protect teachers whose instructional practices are harming children. A teacher with poor value-added scores could take two years to enter remediation and get as many as two years to improve, but no longer if the scores remain ineffective.

Ensure Due Process. In most peer assistance and review programs, such as in Columbus, the union provides teachers with legal representation, but given the overwhelming body of evidence, no challenge to a PAR decision has ever been overturned. Another option is that the union would relinquish its right to defend the teacher in legal proceedings in return for the key role it would play in the remediation process. Either way, the result is a system with integrity designed to support, but also to dismiss, teachers who fail to improve their instructional practices.

CHALLENGES AND CONSIDERATIONS

Costs

The cost of instituting a peer assistance and review program will depend on local district conditions. An office must be maintained with at least one secretary and consulting teachers who are on full-time release status, so districts must factor in their salaries plus the extended-time stipends. If districts decide to expand peer re-view to all teachers, the decision will also have cost implications (the precise amount depends on how the district implements the program), but the number of observations for experienced teachers would be significantly lower than for new and struggling teachers.

The union does help in a number of small ways, but in participating school systems across the country the program is primarily funded by the school board or central administration. Instead of viewing a PAR program as a new item in the budget, districts should consider how existing resources can be redeployed to bet-ter align with current priorities (see chapter 13). Additionally, many districts im-plementing PAR programs have done so by utilizing grant funds, so districts would be wise to secure support from external sources.

Governance

Some critics may be concerned that PAR will take away the principal's instruc-tional leadership role or undermine union strength. However, these concerns have not yet materialized in districts where the program has been implemented. In today's school systems, building administrators are often overwhelmed by all facets of their jobs, so PAR is typically appreciated. Furthermore, a solid evalua-tion system that includes a high level of support only helps the union do its job. No one has the right to teach, but everyone deserves the kind of support and scrutiny that can lead to success.

To ensure that positive relationships are maintained, consulting teachers should be trained to work closely with principals and help them by taking evalua-tion off their very full plates. Additionally, they should work together to develop strategies for improving intern and intervention teachers' performance. This posi-tive relationship is essential to a successful program.

Districts and unions will need to jointly decide where the PAR agreement will be written. Some districts, such as Columbus, have chosen to include the agreement in the master contract, providing the program with a sense of perma-nence. To ensure flexibility, other districts have developed an agreement that exists outside of the master contract. Either way, the decision should be supported by both union and district officials.[7]

Capacity

Each year districts should project the number of consulting teachers who will be needed. When projections change, it may be tempting to increase loads instead of adding more consulting teachers, but it is essential that the ratio be minimized. This will ensure that every consulting teacher is able to provide sufficient ongoing support for each of their cases.

Building Trust

Peer review may initially be met with opposition from teachers who view it as a threat to solidarity or by administrators who view it as a threat to their power. With time, support will build for the program, but this initial hurdle can be overcome if districts move slowly and ensure that the lines of communication are kept open and program expectations are made clear.[8] Educators may also initially question whether it is possible for a mentor to simultaneously serve as an evaluator. However, with training in building relationships and setting expectations, consulting teachers can be taught to fulfill both roles. Since the process is systematic and data-driven, it increases the likelihood that both parties involved will come to the same conclusions.

CONCLUSION

The process of peer assistance and review has proven to be successful in changing the culture of many school systems for more than a quarter of a century. Not only is the program focused on high standards for student learning, but it emphasizes the importance of creating a professional conversation around improved instruction. In doing so, it builds a solid partnership between unions, teachers, and administrators, and encourages them to work collaboratively to improve the quality of teaching and accelerate student learning.

CHAPTER THIRTEEN

Strategic Professional Development Review

REGIS ANNE SHIELDS

KAREN HAWLEY MILES

Expanding professional development to ensure that teachers acquire new knowledge and skills may be expensive. Therefore, before determining whether additional investments are needed, it is necessary to determine not only the current investment level but also what that investment is buying. Districts often spend significantly more on professional development than they think, and these fragmented efforts too often lack the coordination, focus, and school-level support needed to implement research-proven strategies.

A strategic review of professional development spending will allow districts to understand their total investment for teachers and principals in terms of both magnitude and alignment with district priorities and best practices. Armed with this information, districts can make informed decisions on redirecting current investments to more aligned strategies and leveraging funds for additional investments.

Education Resource Strategies, Inc. (ERS) is a nonprofit that has worked extensively with urban public school systems to rethink the use of district and school-level resources—people, time, and money. Its working partnerships with school systems bridge research and practice by supporting clients with Web-based tools, research and training, and diagnostic analysis tailored to their district, and by outlining strategies that are actionable and transformational both within and beyond the districts in which they work. In this chapter, Regis Shields, a director of ERS, and Karen Hawley Miles, the founder and executive director of ERS, discuss how to develop the capacity to carry out these strategic professional development reviews at the district level.

INTRODUCTION

The Operation Public Education (OPE) framework recognizes the value of increasing a teacher's or principal's capacity by investing in his or her knowledge and skills, both as an individual and as part of a team of teachers, a school, and a district. The implementation of the critical professional development components of the OPE framework—including supports for new teachers, collaborative planning time, and peer assistance and review—will require districts to rethink their professional development strategies. Districts will need to ensure that other district professional development initiatives align with and support these OPE components and that these components are adequately funded.

The professional development strategic review designed by Education Resource Strategies facilitates school district efforts to allocate scarce professional development resources to the district's most pressing priorities in ways most likely to improve student performance. In doing so, the strategic review highlights whether districts are investing across the career cycle of teachers and principals, matching professional development support with school needs, distributing resources across content areas, organizing to provide teachers with collaborative planning time and expert coaching, and adequately supporting professional staff development efforts.

A strategic professional development review has three major components (see figure 13.1):

1. *Consensus Building.* Building a shared understanding among all relevant stakeholders of professional development needs and priorities
2. *Mapping and Measuring Current Investment.* Detailing and measuring the current investment in professional development
3. *Strategic Planning and Resource Reallocation.* Reallocating investments to create a multiyear professional development strategy that aligns with best practices of staff development and systemwide priorities

When developing a professional development plan, most districts fall short of or completely omit the mapping and measuring phase—the foundation for all subsequent work—because they often lack the expertise, time, framework, and tools to complete this task. While the consensus-building and planning phases are

FIGURE 13.1

The professional development strategic review process

of critical importance (and we will touch on each briefly), this chapter will focus primarily on the mapping and measuring phase of the strategic review, thus seeking to provide districts with a framework and tool for effectively mapping and measuring their professional development.[1]

CONSENSUS-BUILDING PHASE

Building a shared understanding of systemwide professional development priorities, opportunities, and challenges is critical to a successful long-term strategy. It ensures that all relevant stakeholders own the district's focus and approach and greatly increases the likelihood that they will act in ways that align with this strategy. Consensus building is not a one-time event; it occurs throughout the strategic-review process, from the initial decision to undertake the review through the development of the strategy. Without understanding the critical nature of how rethinking investment in capacity building contributes to student success, participation may devolve into a compliance activity.

School districts tackle this task in many different ways, depending on professional capacity, culture, and community involvement practices. At its core, this process should involve all stakeholders who will be affected, including teachers representing different grade levels and subject expertise, principals representing different grade levels and school types, and teachers and principals unions or associations. The process should be led by the superintendent and his or her cabinet to signal that the outcome of this process is the heart of the district's plan for student success.

MAPPING AND MEASURING PHASE

Before districts can begin to create a strategic professional development strategy, they must first understand their starting point: how much are they currently investing and what are they buying? This process requires compiling a comprehensive inventory of all professional development activities and categorizing each dollar invested so that spending can be mapped to understand its alignment with district priorities and research-based strategies.

Districts should begin the process by identifying all professional development initiatives, which is not as simple as merely reviewing the district budget and tagging line items. Professional development can be spread over many departments and/or combined with other activities, and is sometimes not identified with any specificity in the budget. In addition, district budgets rarely include sufficient detail about the purpose or topic of the initiatives to accurately map investments in ways that inform whether the professional development is strategic.

To accurately identify all professional development activities, districts must collect data from a number of different sources. The primary data sources are the district's strategic plan, adopted budget, payroll data, human resource information, student enrollment data, school performance and demographic information, school improvement plans, and all relevant contracts.[2] This information will often need to be supplemented with interviews with key district staff, individual initiative budgets, and lists of all personnel involved in the planning, delivery, and implementation of professional development. School district information systems are not perfectly aligned, and districts should take care to reconcile and validate information from the different data sources.

Once all professional development initiatives have been identified, districts must code each initiative in ways that will allow mapping against priorities and research-based staff development strategies. The ERS coding tool provides a framework for this mapping and is guided by the following five questions:[3]

1. How much is the district spending on professional development?
2. What does the current spending buy?
3. Who controls and manages how the dollars are spent?
4. How is the professional development funded?
5. How is spending allocated across schools?

The findings uncovered by answering each of these questions should serve as the foundation for districts when building consensus and shared understanding around the opportunities, gaps, and challenges of current professional development investment and developing a systemwide professional development strategy.

How Much is the District Spending on Professional Development?

When districts think about their investment in professional development, they often think narrowly. They look to the activities of the professional development office, such as workshops and courses, as well as big-ticket items, such as content coaching or new teacher mentoring. This narrow perspective results not only in an understatement of the total investment but also in a lost opportunity to consolidate and tightly align all professional development investment around focused district priorities that reflect both student and teacher needs.

For a more proactive, inclusive approach to professional development, districts need to include (1) all sources of funds, (2) teacher contractual time, (3) all types of spending, and (4) nontraining investment (see table 13.1).

All Sources of Funds. Professional development is typically supported by multiple funding streams, including federal, state, local, and private funds. Many districts

TABLE 13.1

Capturing all investment in professional development

Sources of funds	Teacher time	Types of spending	Non-training investment
• Federal funds • State funds • Local or general funds • Private foundation and grants • In-kind contributions or partnerships	• Contract time • Required regularly collaborative planning time	• Staff and administrative time • Consultants • Stipends • Substitutes and coverage • Materials • Travel and conferences	• Education lane increments • Sabbaticals • Tuition reimbursement

do not have an "all-funds" budgeting practice, with state and local funds sometimes being managed completely separately from categorical or federal funds, often in completely different departments. To further complicate matters, private grants and community partnerships are often managed and accounted for in the specific departments responsible for raising the funds and conducting the activity. This fragmentation creates a challenge in tracking down all investments and also results in silos of professional development activities with little integration or coordination across departments. Districts should keep in mind that a comprehensive picture of professional development spending requires looking across all of these types of funds.

Teacher Time. Many districts include in their calendars full or half days for teachers that are specifically dedicated to professional development. Even though teachers negotiate extra salary dollars to cover these days, districts do not typically consider the cost of these days as a professional development expense. This is even the case when these days are the primary means of delivering districtwide professional development initiatives, such as the implementation of a new curriculum or literacy initiative. Including this cost is important because it highlights the fact that this teacher time is often one of the largest expenditures in professional development and puts a premium on making sure it is used effectively.

Another large district investment is in school-based teacher collaborative planning time—regular time scheduled during the work week when teachers meet in strategic groups to work to improve practice. If this time is mandated by district policy and plays a critical role in a district's professional development delivery strategy, such as when it is paired with school-based content coaches, its cost should also be included.

All Types of Spending. Districts should include all types of spending that support an initiative, such as consultant fees, travel, teacher stipends, materials, and substitutes or coverage. Some of this information is difficult to collect, such as spending on coverage, as it is rarely tracked as professional development. Districts should also include the percentage of administrative time that is devoted to managing, developing, and delivering professional development.

Nontraining Investments in Skills and Knowledge. Teachers participate in many activities originally intended to improve content knowledge and pedagogical skills, which are typically overlooked by districts when they are considering their portfolio of professional development activities. These activities, including items such as tuition reimbursement and sabbaticals, are often considered more as benefits or entitlements by both districts and teachers. The largest of these items is education salary increments that are part of many teacher-compensation structures and codified in union contracts. Because control over the content and focus of this category of spending is often determined by the individual participant, districts miss an opportunity to align a large investment with district priorities and needs. This missed opportunity is compounded by the fact that these salary increments, once achieved, are earned over the life of a teacher's career. OPE's proposed compensation structure eliminates salary education credits altogether and gives teachers a salary "bonus" only at the time of educational attainment.

What Does the Current Spending Buy?

This seems like an obvious question. Once a district has identified the total investment in professional development, all the activities should be identified. However, the devil is in the details. To understand whether the investment is strategic, the inquiry does not end at identification. For each initiative or agency, districts must understand the (1) target, (2) purpose, (3) topic, and (4) delivery strategy. Looking collectively at all investments will highlight activities for enhancement, elimination, and expansion (see table 13.2).[4]

Target. School districts should invest in developing professional capacity both in the context of a school-level or districtwide instructional program and in the context of meeting the individual career needs of teachers and principals. A strategic review provides insight into whether and to what extent a district is targeting professional development investment in these two critical areas. By identifying the target of the investment, districts also gain insight into the balance of their investment between teachers and principals in relationship to their priorities and needs.

TABLE 13.2

Understanding professional development activities[a]

Target	Purpose	Topic	Delivery method
School	*School target*	• Arts	• School-based
• Whole school	• Restructuring	• Assessment	coaching
• Teams of teachers	• Instructional	• Bilingual	• District depart-
	improvement	• Character	ment training
Individual career	• Program support	• Counseling	• Individual
growth	• Special	• Foreign language	workshops
	populations	• Gifted	• Externally pro-
• Teachers		• Health	vided courses
• Principals	*Individual career*	• Instructional	• Training academy
	growth target	strategy	• Mentors
		• Math	• Comprehensive
	• Induction	• Leadership	reform models
	• Continuing	• Literacy	• Consultants
	education	• Safety	• Salary increments
	• Recertification	• Science	
	• Leadership	• Social studies	
	development	• Special education	
	• Support for strug-	• Standards	
	gling teachers or	• Technology	
	principals		

[a] More detailed information on coding professional development activities in each of the areas can be found on our website at www.educationresourcestrategies.org.

Purpose. It is also critical that districts understand the purpose of the investment to determine if their investment strategy is focused and strategic. When investing in the individual growth of teachers and principals, specific career transition junctures should be the focus of a district's investment, including induction, leadership opportunities, recertification into high-need subject areas, continuing education for individual performance skills and knowledge, and support for struggling professionals. With limited resources it is not always possible to invest equally across each stage, but it is important for districts to understand the balance of their investment across the cycle to ensure that this balance makes sense in terms of district needs and priorities.

Topic. Districts should utilize the strategic-review process to determine how focused or thinly spread the total investment is across topics. Districts that offer thirty or more professional development topics actually may have less of an impact on teaching and learning than districts focused on key areas of need. There are many topics and kinds of training worthy of professional development investment, but districts should focus on depth over breadth.

Delivery Method. Finally, districts should code all professional development by how it is delivered so that they can reflect on whether the method of delivery is the most effective or whether it can be done in a more job-embedded manner. A district can see whether they are relying heavily on ineffective stand-alone workshops for the delivery of their professional development or on more research-based practices that are job-embedded, such as content coaching and mentoring. While the choice of delivery method is sometimes dependent on the target and topic of the activity, it is essential that professional development be delivered in a way that has the most potential to have an impact on teaching and learning.

Who Controls and Manages How the Dollars Are Spent?

To understand why current professional development activities are often fragmented and uncoordinated, districts must understand who controls funding. When departments and offices are provided generic budgets for professional development, thereby spreading spending decisions across multiple departments, there is little chance that a comprehensive and integrated professional development strategy will emerge.

Knowing who manages the money will help districts determine who should be held accountable for effective implementation. This question focuses on a district's system for evaluating and improving professional development activities. As an example of how these questions are applied, we can look at a typical example of a school-based content coaching initiative. In many districts that have adopted this strategy, the decision is made centrally and each school is allocated a content coach. This coach often reports to and is evaluated by the principal. In this scenario, the district "controls" the spending while the principal "manages" the spending. When control and management are split, districts should pay close attention to accountability structures.

How Is Professional Development Funded?

To make long-term plans, districts must understand how professional development activities are funded. The ERS coding tool provides a framework for reviewing and analyzing professional development investments by (1) source—federal, state, local, or private; (2) type—nonrecurring funding stream or grant; and (3) flexibility of use. Reviewing the source and type of funding allows districts to understand both the predictability and sustainability of the funding supporting critical professional development initiatives. Heavily relying on external funds or competitive grants with unpredictable revenue streams or stated end dates to support professional development places the sustainability of a long-term professional development strategy at risk. In addition, many professional development activities are supported by funds with restrictions on use. Districts must develop a clear understanding of the flexibility of the use of funds in order to use them more effectively to support a strategic-development plan.

How Is Investment Allocated Across Schools?

As districts seek to create a system of high-performing schools rather than pockets of successful ones, it is critical that they understand the type and amount of professional development investment that is allocated across schools, and if that allocation makes sense in terms of each school's teacher and leadership capacity and student performance. Districts allocate professional development resources to schools in a number of different ways. They allocate dollars directly to be used at the individual school's discretion; they allocate specific resources to schools that directly support a systemwide initiative, such as content coaches or mentors; and they place specific programs at schools that have significant professional development support components, such as Reading First, or comprehensive reform models. Districts should utilize the strategic professional development review to quantify professional development spending by school and highlight any inequities in how district policies are playing out at the school level. This process will determine whether district professional development is matching school needs and provide the needed foundation for the district to consider both the amount and type of support each school requires.

THE STRATEGIC PLANNING AND RESOURCE REALLOCATION PHASE

The professional development map serves as the foundation for the strategic planning and resource reallocation phase. This phase culminates in a multiyear, focused professional development strategy that is tightly linked with the system's strategic plan, supporting and facilitating major reform efforts such as curriculum and assessment development.

Adding the word "strategy" rather than "plan" after the words "professional development" changes the discussion dramatically. A strategically designed professional development system targets scarce resources to a district's most important priorities in ways most likely to improve student performance. This short definition embodies two critical elements that form the foundation of a strategic professional development system: (1) targeting the district's most important priorities, and (2) incorporating best practices of teacher and principal development.

Professional Development Targets District Priorities

A good systemwide professional development strategy directs scarce resources to a district's most important student performance priorities, to teacher and principal capacity needs, and to schools that can benefit the most. It deliberately balances investment in different parts of a district system, making decisions and trade-offs regarding purpose, focus, and target—for a whole system. Decisions and trade-offs are made with a long-term perspective—understanding that building skills and knowledge is not something that happens in a year but over time.

Determining priorities and then aligning investments requires a careful analysis of student performance, school needs, and principal and teacher capacity measured across multiple indicators. Table 13.3 provides some categories of information that serve as a foundation for determining a system's professional development needs. This information must be detailed enough to provide concrete help in the specific areas in which students, teachers, and principals need to improve. Measuring, collecting, and disseminating information of the type detailed in table 13.3 will have significant implications for current practices in many districts, including the way teachers are evaluated. The OPE framework incorporates practices around teacher evaluation that will lead to a more informed understanding of professional development needs at the individual, school, and district level.

TABLE 13.3
Defining system-wide professional development needs

Students	Schools	Teachers	Principals
• Student academic performance • Social and emotional needs • Programmatic profile (special education, English-language learners)	• Distribution of teacher experience • Distribution of teacher quality (as measured by evaluations based on teaching performance standards) • Teaching in areas of certification • Principal and teacher-leader capacity • Student performance results	*Experience* • Less than three years of experience • Hiring estimates *Skills and content* • Measures against teaching performance standards • Student performance results • High-need subject areas • Professional development history	*Experience* • Less than three years of experience • Hiring estimates *Skills and content* • Measures against leadership performance standards • School performance results • Professional development history

Professional Development Is Structured to Improve Student Performance

A strategic professional development system invests in professional development that is designed according to evidence-based principles that detail the kind of activities most likely to improve student performance. While drawing a concrete link between student performance and specific professional development efforts is a difficult task, there is growing consensus regarding what types of professional development have the biggest impact on student performance.[5] Figure 13.2 sets forth a set of professional development principles that ERS has drawn from its work with school districts and from the scant literature to suggest principles for a strategic professional development system.[6]

A district can also look to comparable districts for best practices, as it is often helpful to understand how similarly situated districts are managing their professional development investments. While there is no research that links the balance of investment in a professional development portfolio to improvement in student performance, understanding how investments compare to other districts can provide invaluable guidance in terms of both investment direction and identifying best practices.

COMMON FINDINGS AND IMPLICATIONS FOR PLANNING

During the strategic-planning process, a district should use the professional development map to view the entirety of its investment with an eye to enhancement,

FIGURE 13.2
School system professional development principles

---

1. Invest primarily in school-based expert support for school leaders to implement a coherent instructional design and respond to identified student and teacher learning needs.

2. Ensure effective time and structures for teachers to engage in collaborative learning and planning.

3. Structure career opportunities and compensation to encourage and reward individual professional development.

4. Focus district investment in professional development on leveraged career transition points: entry, leadership, and support for struggling educators.

5. Differentiate professional development and support based on school and educator needs and performance levels.

6. Create accountability for professional development effectiveness by assigning responsibility and measuring impact on classroom practice and student achievement.

---

elimination, and/or expansion. Below we highlight some findings that are typical in many districts that ERS has worked with and the implications of those findings for creating a comprehensive professional development strategy. How districts tackle these common findings in the planning phase will vary by district, depending in part on available financial resources, flexibility of union contract provisions, teacher capacity, student need, and political will.

Include All Forms of Spending

Districts spend more than they think on professional development, and the most costly items are teacher time set aside for professional development and salary increments based on the accumulation of credits or educational attainment. In the districts analyzed by ERS, annual spending on professional development initiatives (not including contractual teacher time or salary education increments) ranged from $5,000 to $9,400 per teacher, or from 2.1 percent to 5.5 percent of the total operating budget. Because districts generally define professional development narrowly, districts analyzed initially understated their total investment. Teacher time—usually in the form of full or half days allocated throughout the year—comprised 20 percent to 60 percent of total spending on professional development, not including education salary increments. In districts studied by ERS, investment in salary increments comprised up to 41 percent of all professional development spending.

The perception of low spending on professional development often gets in the way of "thinking big" about what is possible if leaders are willing to challenge the current use of district resources. Providing expert coaching at the school and classroom level is labor intensive and therefore expensive. In the context of a $400,000 budget it seems impossible; in the context of nine million dollars, it can become a reality.

Even though districts spend more than they think, some districts do underinvest in professional development. Unfortunately, in difficult budget times, nonclassroom activities and those activities deemed not essential to keeping schools open tend to be the first thing on the chopping block, with professional development often a prime candidate. For these districts, current professional development spending might not be adequate to support a new strategy, especially if some professional development activities are funded through restricted sources. While there is not a "right" level of professional development investment, an accurate understanding of the total investment can highlight the need to identify opportunities for the redirection of funds as districts review all investments—including those outside of current professional development spending—in the context of shaping a districtwide strategic plan.

Highlighting both teacher contract time and education salary increments in the professional development strategic review not only puts a premium on making sure these investments are used effectively as currently structured, but also allows the district to consider other ways the resources might be used. In many districts there is little support or guidance for using contractual time effectively, no accountability to link activities to improved student performance, and, when controlled by the central office, little differentiation based on school capacity or need. As there are often loose policies for how education credits can be earned, this type of investment is often not aligned to district, teacher, or school needs and is not responsive to changing needs.

Districts may want to consider how to convert this investment in teacher time into more flexible school-based time, where strategically grouped teachers can work together on a regular basis with expert support. Or districts may want to rethink the entire teacher-compensation structure and use funds currently devoted to salary education credits to compensate teachers for leadership responsibilities or expertise in high-need areas.

Invest in Both Organizations and Individuals

Districts tend to invest predominately in professional development activities that focus on improving teaching quality in the context of district or school priorities, with an emphasis on school-based coaching. Five districts recently analyzed by ERS focused from 64 percent to 82 percent of spending on professional development initiatives that targeted organizational priorities rather than individual growth opportunities.[7] From 30 percent to 60 percent of this investment supported school-based teacher leaders or coaches. The investment in individual growth tends to be focused predominantly at the outset of principal and teacher careers and very little at other critical career junctures. Almost all districts studied have no targeted professional development for supporting struggling professionals and very little professional development invested in leadership training.

Districts need to invest in developing skills in both the context of organizational needs and in the context of individual careers. In the past, many districts targeted investment primarily in areas that emphasized the individual career needs of teachers, with a large percentage of dollars allocated to continuing education activities, such as volunteer course offerings, workshops, and tuition reimbursement. Over the past ten years there has been a shift toward a more evidence-based approach, with districts making a significant investment in professional development activities that support school-based, job-embedded learning, such as comprehensive school reform models and school-based content coaching initiatives.

The professional development strategic review lays out the investment along critical career junctures of teachers and principals—induction, continuing education, recertification, and remediation—allowing districts to understand how they are prioritizing. With limited resources available, it is a far more effective strategy for districts to concentrate investment in areas of high need rather than to touch lightly upon each career juncture.

Evidence shows that investing in new teacher induction programs that include job-embedded mentoring improves teacher retention (see chapter 11). Teacher mentoring programs can suffer from a lack of long-term planning and sometimes inequitable and insufficient funding. Districts should guard against new teachers receiving different supports and services depending on the school site, pathway into the district, or date of hire.

Develop Multiyear Funding Plans

Districts rely heavily on external funds to pay for professional development, and a large portion of these external sources are nonrecurring. We are seeing districts rely increasingly on external funds to support professional development activities, including Title I and Title IIA, federal competitive grants such as Reading First, grants from private foundations, and partnerships with local colleges and universities.

A challenge for districts in implementing a professional strategy is the temptation to allow funding streams to dictate professional development priorities. This is particularly true in lean budget years. Districts need to seek funding based on their priorities and not, as is often the practice, chase funding based on availability. While urban districts have enormous needs, the solution is not to answer every need with a different grant, as multiple grants and funding sources are partially to blame for the fragmentation of professional development efforts in districts. Districts need to be thoughtful and to develop multiyear plans, which target sources that support their priorities and contemplate the continuation of professional development activities after the end of the grant or funding period.

Allocate Resources Based on School Need

School-level allocation of professional development resources is often not differentiated based on school capacity or closely linked to student or teacher needs. When district professional development is tracked to the school level and monetized, professional development spending per teacher varies widely across schools. When analyzed on a school-by-school basis, there is often very little relationship between school, teacher, or student need.

Districts need to be comprehensive in looking across all initiatives to understand whether professional development resources have been allocated to schools in an equitable manner. There are three important drivers of variation in school-level investment: (1) certain resources are targeted to support low-performing schools; (2) particular resources, such as content coaching, are distributed equally across schools, regardless of school size or number of teachers; and (3) instructional program placement (such as Reading First) is targeted to specific grade levels, subsets of schools, or regions.

Districts may want to consider differentiating school professional development based on (1) school performance and (2) teacher and leadership capacity. High-performing schools with high-capacity leaders may need more flexibility and autonomy in implementing professional development that is aligned to their individual needs. Receiving funds rather than specific programs may be a more effective strategy for these schools. On the other hand, low-performing schools without leadership capacity may require more technical assistance from the central office or other external support.

CONCLUSION

If high-quality teaching is the most important job of schools, then it follows that districts have a critical role in ensuring this quality and developing it. There are those who argue that schools might be better off without district involvement in most activities. However, a system that views recruiting, developing, and rewarding teachers and building high-capacity teaching teams as its most important job could improve more than just an individual school. A district has the scale to invest in activities such as finding the best teachers and developing new and struggling teacher supports that respond to school-level needs that vary over time. A system has the ability to create career paths and leverage teacher expertise in ways that single schools cannot. Only a system can insist on improved performance and act to ensure that teachers in a poorly performing school get the support they need.

We have found that school systems already invest significant dollars in these activities but that they do so without an overarching strategy and without aligning all of the pieces of human capital development. The professional development strategic review gives districts a way to begin this discussion. Connecting the discussion to the use of resources makes it especially powerful and actionable because it highlights the difference between stated priorities and actual investment, and pinpoints places where dollars can be reallocated to support a more strategic effort. In the end, districts may find that they need to invest significantly more to build teacher and leadership capacity. However, they will be better able to do so in the context of a clear vision that makes the best use of existing resources.

PART IV

Piloting
the Framework

Pilot Overview

THEODORE HERSHBERG
CLAIRE ROBERTSON-KRAFT

We expect that many school districts will adopt subsets of the components drawn from the new reward structure and support for educators. Some may choose value-added assessment and the necessary training for the use of the growth metric, along with a program of multiyear mentoring for new teachers. Others may be attracted by the benefits provided by the OPE career ladder and include it, along with peer assistance and review and the sophisticated observation rubrics, to evaluate teachers and administrators. Still others may focus on the value of supporting their teachers with formative assessments, as well as providing consulting teachers, mentors, and ample time to participate in learning communities in which they can develop the necessary skills to use data to drive instructional decisions. Hopefully, all will recognize the importance of embracing a professional union model in which teachers enjoy an expanded role and share key decisions with administrators about how to improve instruction and academic outcomes.

However, discussion in the final section of this volume is devoted to the issues involved in a pilot of the *entire* OPE framework. Imagine the kind of student learning results that might emerge if a district embraced comprehensive school reform—that is, when all the components known to contribute to success were implemented at the same time. Such a pilot would benefit from the synergies that arise when all the components simultaneously reinforce each other within a system that aligns rewards with the goal of increased student achievement.

The most comprehensive effort to date in the United States to change the way an entire school district pays and provides professional development for its educators is the ProComp program developed by the Denver Classroom Teachers Association and the Denver Public Schools. This experience provides important lessons to inform a pilot of the OPE framework:

- Comprehensive rather than piecemeal reform is possible in a large and complex school district.
- A neutral third party can be an effective partner in keeping the pilot moving forward.

- Remaking the compensation system provides an occasion for broader change because it focuses everyone's attention.
- Reform succeeds when pursued in two separate phases—one devoted to design supported by private foundations, the other to implementation supported by the public sector.
- Tying implementation of the reforms to sufficient funding to support them in practice provides incentives for educators to agree to the reforms and for the public to pay for them.
- When "everyone" is on the same page—that is, when the mayor, city council, chamber of commerce, school board, superintendent, and teachers unions unite in saying that the proposed reforms will be good for the city and for the children—voters will be more likely to approve an increase in their taxes to support fundamental changes in how schools compensate their educators.[1]
- And, from the perspective of OPE, if citizens were willing to provide a 12 percent increase in teacher compensation based on system changes that are modest relative to those in the OPE framework, it is possible that even greater support would be available from state and federal governments in return for more extensive and fundamental change.

PILOT DESIGN PRINCIPLES

Distinct Phases and Appropriate Time

The process OPE envisions for a pilot of its framework consists of two phases: design and implementation. Phase one is devoted to reaching agreement on the many specific details of the framework so that everyone involved can understand what the reforms will look like when fully embedded in the culture and practice of the district. This phase may run from twelve to eighteen months, depending on the speed with which participants can finalize all the design elements. Phase two consists of the framework's rollout and may run for a period of five to seven years—an estimate of the time required to gauge its effectiveness in increasing student achievement.

Joint Leadership

Teachers and administrators participate in equal numbers throughout the pilot as members of a steering committee that will guide the entire process and approve its final form, and as members of the working groups charged with specifying the details of how each component will work as part of the larger framework. In what is arguably the most important initial decision, both sides must agree on a project director to guide the complex design process. Although able candidates may be recruited from outside the district, someone known and respected by both the administration and the teachers union, and who is already familiar with the district, may be the best choice. A memorandum of understanding signed by the superintendent, the school board, and the teachers union should establish at the outset the respective responsibilities that each party will assume throughout the pilot.

Capacity

A neutral third party—a role played by the Community Assistance and Training Center (CTAC) in Denver—can help the district organize and monitor the pilot's progress. To ensure that all steering committee members understand the entirety of the project they will lead, it is recommended that they attend multiday mastery institutes. At these retreats, national consultants—prominent educators, such as those contributing to this volume—would introduce the respective components of the framework, identify the decisions that need to be made locally, and sketch out the work that lies ahead in order to help reach agreement on the final version of the reforms. These experts should also be available to assist the working groups responsible for each component of the framework. Partnerships with local colleges or universities can play a valuable role here, providing both graduate students to serve as research assistants and knowledgeable faculty to advise district working-group participants.

Key Design Features and Local Flexibility

A pilot of the full OPE framework must be true to its key design features. Local educators will determine the final shape the reforms will take in their district, but they must include all the framework components. It may be helpful to think of the district as a vehicle on an eight-lane highway that can move freely from lane to lane. In this analogy, the foundation and public sector representatives who provide funding for the pilot function as traffic cops, ensuring that the district does not leave the "road to reform." The essential signposts include:

- Professional unionism characterizing labor-management relations, and teachers as full partners in reform with an equal say in the decisions that affect their classrooms—for example, curricula, professional development, and assessment not mandated by the state
- Value-added assessment, providing a fair and accurate empirical component for use in educator evaluation and compensation
- Sophisticated observation protocols for teacher and administrator evaluation
- A career ladder up which teachers and administrators can climb, based on their classroom and school success

- A system that provides educators whose effectiveness cannot be measured by formal value-added methodologies with a means of moving up the career ladder
- A program to train educators adequately in the use of the growth metric
- Peer assistance and review, which includes both mandatory remediation to help struggling educators improve their practice and a process to dismiss those unable to do so, with fairness and integrity
- Multiyear mentoring of new teachers
- Expanded opportunities for professional development
- Integrated assessment, where formative assessment is purposefully connected to the high-stakes tests
- A review of district spending
- Adequate time and flexibility in the school calendar for teachers to participate in learning communities and professional development

Despite a book-length elaboration of the framework's components, the fact is that a great many decisions remain for local educators to make. Because all the items on the above list are generic, the district has to determine precisely how it will operationalize them: When implemented, what will they consist of and how will they work in the district's schools? It is useful to think of the framework as a newly constructed home that is not yet ready for its owners to occupy. From the street it may look finished, but an inside tour reveals an unpainted dining room, a kitchen without countertops, and incomplete electrical wiring. These decisions are for district administrators, teachers, and the local community to make.

Districts that agree to pilot the OPE framework in its entirety will have to pay special attention to two remaining issues: communications and evaluation. Success will hinge on the degree to which the district can communicate the progress of the reform effort, both inside and outside the district (see chapter 14). Careful evaluation research can also begin to sort out the separate contributions each component makes to overall student-learning gains (see chapter 15).

THE ROLE OF TEACHERS UNIONS

A state could impose the OPE framework on one, several, or all school districts, but this would certainly undermine any evaluation of its effectiveness. The proposed reforms are far more likely to succeed if educators are willing participants. The design phase should be followed by a ratification vote by teachers, as it was in Denver. If teachers are fully informed, the framework should win their support because it was designed to place them in the vanguard of change. More than a decade ago, Albert Shanker of the American Federation of Teachers (AFT) and Bob Chase of the

National Education Association urged their colleagues to move in a more progressive direction. The heirs to this tradition include the Teacher Union Reform Network, the Tom Mooney Institute for Teacher and Union Leadership, and the AFT's new Innovation Fund. As this volume makes clear, the OPE framework provides teachers with a significantly expanded role in the nation's schools, fully commensurate with their efforts as knowledge workers in a century that will place more value on the development of human capital than at any time in history.

A good-faith pilot of the OPE framework needs the support of teachers and, especially, of progressive union leaders who recognize the potential of this approach to transform the profession and elevate teachers to a more highly respected position in American society. The interests of rank-and-file teachers would be well served as part of a quid pro quo that provides new funding in return for their acceptance of new individual-level accountability. No teachers would earn less than they would in the current system, and new funding would underwrite higher compensation for outstanding performers. This move would prove especially helpful, now that taxpayers, because their confidence in the nation's public schools is eroding, are reluctant to support much beyond cost-of-living increases. Teachers' interests would also be well served by new funds to support professional development, which would help all educators improve their craft. Peer review would place teachers on the level of other professionals who govern their own ranks, and they would become full partners in reform by sharing equally with administrators all major decisions affecting their classrooms. The only educators whose jobs would be at risk would be a small minority of teachers whose instructional practices continue to ill serve children, despite being provided reasonable time and supports to improve; it is precisely these colleagues whom the large majority of teachers repeatedly tell pollsters they don't want in their profession.

The interests of union officers and paid professional staff may initially be threatened by the OPE framework, as they may be concerned that their roles would cease to exist if teachers embraced a professional union model. The fear is that many dues-paying members would be lost if (1) a single contract negotiated through the collective bargaining process no longer determined everyone's salary, and (2) dismissal judgments rendered by a combined panel of teachers and administrators meant that union representation in due-process hearings failed to protect members whose instructional practice was consistently ineffective.

These fears need not be realized. Rank-and-file teachers are highly likely to remain dues-paying members because (1) they see the important role that collective bargaining will continue to play in compensation, and (2) they need to be well represented in discussions about issues that are central to their classrooms—curricula, professional development, and assessment—and to improving student-learning outcomes.[2]

To the extent that any jobs will be lost, however, OPE suggests a strategic course of action for unions that could very well result in an increased number of staff positions, albeit of a different sort. As the cognitive challenges of classroom teaching grow in the twenty-first century, school systems will be investing substantial funds in professional development in order to continually upgrade the human capital of their faculties. Who better than unions to train teachers to improve the quality of their instruction? This represents a major growth opportunity for institutions that are in the business of organizing teachers and meeting their professional needs.

The final point to keep in mind is that no one is asking that fundamental reform be embraced everywhere at once. The leadership of our national teachers unions, rather, is asked only to allow—or, far better, to encourage and support—several pilots of the OPE framework in order to learn whether the expected gains in student learning will be realized.

CHAPTER FOURTEEN

Communications

SHEPPARD RANBOM

For districts undertaking comprehensive reform, a communications plan is indispensable to keep educators inside the district and key external constituencies aware of the purpose of the pilot and the progress being made. The success of the Denver ProComp system, in which voters approved a new tax to increase total teacher compensation by $25 million, amounting to a 12 percent increase in the district's budget, rested to a considerable extent on the "buy-in" at the outset from the mayor, city council, chamber of commerce, as well as the school board, superintendent, and teachers union.

In this chapter, Sheppard Ranbom, founder and president of Communication-Works, a Washington, D.C.—based consulting firm specializing in issues of public education, discusses the key considerations for districts interested in developing a comprehensive communication strategy. The strategies presented here are derived in part from lessons learned in places that have introduced new performance pay programs, such as Charlotte-Mecklenburg in North Carolina, Denver, New York City, and the state of Minnesota, and from the author's experience in promoting improvements in teaching, learning, and policy development.

OVERVIEW

Efforts to gain acceptance for reinventing teacher evaluation and compensation require carefully planned outreach to educators and the public. Leaders must understand the attitudes of key audiences, articulate the purpose and benefits of the proposed changes, build support as they forge the model, consistently share information, foster dialogue, and seek feedback.

Put simply, communicating significant change in teacher evaluations and rewards starts with building trust to gain traction. District officials need to demonstrate by their actions that the new system is not another top-down initiative but one designed and implemented with equal representation in planning and decision making between district leaders and teachers. To win support, teachers need equal say in developing the nuts and bolts of the program and regular opportunities to speak out about key aspects of the plan and potential improvements and trade-offs.

The communications effort must consistently solicit teacher input through all the phases of the pilot by conducting ongoing opinion research (via focus groups, in-depth interviews, teacher surveys, regular meetings, and dialogue with teachers). Even after the pilot is approved and implemented, ongoing communications efforts are crucial. Districts and unions need to constantly repeat the big picture, offer details, and reinforce messages that educator performance will be objectively evaluated and that changes will be introduced wisely and fairly following agreed-upon procedures and timelines.

The spirit of collaboration generated from working out new requirements between a district and its educator workforce can be positioned as a major turning point in district improvement efforts. Half of the battle in transforming any organization is recognizing excellent performance and putting the right talent in the right place to make a difference. Communications efforts can demonstrate in symbolic and substantive ways how leaders who are typically in conflict can instead work together on a common cause and initiate new norms of behavior that signal a new day for public schools.

Districts that have made changes typically make clear that union and district, administrators and teachers, school district and community are on the same page, student improvement comes first, and teachers are leading the way. It is crucial that public officials used to taking the spotlight give teachers the lion's share of credit for their willingness to accept new standards and measures of accountability.

Approving a new compensation plan will be a pyrrhic victory if civic leaders fail to build on momentum from the initial implementation to ensure long-term sustainability for the effort. Districts must address this problem from the outset by ensuring that there is foundation funding for the pilot and by securing state funding for salary increases and for the cost of expanded professional development for the first five to seven years of the program. Because of the need for ongoing financial support, district and union officials should continually reach out to policy makers and the public.

This chapter describes how leaders can go about developing a strategic communications plan that can serve as a common road map to move an initiative, such as the Operation Public Education (OPE) framework, forward successfully. It addresses the key elements in the plan:

- *Goals and objectives* the initiative seeks to accomplish and the methods to gauge success
- *Campaign staging* that organizes the outreach effort into different phases of activities to help guide the successful plotting and timing of communications activities

- *Audiences* that are crucial to the success of the effort, their primary concerns, how they think about teacher evaluation and compensation, and what will motivate them to support the reforms
- *Challenges and solutions* that anticipate what the major problems will be and gain insight into what will work to remedy them
- *Messages* targeting teachers, school leaders, unions, businesses, parents, the community, and elected officials at both local and state levels; part of the messaging process includes developing a name for the initiative that will resonate with educators and the public
- *Naming the initiative* to succinctly capture the focus of the effort and attributes it seeks to convey
- *Case-making materials* that present key information and messages in formats audiences will pay attention to
- *Strategies* that help address key challenges and meet the initiative's goals
- *Launching the initiative* with a plan that ensures an effective start to reform
- *Tactics to spread the word* and specific activities that are used to put strategies into action, including the specific launch plan
- *An implementation plan,* which includes a timeline for action that addresses what needs to be done by whom and when

DEVELOPING THE COMMUNICATIONS PLAN

In managing communications, as in managing change, leadership counts. School and teacher leaders note that communication efforts need a strong direction based on a clear plan of action. Districts should establish a steering committee to set goals and establish principles governing how the district will communicate about the effort, mediate concerns, and speak with one voice. Hiring independent communication consultants can also help to expedite the process of developing a plan by ensuring that important decisions are made and key issues are anticipated and fully addressed. The following sections will provide districts with essential elements for their comprehensive communication plan.

Goals and Objectives

In this part of the plan, districts should identify specific objectives that can be used as indicators of success. Table 14.1 offers a very broad picture of possible goals and objectives for each phase of the project.

Campaign Staging

The communications plan needs to be somewhat flexible and to be updated month by month; it must be a "living document" that will change through the life

TABLE 14.1
Goals and objectives for each phase

Objectives	Measures
Short term	• Make x presentations and speeches
• Secure funding for planning	• Publish x articles
• Develop plan	• Convene x groups y times
• Develop information materials	
• Build alliances	
• Launch planning process	
Intermediate	• Introduce legislation, policy changes
• Build consensus	• Create coalition of x active supporters from y target audiences
• Secure approval for plan	• Assess action
• Bolster community support	• Provide media coverage and polling reflects strengthened support
• Launch implementation	
• Announce midcourse corrections in ways that will further build support	
Long term	• Legislate policy shift
• Achieve goals for student achievement	• Student growth meets proficiency target
• Demonstrate link between achievement and teacher performance	• Increased resources by $x

Source: Copyright © 2008 CommunicationWorks, LLC.

cycle of the initiative to respond to new challenges and concerns. Because the design of the program may vary, depending on particular communities, planning will not follow a cookie-cutter model. Whatever the exact design, districts should plot out their communications activities in three phases.

Design and Building Ownership. Communications activities in this phase should begin with a comprehensive planning effort to identify how district and union leaders will ensure that information reaches key audiences, communicate why the change is in the interest of these audiences, and identify steps that will be taken to address common fears. This phase might include a "soft launch," where the union, district, and civic leaders announce the agreement to work together to develop a new model, and will include comprehensive efforts to understand the attitudes and concerns of teachers and the public.

Ratification and Approval. Theoretically, ratification of the plan could occur during the pilot effort, but teachers will probably sign off only after they can study the details of the plan. Most likely, as in the case of Denver's ProComp initiative, teachers will vote during the second phase. Ensuring that the plan has adequate buy-in from teachers requires broad dissemination of information about all details of the program, development of dissemination tools to reach members, and more discussion and dialogue. Even when there appears to be significant buy-in from teachers, there are always many unanswered questions and teachers new to the district. Upon ratification, districts should make a high-profile public announcement.

Ongoing Communications, Reporting, and Midcourse Corrections. Observers note that communications efforts need to be stepped up, not slowed down, during the implementation phase. That is because teachers are likely not to fully understand what they voted for and may feel that their concerns are being glossed over. Equally important, new educators are constantly coming into the district and need to understand the policies and procedures. In order for the initiative to be sustainable, districts must ensure that it is made public, and regular reporting on progress must be built into the plan.

Audiences

As part of the communication plan, districts need to look closely at the concerns and needs of key audiences, the desired actions sought from these groups, and ways to encourage these actions. Table 14.2 underscores the typical concerns of

TABLE 14.2
Concerns of key audiences

Audience	Concerns and needs	Desired action
Teachers	• Motivated by mission, not money. Want to make a difference but also care about working conditions, the quality of leadership in their schools and professional development opportunities, compensation, and transparency of evaluation efforts. • May distrust evaluation plans that give principals who are not instructional leaders a large role in evaluation. • Need immediate and regular updates on specifics of the program.	• See effort as means to improve schools and teaching and provide incentive pay. • Advocate for initiative and share information within school and across networks. • At minimum, remain neutral toward the changes.
School leaders	• Concerned with achieving AYP, supporting teachers, demands on their own workload. • Need to know how the effort can help advance improvement strategies and improve their own and teacher practice. • May hesitate to support the evaluation process until they have ample time to improve their teacher corps. • Need information about program, participation, benefits, and process.	• Understand the new model, disseminate information in their schools, and explain changes in evaluation methods and professional development. • Receive guidance and support from district to work with teachers to meet new evaluation standards. • Support new leadership roles for teachers.

continued

TABLE 14.2
Concerns of key audiences, *continued*

Audience	Concerns and needs	Desired action
Unions	• Concerned about methods used to recognize and measure teacher performance. • Seek ways to improve teaching and learning conditions in schools and principal leadership. • Need to show they are playing an increasing role in raising student achievement and are developing teachers as leaders. • Want to keep support of members and increase membership and clout.	• Exercise full partnership in all aspects of the initiative. • Gather regular input from and facilitate dialogue within membership. • Clarify program, advance its adoption, and communicate with members and all teachers.
Business	• Concerned with raising standards, bolstering teacher quality, and strengthening accountability, all of which affect ability to hire well-educated workers and locate in high-growth, stable communities and neighborhoods.	• Provide support for school and city leadership. • Offer resources to launch local campaign to win over public opinion for increased levies for teacher pay.
Parents and community	• Care about school safety and improving the quality of the school environment. • Want to see improvements in district performance and to increase their children's chances for success. • Want to take action to do what's best for young people and to ensure that their children have quality teachers. • Strongly support teachers and believe that teaching is a profession that provides great benefit to society. • One subset of this group are parents from low-income communities, who may often feel neglected by public school systems and concerned that their children lack access to high-quality instruction.	• Secure support from parent activists and PTA organizations, who can be a major ally. • Change views on district and union roles in promoting school improvement. • Recognize that teachers are leading the change effort and support increases in pay for teachers and additional resources for professional development. • Parents in low-income communities can be a source of urgency for adopting changes and seeking new public investment.
Elected officials (local and state)	• Strengthen accountability for education, improving results and increasing return on investment. • Improve public education at a time when budgets are tight and when there are many competing interests.	• Provide funding for pay increases, professional development, and other costs. • Help identify and recruit foundations to fund the pilot. • Support adoption of model and give credit to teachers for supporting the new system and draw attention to positive changes in the district as a result of the new methods.

key audiences and what leadership teams might ask for to build buy-in and support for their efforts.

In addition to identifying audiences, the communications plan should map out existing networks that reach key audiences, identify areas where their interests might overlap with those of the initiative, and select leaders from each group who can be champions for the effort.

Experts say that introducing new performance measures and pay incentives requires significant and ongoing analysis of public and teacher attitudes to win acceptance. Districts should use opinion research (conducted through surveys, focus groups, and in-depth interviews, all of which can be tracked over time) to better identify what teachers perceive as wrong with current performance and evaluation systems, how the system might be improved, which aspects of the plan they like and dislike, what kinds of incentives are most useful, and how teachers might respond to potential trade-offs. Survey work is particularly important to ensure that people get what they want most.

Challenges and Solutions

Mapping out the specific challenges and potential solutions provides a useful road map for identifying strategies and tactics for the communications effort. Table 14.3 identifies some common challenges and potential concerns that districts should address in the communications plan.

Messages

"How we frame the compensation issue is as important as the details of the changes that are proposed," writes Joan Baratz-Snowden, president of the Education Study Center, in *The Future of Teacher Compensation*.[1] The changes being promoted must be about more than pay. New evaluation and compensation systems provide districts with an opportunity to maximize the skills and talents of their personnel. Performance pay creates more effective ways to help change the public and policy discussion about education spending. In communicating about the programs, districts and unions should draw significant attention to key themes.

Giving the Public What It Wants

Raising achievement for every student in every school. Rather than having parents, administrators, teachers, union leaders, and city and state officials working at odds, the new compensation and evaluation plan puts everyone on the same page. The plan enables everyone to focus on and be rewarded for their efforts to increase the achievement for every student in every school.

We're holding everyone accountable. Just as the education system has been raising standards to hold all students accountable for their performance, we're

TABLE 14.3
Common challenges and solutions

Challenge	Solution
Opposition from teachers who likely: • feel that their voices are not heard. • do not understand enough about or reject the proposed changes in their evaluation and compensation. • are concerned about fairness and transparency and distrust new approaches to measure their performance. • disagree with key elements of the proposal.	• Demonstrate that initiative is a true partnership between the school district and union and create a leadership team comprised equally of teachers and district representatives. • Provide regular and ongoing opportunities to discuss the program with teachers through union-sponsored events and briefings, district events, and giving opportunity for constant dialogue. • Constantly gather attitudinal information from key audiences about key aspects of the program. • Build support and advocacy among principals and teacher leaders for teacher participation. • Create school-based advocates, including a teacher from every school. • Draw attention to incentives, professional development benefits, and opportunities for new leadership roles. • Promote transparency through timely updates for educators. • Develop tools and materials to address educators' specific questions.
Educators and local leaders reject concept of plans developed outside the district (such as the OPE plan) out of hand because it is not truly home-grown.	• Emphasize that decisions will be made at local level through teacher work-group process.
Key players (union, school officials, mayors) have history of animosity in dealing with each other and with key players.	• Identify what's in it for everyone—quid pro quo that creates more pay and better professional development in exchange for performance measures. • Bring in leaders from other districts to discuss how effort brought them together and how issues were resolved. • Encourage funders and public officials to bring people together for benefit of community. • Encourage effort as an opportunity to break the gridlock and as vehicle for building new support for public schools.
Resistance from lawmakers to pick up tab for additional resources.	• Work with foundations, business community, local leaders, and union officials to make case to lawmakers for support. • Emphasize that money is tied to performance and that this is a unique opportunity that holds the key to higher performance for schools. • Present polling data demonstrating broad support from voters and teachers. • Use media (e.g., editorial page endorsement) as lever.
Initiative has limited amount of time to win support.	• Do not oversell program. • Ensure progressively expanded outreach effort to generate awareness and use of resources. • Make delivery of resources and products easy to access and provide strategies for replication. • Build partnerships to help expand use and awareness.

Source: Copyright © 2008 CommunicationWorks, LLC.

holding ourselves accountable, too. The best way to raise performance for all students is for every educator to demonstrate what he or she is doing to make this happen.

Teachers lead the way. The new accountability system was built by teachers, for teachers. The teacher evaluation and compensation plan could never have been put in place unless teachers were willing to put themselves on the line for the benefit of all young people. It's a giant leap that puts teachers truly in charge of their own professional advancement while they help students reach proficiency.

Creating Benefits for Teachers

A politically viable and economically feasible system for evaluation and compensation. The OPE approach evaluates teachers and school leaders based on student growth and peer-review observation in equal proportion. This balanced approach offers a fair and effective method for evaluating and compensating educators based on performance.

A more intellectually stimulating and rewarding environment in which to work. This system expands professional development and provides mentors and consultants so teachers have ample time and support to gain new knowledge and to try out new skills. Schools become learning communities, teachers are no longer isolated, and the profession provides greater satisfaction as teachers see the results of their efforts in higher student achievement.

A fairer way of measuring performance for educators in low-income schools. The OPE framework uses value-added assessment to track the growth of individual students from year to year, not their achievement. This outcome measure reveals the extent to which educators have succeeded in helping their students move forward, regardless of where the students started. When schools are ranked in this manner rather than on the basis of raw test scores, teachers can be defined as successful by virtue of having "stretched" their students beyond what could be reasonably expected, based on their past academic achievement.

An accountability system that treats administrators and teachers equally. The OPE framework links administrator pay to performance in much the way that it does for teachers. The system determines how effectively leaders promote high achievement for all students, use student-learning data to make decisions, and build a school culture of high standards and continuous professional development.

Strengthening the Hand of Teachers and Unions

> *An expanded role for teachers and unions.* The OPE framework creates a new quid pro quo, where teachers accept accountability as individuals in return for a significantly expanded role in public education.

The communications plan should include a list of core messages that advance these themes and, because audiences often look at issues from different perspectives, a list of messages for key constituencies.

It is important to note that messages are often only as good as the messengers that carry them. Denver's ProComp system garnered support among teachers because one of the spokespeople for the program was a long-time classroom teacher and union activist, Brad Jupp, who was able to identify key components of the plan to pitch to teachers. Districts should consider having an experienced teacher make public statements endorsing the plan, from its inception through the various stages of implementation. This move will substantiate claims that the teachers are indeed being given a voice and that their interests are at the heart of reform.

Naming the Initiative

Developing a name for the project can communicate key attributes of the initiative that helps build buy-in. The communications plan should identify possible names for the initiative and test these names with educators. Key words that have positive resonance include teacher, professional, growth, quality, compensation, effectiveness, achievement, alliance, partnership, and compact. By coming up with a list of words that reflect the purpose and attributes of the initiative, planning groups can create names that characterize their particular effort. From the list below, for example, teams can come up with any number of variations:

- Quality Teacher Compensation (QTC) Partnership/Plan/Compact
- Compensation Plan for Student Growth (CPSG)
- Quality Teacher Compact (or Quality/Effective Teacher Compensation)
- Teacher Compensation Compact (TCC)
- Student Growth Partnership (SGP)
- Compensation for Improved Student Achievement (CISA)

Districts should consider organizing words into an acronym that sends a message by itself, for example, Professional Evaluation and External Review (PEER) Plan or Professional Evaluation and Education Reform Compensation Plan (PEERComp). The very process of developing names can help the leadership team focus on what matters most in their community.

Case-Making Materials

Districts should develop specific case-making materials and products that could be produced to carry the messages to educators and the public:

- *Frequently Asked Questions.* A FAQs document should be prepared for both teachers and the public and be continually updated as new questions emerge. It is often helpful to prepare this document first to ensure that communications efforts naturally focus on addressing key issues and concerns. Information from FAQs can be further elucidated across all pieces.
- *Fact Sheets.* These documents should identify the key changes in areas of most concern to educators and describe the substance of key areas, including

    [Name Initiative] and Teacher Professional Development

    [Name Initiative] and Teacher Compensation

    [Name Initiative] and Teacher Evaluation

- *Supporting Quality Teaching.* This document should explain why the public must invest in supporting the program.
- *[Name Initiative]: What's in It? and What's in It for You?* This type of document should identify key contents of the plan and how the provisions will affect teachers.
- *Teacher Compensation and Evaluation: Current and Alternative.* This is a side-by-side comparison that should identify the differences between current requirements and proposed changes.
- *Rewarding Effectiveness: A Guide to Proposed Changes in Compensation and Evaluation.* This piece, created around the time of ratification, should identify in detail key aspects of the program, specific new requirements, rationale for changes, and even identify concerns that still may linger in teachers' minds and how they are planned to be dealt with in implementation.
- *Straight Talk about [Name Initiative].* This communications piece might be produced in the form of an e-newsletter that is released twice a month or more frequently. The e-newsletter might include regular updates about what is happening with the initiative, drawing attention to upcoming meetings and decisions and chronicling what happens at planning meetings. It could also focus on components of the emerging compensation plan and provide clear and unvarnished information on key aspects of negotiation and agreement. The document should include teacher voices and perspectives. As the initiative matures, it can include pieces on the status of implementation as well as reminders about deadlines and opportunities. The document could also provide information about public events and how key constituencies have been involved in the effort.

- *Extra Credit.* This element could be developed as a tabloid newspaper or newspaper supplement that would include a compilation of case-making information and *USA Today*–like graphs, as well as brief stories that will make the case for funding support. The piece could be distributed by a local daily or weekly newspaper and handed out at meetings and presentations.
- *Talking about Teacher Quality: A Discussion Guide for Community Dialogue.* This suite of materials would provide community leaders with templates and tools for having community meetings. It might include meeting agendas, discussion points, overheads or PowerPoint slides about key elements of the program and how it will benefit the community, and tips on moderating a meeting.

Strategies

After mapping out objectives, target audiences, and messages, the next step is to identify key strategies that will work to build support. Following are some strategic considerations to keep in mind:

- Build a compelling case for how the plan will help local teachers, parents, and students.
- Share information across existing networks.
- Leverage existing communications opportunities and available resources.
- Enlist prominent leaders.
- Build alliances with education, community, faith-based, minority-serving, and business groups, and others.
- Use peer-to-peer communications and ongoing dialogue throughout the campaign.
- Model the kind of engagement required.
- Be a resource for the media and provide ongoing, timely, and trustworthy information at key stages and across a broad range of outlets.
- Demonstrate results, progress, and momentum.

Launching the Initiative

The initial announcement of the planning grant is a unique opportunity to draw attention to the purpose and goals of the effort, how and when it will be accomplished, and the partnership that will be required to be successful. That announcement could be made into a blockbuster event if state lawmakers are ready to commit to providing additional resources as a quid pro quo for teachers willing to enter into the new accountability plan. These two efforts could easily be announced simultaneously or separately.

Communications should emphasize equality in decision making between teachers and district leaders and a commitment to openness and transparency in the planning process. The steering committee should only draw attention when there is agreement. Union officials in particular need to formally survey the issues, interests, and concerns of their members, and solicit constant feedback. They also need to set up ongoing briefings, discussions, and dialogue every step of the way about what is being discussed and potential directions for all elements of the plan.

Tactics for Spreading the Word

Districts should utilize the following tactics to build understanding and ongoing support for the initiative:

- *Establish and advertise an accessible campaign-style Web site* that is a repository for crucial information. The site can serve as a one-stop resource page and could include everything from an initiative handbook and newsletter, media coverage, information on work groups, frequently asked questions, briefing documents on professional development and evaluation, and a salary calculator.
- *Continually push information to educators via the Internet*, including using listservs and regular reporting on the site through blogs and postings.
- *Create close relationships with news reporters and media outlets.* Reporters are looking for good information and analysis from trusted sources and want to be treated fairly and equally when news breaks.
- *Produce public service ads* for radio, newspapers, community newsletters, and—if possible—broadcast pieces that could be shown on television. Producing pieces for cable stations and cable providers is a particularly cost-effective means of getting the word out.
- *Produce posters for distribution in schools* that are designed to build support for the initiative and draw educators to the Web site and suggest where they can get more information.
- *Train teachers and other advocates* to talk about the program and give them tools to help them make presentations.
- *Use district and union communication vehicles and those of professional educator networks* to disseminate information about the program to teachers, teacher leaders, and principals and their networks. This effort includes ensuring that the program is featured as part of district professional development days, and using the district's TV network as a platform to provide information and broadcast teacher dialogue about the plan.
- *Continually highlight successes.* At the beginning, this aspect might focus on posting lists of partners and endorsers and quotes from leaders of groups influential with teachers and the public. Later, this might come in the form of an annual report to teachers, staff, and the community. In communicating progress, be honest about challenges, but do so in a way that honors what the system is doing for students.

Implementation Plan

Once districts have mapped out strategies and tactics, they should evaluate these activities based on the time it takes to implement, capacity to deliver, their likely impact, and other factors. The initiative should develop a detailed work plan that identifies tasks, assigns responsibility for implementation, and sets clear deadlines.

CONCLUSION

Leaders must recognize that the most successful communications efforts typically come around the best-designed programs. It is hard to sell something that is poorly designed or does not meet the needs of educators and the community. The communications plan is just the first step, but, as the Asian proverb says, "The first step takes you halfway there." Addressing each section of the proposal carefully and thoughtfully can help put districts on solid footing, provided there is strong leadership from the planning team, shared ownership, and a commitment to transparency and consistent communications to key audiences who have a stake in the outcome.

CHAPTER FIFTEEN

Evaluation

JEFFERY H. MARSHALL

LAURA S. HAMILTON

JULIE A. MARSH

DANIEL F. MCCAFFREY

BRIAN M. STECHER

Whether districts adopt the Operation Public Education (OPE) framework in its entirety or a subset of its components, it is essential to create a "culture of measurement"— that is, districtwide awareness of the need to respect and support the collection of all appropriate data necessary for a thorough evaluation of the reforms. Although the individual components in the OPE framework have a positive impact on student learning, little is known to date about what happens when they interact with one another and how the results might vary across districts with differing socioeconomic and demographic profiles. Knowledge gained from good evaluation research about which components work best in what combination would be of great value, especially in an era characterized by limited resources.

This chapter helps districts piloting a comprehensive approach to reform develop strategies for program monitoring and evaluation activities. Researchers at RAND— Jeffery Marshall, Laura Hamilton, Julie Marsh, Daniel McCaffrey and Brian Stecher— outline the challenges and requirements for a thorough qualitative and quantitative evaluation of a pilot. Their discussion emphasizes the conceptual issues in evaluation work of this nature and highlights the importance of defining an evaluation vision adequately aligned with each district's needs. They review the specific activities that districts can undertake to monitor and evaluate the use of assessment data in the classroom, explore more general issues related to evaluating the overall impact of a comprehensive effort, and identify specific actions districts can take to facilitate this kind of work.

SIGNIFICANCE

Evaluation is an important part of any large-scale education reform effort. It is broadly defined as systematic data collection, analysis, and reporting to meet the needs of a range of stakeholders. This process often begins with formative evaluation activities that help program designers and districts monitor and improve the implementation. For example, teachers can be surveyed to get their perceptions about the effectiveness of teacher-training activities, which are then modified based on the survey feedback. The program designers and districts—or other stakeholders, like state legislatures—may also wish to know more about the overall impact of the reforms. This need calls for summative evaluation information that helps isolate the overall effect of the intervention on outcomes such as student achievement. The distinction between formative and summative evaluation activities is not always clear, however, and in some cases the same information can be used to address both types. Projects with incomplete evaluation resources not only run the risk of falling short of their immediate goals, but long-term survivability may also suffer if there is no way to demonstrate the overall impact of the reforms.

OPE envisions a comprehensive transformation of public education that leads to high levels of academic performance for every student. Compared with other interventions, an evaluation of a system like OPE may seem unnecessary because the cornerstone of the approach is evaluation, as evidenced by the value-added system for measuring student learning (chapter 3) and the use of classroom observation data (chapter 4) to inform the teacher peer-review process (chapter 12). However, even a system of evaluation needs to be evaluated, and the existence of these different strands of data does not guarantee adequate guidance and support for integrating this information or making the best use of it for the purpose of improvement or to judge impact. Furthermore, there may be aspects of the reform that do not come with built-in mechanisms for generating relevant data. These potential complications highlight the need to define an evaluation plan that is implemented alongside (if not before) a comprehensive reform effort such as OPE. The purpose of this chapter is to help districts develop precisely this kind of enterprise.

BASIC PRINCIPLES OF EVALUATION

The field of evaluation is vast, and it cuts across many research disciplines and areas of inquiry. There are evaluations of programs, policy, personnel, technology, and even evaluations of evaluation work. Because of this diversity, the task of defining basic, "universal" principles is somewhat problematic. Nevertheless, based on our experience, we can provide some guiding principles for evaluation work in the field of education.

According to our ten basic principles, effective evaluations accomplish the following tasks:

1. *Engage stakeholders in planning the evaluation.* Stakeholders include those who have a role in conducting the program and those who have an interest in its outcomes. When such stakeholders are engaged from the outset, the evaluation design is more likely to ask the right questions and meet people's needs.

2. *Think about how the results will be used and incorporate the needs of users in the evaluation design.* For example, if the evaluation is going to be used for midcourse corrections, data on implementation must be available in a timely manner. If it is going to be used for downstream decisions about program effectiveness and continuation, the research design must support strong inferences about cause and effect.

3. *Design evaluation activities to reflect the program's theory of action.* A program's theory of action spells out the intended actions and results before a specific intervention is actually implemented (see next section). Therefore, the evaluation work must be aligned with the theory of action in order to provide relevant information for monitoring the program, as well as to identify areas for improvement.

4. *Collect data about program processes (e.g., participant opinions, classroom observations, etc.) that can be used for formative purposes—that is, to help designers and implementers monitor the program and allow them to make performance-enhancing changes when necessary.* It is a mistake to think of evaluation work only as an end-of-program activity. Useful evaluation activities can be undertaken throughout the life of the intervention or program.

5. *Collect summative data that can be used to evaluate the overall impact of the program.* These sources of information make it possible to consider to what extent the program has achieved its main goals in terms of outcomes, such as student achievement.

6. *Begin the evaluation work as early as possible, before the actual program is implemented.* An early start to collecting evaluation data will aid the formative activities by allowing for more precise monitoring of the immediate impact of the intervention. It will also allow for collection of baseline data to improve summative evaluations.

7. *Promote efficiency by addressing the most important questions without trying to do too much.* Too much data can overwhelm stakeholders and result in a mass of information that nobody uses. But it is also possible to undershoot and end up with insufficient information to address the main questions.

8. *Obtain feedback from participants and stakeholders (if possible) throughout the process.* Ongoing feedback allows for updating and making adjustments to

the evaluation design as needed. When the evaluation work lasts for more than one year, it is important to get feedback from participants not only about the program, but also about the program evaluation process itself.

9. *Ensure that data are reliable and valid.* This goal can be a challenge for some sources of data, but quality information is a necessary—although insufficient—ingredient of an effective evaluation system.

10. *Rely on multiple sources and types of data (principle of triangulation).* The results of the evaluation will be more robust when based on consistent information provided by multiple sources.

These principles will serve as the basis for the more specific evaluation plan developed in this chapter.

PROGRAM THEORY OF ACTION AND EVALUATION DESIGN

The program theory of action is a conceptual summary that specifies program interventions and outputs together with the causal mechanisms that link them.[1] For example, in the case of OPE, the overall program theory envisions higher student achievement (the output) resulting from improvements in teaching practices (mechanisms) that are produced by a range of program interventions. These improvements in teaching practices—which can also be thought of as intermediate outcomes—include more effective instruction and pedagogy through better use of assessment data. The program interventions emphasize greater monitoring of teacher performance and accountability of teachers and principals, which are tied to performance incentives, and increased support and training for teachers and administrators in a number of areas.

The OPE framework will not likely be adapted in identical form by all participating districts. It is safe to say that each district accepts the basic premise of the approach, but the very comprehensiveness of OPE means that districts will have considerable input into how it is implemented. They will also have some say in terms of prioritizing the interventions, and with this discretion comes the need for each district to clearly define what it expects to accomplish and how it expects to achieve it.

No template can guide this planning process, but in general, districts need to address three sets of questions up front: One, what are the most pressing needs facing the district and how do individual components address these areas? Two, what is the current capacity to implement each component? Three, how do the different elements fit together and what is the best way to create synergies across components? This last issue is probably the biggest challenge facing districts implementing a comprehensive approach, such as the one proposed by OPE. Each individual component has something to offer on its own, but overall success will depend to a large degree on how well the various components work together.

These dynamics also have implications for the evaluation work. The evaluation questions have to address what is happening within each component (e.g., are teachers receiving professional development?), but they also have to address separate questions about links between components (e.g., is professional development tied to teaching deficiencies?).

When participating districts choose the components they want to emphasize and begin to think about how these elements will work with one another, they are defining their own individualized program theory of action. This task of defining an evaluation plan based on a program theory of action may seem unwieldy or abstract and largely of an academic nature, but this process can provide an excellent opportunity for each participating district to build agreement among the various stakeholders on the key goals and strategies. This process will not only aid the evaluation of the reforms, but, more important, it will force each district to think about the specific mechanisms that link the various inputs with outcomes, such as teacher performance and student achievement. Districts should avoid a checklist mentality where they are simply implementing someone else's plan, because this deprives them of the deeper understanding that comes from going through the design process.

The evaluation work should revolve around two general categories of activities. The first category can be termed "implementation evaluation." This process begins with basic program monitoring ("counting the beans"). For example, districts will want to know how many teachers have passed through the peer-review process, how many students have been evaluated through value-added analysis, etc. Although this kind of information does not provide evidence of the quality of implementation, it is useful for general summaries of implementation and to identify program components that appear to be lagging behind.

Implementation evaluation activities also include checking on intermediate outcomes. For example, the district may wish to know more about the quality or effectiveness of the training teachers receive for the use of student assessment data. One strategy is to develop a classroom-observation protocol that looks for observable improvements in teacher behavior (e.g., more personalized instruction of students). Or, district personnel could simply observe the training sessions themselves and get feedback from participants about the quality and their reactions to it. Both are examples of data-collection activities that help the district more fully understand the critical question: what is happening? Information from each source can then be used to make adjustments in the teacher-training activities.

The second category of evaluation activities focuses on the overall program outcomes. For an approach like OPE, this category mainly refers to student achievement, and these outcomes are distinct from implementation outcomes because they are not directly affected by the program's inputs. For example, teacher training in the use of assessment data does not improve student achievement directly; it does so indirectly through a classroom teaching mechanism that results from the training. The overall program evaluation work is inherently summative, as the results are likely to be used toward the end of the program cycle to make judgments about the overall effectiveness. For comprehensive reform efforts, the summative work is often carried out by an outside contractor. Nevertheless, even when the district is not responsible for carrying out these summative evaluation activities, they are likely to be involved in the generation of the data that will be required.

Before undertaking evaluation work, each district will need to carry out some institutional planning. In the larger school districts, an evaluation (or research) office is likely to already be in place; this will be a natural home for the various monitoring and evaluation activities. In smaller districts, a different entity such as a committee may need to be created or an outside contractor brought in. However, it is important to go beyond simply empowering a few individuals to be in charge of evaluation. Their work will require extensive coordination with various departments to ensure that the correct questions are asked, preferably before the reform process is started. This means having open lines of communication and a commitment from other entities in the district to support these activities.

In sum, a range of evaluation activities can be implemented, but this process requires thinking beforehand about data-collection mechanisms and the kinds of questions that need to be asked (see figure 15.1). It also requires extensive coordination across activities. This process brings us to the central complication in defining an evaluation plan for districts implementing a comprehensive theory of action: the sheer scope of the reforms. The OPE framework is not made up of a single intervention with a correspondingly simple program theory of action. It posits a transformation of the existing teaching and learning environment with wide-ranging intermediate outcomes that will, in turn, affect student achievement.

OPE EVALUATION SPECIFICS: ONE EXAMPLE

In this section we focus on one of the key elements of OPE from the perspective of evaluation: teachers' use of assessment data. In particular, we look at the kinds of data collection that might be needed to monitor the implementation of this component and to judge its impact on student outcomes.

Figure 15.2 includes an evaluation overview for the use of assessment data in the classroom. One of the ways OPE envisions transforming the teaching and learning environment is by providing teachers with extensive information about student performance, backed by training about how to use this information to

FIGURE 15.1
Evaluation question examples

"Up-front" questions on evaluation work itself:
- Do evaluation personnel know their roles?
- Are data being properly entered? Is the coding scheme useful for matching students with teachers, teachers with schools, etc.?
- Are teachers and administrators filling out surveys correctly? What is the response rate? What changes would they like to see in these processes?

Questions about "intermediate" OPE outcomes:
- Are teachers and administrators receiving training in the use of assessment data for instruction? Do they like the training? What changes do they recommend?
- Is there evidence that teachers are using assessment information to guide individualized (student) instruction?
- Are those teachers identified for remediation receiving additional training?
- How responsive are school personnel to the peer review process?

Program impact questions:
- Are there observable changes in teaching behaviors over time that differ from what would have occurred if OPE had not been implemented?
- Have student achievement levels improved over time compared to what would have occurred without OPE? All else being equal, are these improvements larger in classrooms where teachers are most faithfully implementing the OPE vision?
- Is there evidence of program impact in other outcomes, like graduation rates, daily attendance, or postsecondary enrollment?
- How sustainable is the program? Are schools buying into the OPE framework? Are evaluation personnel capable of continuing the work?

FIGURE 15.2
The OPE treatment: using assessment data in the classroom

OPE treatment	Intermediate outcomes	Evaluation activities
<ul><li>Value-added training for teachers</li><li>Value-added in the classroom</li><li>Student growth and performance objectives</li><li>Assessments</li></ul>	<ul><li>Development of individualized student growth objectives (SGOs)</li><li>Collaboration among teachers, team leaders, administrators, etc., to determine objectives</li><li>Conceptual understanding of value-added</li><li>Understanding of value-added reports' ability to transform into targets, objectives</li><li>Syncing of students by performance</li></ul>	<ul><li>Monitoring of individualized assessment activities (evidence of SGOs, coordination, etc.)</li><li>Monitoring of teacher support and training</li><li>Analysis of use of value-added reports</li><li>Teacher-perception surveys about effectiveness of training</li><li>Classroom observations</li><li>Review of student outcomes</li></ul>

---

guide their instruction. These (expected) program interventions make up the OPE treatments, which are listed in column 1.

The middle column in figure 15.2 identifies some of the intermediate outcomes that are expected to result from the various program interventions. The most immediate outcome concerns the teachers' (and administrators') conceptual understanding of the assessment system in place (e.g., the difference between measures of growth versus absolute achievement) and their familiarity with the kinds of individual student reports generated by value-added assessment systems. Teachers should also be developing and monitoring individualized student-performance objectives based on value-added assessment evidence, as well as their own classroom-based assessments. This work is supposed to be collaborative; team leaders, department supervisors, and other administrators are all involved in these efforts in some manner.

The critical element in this sequence is how teaching is affected by the existence of personalized growth objectives and extensive assessment data. Space does not permit a full discussion of how teaching strategies can be modified to take full advantage of the information provided by state-of-the-art data systems (see chapter 9). Besides, each district needs to define these parameters as part of its program theory of action, paying particular attention to teacher capacity and the ability of support systems to keep up with the training needs. Nevertheless, the OPE emphasis on assessment data is likely to lead to changes in teaching behaviors, so from an evaluation standpoint, this outcome (what teachers are doing) is clearly one of the main intermediate outcomes to be evaluated by OPE districts.

The right-hand column of figure 15.2 provides some examples of evaluation activities that districts can implement to address these questions. These include fairly basic monitoring activities, as well as teacher surveys that allow teachers to weigh in on the quality of the training they have received, the support they are getting from other teachers and administrators, the perceived effects the reforms are having on processes in their classroom, and additional support they need to use these tools more effectively. Reviews of student outcomes might also be important for formative assessments as a means of assessing which components and activities are showing signs of working as designed, and which components might not be yielding desired results and need modification. Classroom observations can also be used to assess teacher behaviors (see chapters 4 and 12). These examples demonstrate how districts will have to make explicit links across components, in this case to make sure that the numerous classroom-observation activities are coordinated with the main evaluation questions. This will minimize the potential burden on teachers and maximize utility for all potential users of this information.

The purpose of this section was to provide participating districts with specific examples of evaluation activities. The area we chose to focus on—the use of assessment data—is likely to be central to any district's approach to reform. The overview is not intended to be exhaustive; individual districts will still need to fill in specifics on their own. But hopefully these kinds of details will help participating districts get a better feel for what evaluation work looks like.

ESTABLISHING A TREATMENT EFFECT

Based on the discussion in the previous two sections, it is clear that districts can—and must—play a central role in designing and implementing a monitoring and evaluation plan. However, by themselves, the evaluation activities discussed so far are not likely to answer a critical question: is the comprehensive approach an effective intervention overall? In other words, what is the direct effect of participation on outcomes like student achievement? A treatment effect must be established that determines the difference between the outcomes of the district's students when a reform is in place and the outcomes that would have been observed had the district not implemented the reform.[2]

With the OPE framework, it is particularly challenging to measure the impact of the program relative to what would have happened if the program had never been implemented. Districts participating will have chosen to do so, rather than being randomly assigned by state education offices. In some cases, districts may respond to a perception of underperformance by determining to shake things up and get more out of existing capacity. But other districts may already be performing well and instead see an opportunity to take their performance to another level. What this all means is that we have no simple and clear manner of establishing a control group against which to compare districts implementing the OPE framework.

These conditions characterize almost every ambitious education intervention. Districts need to be aware of these issues and their potential consequences down the road, as legislators, policy makers, and researchers ask tough questions about the program's overall effectiveness. To anticipate these issues, we have identified some additional activities for districts to consider as part of their monitoring and evaluation planning. One option for establishing a treatment effect is to exploit variations in extensive, longitudinal data. To implement these methods, detailed data are collected for several school years prior to the reform and then during the implementation of the program. Outcomes during the implementation period are then compared to outcomes from the baseline period.

Districts should also consider gathering some additional sources of student achievement data. There are limits to what standardized tests can measure, even in systems that use value-added assessment. The most common criticism is that standardized tests can only address a limited range of cognitive skills and content, as discussed in chapter 8.[3] Districts should therefore utilize additional testing modalities to provide information on skills that are not captured by traditional assessments. The overarching goal should be to develop a more refined picture of individual performance based on multiple sources.

Districts should also introduce other measures of overall performance in addition to student test scores. Some examples are enrollment rates in college-preparatory and advanced courses, grade completion and graduation rates, student and teacher absenteeism, enrollment in postsecondary education, and student engagement and motivation. The overarching purpose, once again, is to provide a broader picture of student performance—or triangulation—that will aid in the establishment of a treatment effect.

IMPLEMENTATION GUIDELINES

It is clear there is no single template for implementing comprehensive reform. Each participating district will create its own plan of action, and the evaluation plan will need to be tailored to meet the needs of each approach. Because of this variation, we are reluctant to map out a specific plan of action for beginning the evaluation work. This chapter has already touched on some general themes about how this work should progress, with extensive discussions up front about the purposes of the evaluation, consultations with different participants and stakeholders, and establishment of clear lines of authority and responsibility. In this section we augment these general considerations with some more specific actions that districts can take, both early on and throughout the period of implementation, to facilitate the evaluation work.

These ten suggestions for districts include the following:

1. *Identify key questions, outcomes, and indicators for the evaluation, and map to data-collection activities.* Focus the evaluation early on by specifying the questions the evaluation seeks to answer, along with the expected outcomes and possible indicators derived from the theory of action.
2. *Develop capacity of central office staff for collecting and analyzing data.* Even in districts with specially designated offices of evaluation (or research), it may be necessary to upgrade capacity for data collection and analysis.[4]
3. *Develop teachers' and school administrators' capacity for talking about data.* The data-collection and analysis training need not be focused exclusively on district personnel who work in evaluation. Teachers and administrators may also benefit from training that helps them understand more about these processes, especially regarding how the information can be used.[5]

4. *Set aside time for teachers and administrators to discuss data collection, analysis, and findings with evaluation personnel and with each other.* One general purpose of these activities is to familiarize staff with the evaluation processes. Involving staff is especially important at the beginning of the implementation period in order to alert them to ways they can help facilitate these activities.

5. *Assign individuals to filter data and help translate data into usable—or user-friendly—information.*[6] For example, at the school level, individual teachers and coaches who are more comfortable with student achievement reports can work with other teachers to interpret these data. At the district level, administrators can help by completing initial analysis and summarizing results in easy-to-understand tables and graphs.

6. *Consider partnerships with external organizations that have evaluation capacity.* The most likely candidates are universities that may be willing to help with various aspects of the evaluation, perhaps in exchange for access to data that can be used for original research.

7. *Invest in user-friendly data-management systems or data-warehousing technology.* Foley et al. describe how useful it has been for individual school districts to have created effective systems, which they use to manage large amounts of data collected for both formative and summative purposes.[7]

8. *Consider online survey options like Survey Monkey and Zoomerang.* These are relatively inexpensive options for administering surveys, especially for teachers and administrators.

9. *As part of evaluation planning, have specific conversations about how to ensure high response rates.* Low response rates can be a serious problem for evaluations relying on surveys, and this is a problem that is easily overlooked in the planning stages. Involving teachers and administrators in the planning and discussions up front is one way to help ensure their buy-in.

10. *Consider sampling rather than working with every member of a given population (i.e., every teacher).* District size and the nature of each evaluation question will help determine the feasibility and necessity of sampling. But when done properly, this method can be an effective way to address research questions in a cost-effective manner.

CONCLUDING REMARKS

This discussion about evaluation has covered a lot of ground, especially considering that the OPE framework has not yet been implemented in any school district. This means we have to anticipate rather than react, and there is little question that districts will find some of our ideas more relevant than others. However, we feel strongly that it would be a mistake for districts to view this evaluation work as an extra burden, or as a purely bureaucratic set of actions that they are somehow required to do. The process of setting up a monitoring and evaluation plan is actually an excellent way to help define a vision for reform.

The sooner this begins, the better. Many education reforms have gone awry as a result of a "failure to launch." The OPE framework is so ambitious that getting it off the ground will require a substantial amount of work, and once again, the planning for evaluation can help at the beginning of this process, not just at the end. A number of reforms—many of them possibly quite effective—have proven to be nearly impossible to evaluate in terms of their direct effectiveness. As a districtwide reform, the OPE framework has some built-in complications for this kind of work. But a commitment to measurement from day one (if not before the start of implementation) will help address the kinds of critical questions that come at the end of the program cycle and inform future funding and expansion. Districts undertaking comprehensive reform should see themselves as part of a larger community, and their evaluation efforts will not only help their own district but may also be a form of a public good for others to use and benefit from.

In sum, five points are key for districts to remember. One, the district is ultimately responsible for defining what it will accomplish and how it will reach those goals. Two, the evaluation plan needs to be closely aligned with a program theory of action. Three, institutional support and coordination are critical for creating a sustainable evaluation system; one or two people cannot handle this alone, it needs to be based on a districtwide commitment to measurement (a "culture of measurement"). Four, the actual data collection should begin as soon as possible in order to help establish a pre- and postreform treatment comparison. And five, districts should not assume that the implementation is successful just because teachers and administrators are attending training sessions, participant perceptions are generally positive, or student test scores are going up. The most important test of effectiveness concerns what is happening in the classroom, and this is where evaluation work is so critical for monitoring implementation and establishing the overall validity of treatment effects. It is only through this type of rigorous and comprehensive program evaluation that educators and policy makers can determine what reforms are effective in transforming instruction and increasing student learning.

Notes

Preface

1. Warren Simmons, Michael Grady, and Brenda J. Turnbull, *Research Perspectives on School Reform: Lessons and Reflections from the Annenberg Challenge* (Providence, RI: Annenberg Institute for School Reform, March 2003).

2. Faced with pressing time commitments, Walter Hussman and Gerri House subsequently left the board.

3. Included among these were the National School Boards Association, American Association of School Administrators (AASA), Association for Supervision and Curriculum Development, and the Teacher Union Reform Network. The OPE model was also presented in keynote addresses to the annual meeting of superintendents in Idaho, Texas, and Illinois. Aspects of the OPE model were described in "The Case for New Standards in Education," *Education Week* (December 10, 1997); "Adequacy, Equity and Accountability," *Education Week* (February 19, 2003); "Aligning the System: The Case for Linking Teacher Pay to Student Learning," Education Week (March 29, 2006); "Not Performance Pay Alone: Teacher Incentives Must Be Matched by Systemwide Change," *Education Week* (April 10, 2007); "Value-Added Assessment and Systemic Reform: A Response to America's Human Capital Development Challenge," *Phi Delta Kappan* (December 2005): 276–83; "The Revelations of Value-Added," *The School Administrator* (December 2004); "Value-Added Assessment: Powerful Diagnostics to Improve Instruction and Promote Student Achievement," in Helen C. Sobehart, ed., *2004 Monograph: Leadership in a Time of Change* (AASA, November 2004), 11–22; "Measuring What Matters: How Value-Added Assessment Can Be Used to Drive Student Learning Gains," *American School Board Journal* 191, no. 2 (February 2004): 27–31.

4. President Barack Obama, "Remarks by the president to the Hispanic Chamber of Commerce" (Washington, DC, March 10, 2009).

Chapter 1: Overview of the OPE Framework

1. Louis V. Gerstner Jr., "Bad Schools + Shackled Principals = Outsourcing," *Wall Street Journal* (October 7, 2004), A18.

2. National Commission on Teaching and America's Future, "Policy Brief: The High Cost of Teacher Turnover" (Washington, DC: NCTAF, 2007).

3. National Commission on Teaching and America's Future, "No Dream Denied: A Pledge to America's Children" (Washington, DC: NCTAF, January 2003).

4. Bureau of Labor Statistics, *Current Population Survey* (Washington, DC: Bureau of Labor Statistics and the U.S. Census Bureau) [Data File]. Available from Census Bureau Web site http://www.census.gov/cps/.

5. Cheryl Lemke, "Learning in a Digital Age" (keynote address, Indiana's Future: World Class Schools for the 21st Century, University of Indianapolis, Indianapolis, November 1, 2006).

6. Kate Walsh and Christopher O. Tracy, *Increasing the Odds: How Good Policies Can Yield Better Teachers* (Washington, DC: National Council on Teacher Quality, October 2004).

7. Eric Hanushek, "A More Complete Picture of School Resource Policies," *Review of Educational Research* 66, no. 3 (Autumn 1996): 397–409; Eric Hanushek and Stephen Rivkin, "How to Improve the Supply of High Quality Teachers," in *Brookings Papers on Education Policy 2004*, ed. Diane Ravitch (Washington, DC: Brookings Institution Press, 2004), 7–25; Jonah Rockoff, "The Impact of Individual Teachers on Student Achievement: Evidence from Panel Data," *American Economic Review* 94, no. 2 (May 2004): 247–52.

8. At the Conference on Teacher Accountability (Williamson Conference Center, Horsham, PA, May 16, 2000), William Sanders presented a graph of statewide data from Tennessee that arrayed value-added scores for individual teachers by years in the classroom. He reported that, on average, new teachers add precious little value—a pattern with significant implications for mentoring (see chapter 11), and that teachers with more than twenty years of service, on average, experience a steep decline in productivity. This decrease in classroom effectiveness is undoubtedly due to several factors, including attrition that finds more effective teachers leaving the classroom for higher-paying administrative posts or leaving the profession altogether, but it also suggests burnout. When administrators see this pattern, they often remark that retirement should be mandated after twenty years of service. The problem with that suggestion is that while the variation around the mean in the first two-thirds of a career is relatively small, in the last third it is very large, meaning that early retirement would force some of the most effective (along with some of the least effective) teachers from the classroom.

9. William L. Sanders and June C. Rivers, "Cumulative and Residual Effects of Teachers on Future Student Academic Achievement" (Nashville: University of Tennessee Value-Added Research and Assessment Center, November 1996).

10. William J. Webster, Robert L. Mendro, Timothy H. Orsak, and Dash Weerasinghe, "An Application of Hierarchical Linear Modeling to the Estimation of School and Teacher Effect" (paper presented at the annual meeting of the American Educational Research Association, San Diego, CA, April 1998).

11. June Rivers, "The Impact of Teacher Effect on Math Competency Achievement" (doctoral dissertation, University of Tennessee, Knoxville, 1999).

12. Thomas J. Kane, Jonah E. Rockoff, and Douglas O. Staiger, "Photo Finish: Teacher Certification Doesn't Guarantee a Winner," *Education Next* 1 (Winter 2007).

13. James S. Coleman, "Equality of Educational Opportunity Study" (Washington, DC: U.S. Department of Health, Education, and Welfare, Office of Education/National Center for Education Statistics, 1966); Christopher Jencks, *Inequality: A Reassessment of the Effect of Family and Schooling in America* (New York: Harper & Row, 1973).

14. Daniel F. McCaffrey, Daniel Koretz, J. R. Lockwood, and Laura S. Hamilton, "Evaluating Value-Added Models for Teacher Accountability" (Santa Monica, CA: RAND Corporation, 2003); National Association of State Boards of Education, "Evaluating Value-Added" (Arlington, VA: National Association of State Boards of Education, 2005); Henry Braun, "Value-Added Modeling: What Does Due Diligence Require?" (Princeton, NJ: Educational Testing Service, December 20, 2004).

15. "One can envision VAM results serving as a component of a multidimensional system of evaluation; however, this possibility would have to be evaluated in light of the specifics of such a system and the context of use." Henry Braun and Howard Wainer, "Value-Added Modeling," in *Handbook of Statistics, 26*, eds. C. R. Rao and Sandip Sinharay (New York: Elsevier, 2007), 189.

16. Reg Weaver, "To Boost Students and Teachers, Steer Clear of Merit Pay on the Road to Reform," *Christian Science Monitor* (November 13, 2006).

17. William L. Sanders and Sandra P. Horn, "The Tennessee Value-Added Assessment System (TVAAS): Mixed-Model Methodology in Educational Assessment," *Journal of Personnel Evaluation in Education* 8 (1994): 299–311.

18. William L. Sanders and Sandra P. Horn, "Research Findings from the Tennessee Value-Added Assessment System (TVAAS) Database: Implications for Educational Evaluation and Research," *Journal of Personnel Evaluation in Education* 12, no. 3 (September 1998): 247–56.

19. Thomas Toch and Robert Rothman, "Rush to Judgment: Teacher Evaluation in Public Education," *Education Sector Reports*, (Washington, DC: Education Sector, January 2008): 3–4.

20. *Benchmarking for Success: Ensuring U.S. Students Receive a World-Class Education*. A report by the National Governors Association, the Council of Chief State School Officers, and Achieve, Inc. (Washington, DC: National Governors Association, 2008); David J. Hoff, "National Standards Gain Steam: Governors' Embrace Rooted in Competitiveness Concerns," *Education Week* (March 4, 2009), 1, 20–21.

21. E. D. Hirsch, Jr., "Reading Test Dummies," *New York Times* (March 23, 2009), A21.

22. Ellen R. Delisio, "Pay for Performance: What Went Wrong in Cincinnati," *Education World* (2006).

23. OPE originally reserved this rung for highly effective teachers who also had been certified by the National Board for Professional Teaching Standards. This remains a viable option for districts because although the empirical data do not support the notion that these teachers are significantly more likely than non-Board-certified teachers to have better student learning results, the intellectual process teachers go through to win certification is likely to improve their already highly effective classroom practice. A major additional advantage is the objectivity of an externally certified status.

24. Lauren B. Resnick, "From Aptitude to Effort: A New Foundation for Our Schools," *Daedalus* 124, no. 4 (Fall 1995): 55–62.

25. See the accomplishments of the KIPP Academies in Paul Tough, "What It Takes to Make a Student," *New York Times Magazine* (November 26, 2006), 44(L).

26. Jay McTighe and John L Brown, "Differentiated Instruction and Educational Standards: Is Détente Possible?" *Theory Into Practice* 44, no. 3 (Summer 2005): 234–44.

27. Carol Ann Tomlinson, *The Differentiated Classroom: Responding to the Needs of All Learners* (Alexandria, VA: Association for Supervision and Curriculum Development, 1999).

28. Robert J. Marzano, *What Works in Schools: Translating Research Into Action* (Alexandria, VA: Association for Supervision and Curriculum Development, 2005).

29. Karen Hawley Miles and Matthew Hornbeck, "Reinvesting in Teachers: Aligning District Professional Development Spending to Support a Comprehensive School Reform Strategy," *New American Schools Strategy Brief* 3 (2000).

30. Given the great array of professional development programs and curricula, and the absence of "slam-dunk" evidence to choose among these, OPE did not include them in the framework. Similarly, while most people would agree that parents play a vitally important part in the education of their children, no mechanism has been developed to hold parents legally responsible for what they do or don't do for their children, which is why there is no provision for formal parental accountability in the OPE model. If student learning results were expressed in terms of achievement, there could be no accountability at the level of individual educators, again,

because of the deep biases introduced by family income. But because the student learning results in the OPE model are expressed in terms of growth, the evaluation of educators is unaffected by the parental contribution, regardless of a positive or negative impact. School districts should be encouraged to develop strategies that maximize parental involvement—in some districts voluntary "parent report cards" or "parent contracts" have been successful— but in the OPE model no one is disadvantaged or advantaged in terms of accountability by the level of parental engagement. Students should never be penalized for what they do not get at home; schools have to adjust their practices to compensate for these deficiencies. See the National Coalition for Parent Involvement in Education and the successes achieved, particularly in Hispanic communities, in the work of the United Neighborhood Organization of Chicago.

31. Richard F. Elmore, "Building a New Structure for School Leadership" (Washington, DC: Albert Shanker Institute, Winter 2000).

32. The title of this book is drawn from a column by Jonathan Alter in which he proposed a "Grand Education Bargain." Jonathan Alter, "Obama's No Brainer on Education," *Newsweek* (July 21, 2008), 35.

Chapter 2: Professional Unionism

1. Charles Taylor Kerchner, Julia E. Koppich, and Joseph G. Weeres, *United Mind Workers* (San Francisco: Jossey-Bass, 1997).

2. Julia E. Koppich, "Resource Allocation in Traditional and Reform-Oriented Collective Bargaining Agreements," Working Paper No. 17 (Seattle: University of Washington School Finance Redesign Project, Center on Reinventing Public Education, 2007), 6.

3. Martin H. Malin and Charles T. Kerchner, "Charter Schools and Collective Bargaining: Compatible Marriage or Illegitimate Relationship?" (paper prepared for a labor conference at Claremont Graduate University, Claremont, CA, 2006), 4.

4. Kerchner et al., *United Mind Workers*, 104.

5. Susan Moore Johnson and Morgaen L. Donaldson, "The Effects of Collective Bargaining on Teacher Quality," in *Collective Bargaining in Education: Negotiating Change in Today's Schools,* eds. Jane Hannaway and Andrew J. Rotherham (Cambridge, MA: Harvard Education Press, 2006), 113.

6. Ibid., 113.

7. Julia Koppich and Mary Alice Callahan, "Teacher Collective Bargaining: What We Know and What We Need to Know," *American Education Association Yearbook* (Washington, DC: AEA, 2008), 11.

8. Charles T. Kerchner and Julia E. Koppich, *A Union of Professionals: Labor Relations and Education Reform* (New York: Teachers College Press, 1993); Susan Moore Johnson and Susan M. Kardos, "Reform Bargaining and Its Promise for School Improvement," in *Conflicting Missions? Teachers Unions and Educational Reform,* ed. Tom Loveless (Washington, DC: Brookings Institution Press, 2000).

9. Kerchner and Koppich, *Union of Professionals.*

10. Ibid., 196.

11. Ibid., 197.

12. Ibid., 200.

13. Ibid., 201.

14. Kerchner et al., *United Mind Workers.*

15. Kerchner and Koppich, *Union of Professionals,* 194.

16. Kerchner et al., *United Mind Workers;* Linda Kaboolian and Paul Sutherland, *Win-Win Labor-Management Collaboration in Education: Breakthrough Practices to Benefit Students, Teachers, and Administrators* (Cambridge, MA: The Rennie Center for Education Research and Policy, 2006); Koppich, "Resource Allocation."
17. Koppich, "Resource Allocation," 15.
18. Kerchner et al., *United Mind Workers;* Kerchner and Koppich, *Union of Professionals.*
19. Julia Koppich, "What's a Teacher Worth?" *Education Next* (Winter 2005): 10.
20. Koppich, "Resource Allocation," 11.
21. Ibid., 12.
22. Ibid., 13.

Chapter 3: Choosing a Value-Added Model

1. J. R. Lockwood and Daniel F. McCaffrey, "Controlling for Individual Heterogeneity in Longitudinal Models, with Applications to Student Achievement," *Electronic Journal of Statistics* 1 (2007): 223–52; S. Paul Wright, "Advantages of a Multivariate Longitudinal Approach to Educational Value-Added Assessment without Imputation" (paper presented at CREATE/NEI Conference, Colorado Springs, CO, July 2004), available online at http://www.wmich.edu/evalctr/create/2004/Wright-NEI04.pdf.
2. R. Darrell Bock, Richard Wolfe, and Thomas H. Fisher, *A Review and Analysis of the Tennessee Value-Added Assessment System* (Nashville: Tennessee Comptroller of the Treasury, 1996); Kevin Carey, "The Real Value of Teachers: Using New Information about Teacher Effectiveness to Close the Achievement Gap," *Thinking K–16* 8 (Winter 2004): 3–32; *Evaluating Value-Added: Findings and Recommendations from the NASBE Study Group on Value-Added Assessment* (Alexandria, VA: National Association of State Boards of Education, 2005).
3. The discussion using the matrix is drawn from Theodore Hershberg, "Value-Added Assessment and Systemic Reform: A Response to America's Human Capital Development Challenge," *Phi Delta Kappan* 87, no. 4 (December 2005): 276–83.
4. These studies have been cited in the introductory chapter to this volume.
5. William L. Sanders, "Comparisons among Various Educational Assessment Value-Added Models" (paper presented at The Power of Two, National Value-Added Conference, Columbus, OH, October 16, 2006), available online at http://www.sas.com/govedu/edu/services/vaconferencepaper.pdf.
6. Daniel F. McCaffrey, Han Bing, and J. R. Lockwood, "From Data to Bonuses: A Case Study of the Issues Related to Awarding Teachers Pay on the Basis of Their Students' Progress" (paper presented at the National Center on Performance Incentives Research to Policy Conference, Vanderbilt University, Nashville, TN, February 29, 2008).
7. Sanders, "Comparisons among Various Educational Assessment Value-Added Models."
8. This is the procedure used in the SAS EVAAS Univariate Response Model (URM).
9. S. Paul Wright, William L. Sanders, and Joan C. Rivers, "Measurement of Academic Growth of Individual Students toward Variable and Meaningful Academic Standards," in *Longitudinal and Value Added Models of Student Performance*, ed. R. W. Lissitz (Maple Grove, MN: JAM Press, 2006).
10. The SAS EVAAS Multivariate Response Model (MRM) represents models of this type. For details, see William L. Sanders, Arnold M. Saxton, and Sandra P. Horn, "The Tennessee Value-Added Assessment System (TVAAS): A Quantitative, Outcomes-Based Approach to Educational Assessment," in *Grading Teachers, Grading Schools*, ed. Jason Millman (Thousand Oaks, CA: Corwin Press, 1997).

11. Wright, "Advantages of a Multivariate Longitudinal Approach."
12. Lockwood and McCaffrey, "Controlling for Individual Heterogeneity in Longitudinal Models, with Applications to Student Achievement."
13. Debate continues on whether "teacher effects" persist perfectly into the future.
14. Dale Ballou, William L. Sanders, and S. Paul Wright, "Controlling for Students Background in Value-Added Assessment of Teachers," *Journal of Educational and Behavioral Statistics* 29, no. 1 (2004): 37–66; J. R. Lockwood, Daniel F. McCaffrey, Louis T. Mariano, and Claude Setodji, "Bayesian Methods for Scalable Multivariate Value-Added Assessment," *Journal of Educational and Behavioral Statistics* 32, no. 2 (2007): 125–50.

Chapter 4: Teacher Evaluation

1. Thomas Toch and Robert Rothman, "Rush to Judgment: Teacher Evaluation in Public Education," *Education Sector Reports* (Washington DC: Education Sector, January 2008: 3–4.
2. Anthony Milanowski, Steven Kimball, and B. White, "The Relationship between Standards-Based Teacher Evaluation Scores and Student Achievement: Replication and Extension at Three Sites," CPRE-UW Working Paper Series TC-04-01 (Madison: University of Wisconsin–Madison, Wisconsin Center for Education Research, Consortium for Policy Research in Education, 2004); Robert Pianta, "Spotlight: Classroom Observation, Professional Development and Teacher Quality," *The Evaluation Exchange* XI, no. 4 (Winter 2005/2006), available online at http://www.gse.harvard.edu/hfrp/eval/issue32/spotlight3.html; Herbert Heneman III, Anthony Milanowski, Steven Kimball, and Allan Odden, "Standards-Based Teacher Evaluation as a Foundation for Knowledge- and Skill-Based Pay," *CPRE Policy Briefs* (Philadelphia, PA: Consortium for Policy Research in Education, May 2006).
3. Charlotte Danielson, *Enhancing Professional Practice: A Framework for Teaching* (Alexandria, VA: Association for Supervision and Curriculum Development, 2007), 3–4.
4. Ibid., 3.
5. Charlotte Danielson and Thomas McGreal, "The Design Process," in *Teacher Evaluation to Enhance Professional Practice*, eds. C. Danielson and T. L. McGreal (Alexandria, VA: Association for Supervision and Curriculum Development, 2000), 64–77.
6. Ibid.
7. Charlotte Danielson, *The Handbook for Enhancing Professional Practice: Using the Framework for Teaching in Your School* (Alexandria, VA: Association for Supervision and Curriculum Development, 2008).
8. Ibid.

Chapter 5: Administrator Evaluation

1. Richard Elmore, "Accountable Leadership," *The Educational Forum* 59, no. 2 (Winter 2005): 134-42; Ronald A. Heifetz and Donald L. Laurie, "The Work of Leadership" *Harvard Business Review* 79, no. 11 (2001): 131–41; New Leaders for New Schools, *Key Insights of the Urban Excellence Framework: Defining an Urban Principalship to Drive Dramatic Achievement Gains* (New York: New Leaders for New Schools, 2008).
2. Andrew Porter et al., "Building a Psychometrically Sound Assessment of School Leadership: The VAL-ED as a Case Study" (paper presented at the annual meeting of the American Educational Research Association, New York, March 2008).
3. Douglas Reeves, *Assessing Educational Leaders: Evaluating Performance for Improved Individual and Organizational Results* (Thousand Oaks, CA: Corwin Press, 2008).

4. Another promising administrator measurement tool is VAL-ED (Vanderbilt Assessment of Leadership in Education), which was developed by Vanderbilt's Peabody College faculty members Joseph Murphy, Ellen Goldring, Steve Elliott, graduate student Xiu Cravens, and Andrew Porter, dean of the Graduate School of Education at the University of Pennsylvania.

5. Robert J. Marzano, *What Works in Schools: Translating Research into Action* (Alexandria, VA: Association for Supervision and Curriculum Development, 2003).

6. Meta Kruger, Bob Witziers, and Peter Sleegers, "The Impact of School Leadership on School Level Factors: Validation of a Causal Model," *School Effectiveness and School Improvement* 18, no. 1 (March 2007): 1–20.

7. Given the nature of school administrators' work, other outputs, such as effective teacher recruitment and retention, may need to be factored into the evaluation as well.

8. Joseph Murphy and Neil Shipman, "The Interstate School Leaders Licensure Consortium: A Standards-Based Approach to Strengthening Educational Leadership," *Journal of Personnel Evaluation in Education* 13, no. 3 (September 1999): 205–24.

9. A similar process is currently underway in Prince George's County (Maryland) Public Schools, where the school system is identifying standards, developing rubrics, and creating a portfolio system in collaboration with the local administrators union for administrators participating in the FIRST Program—the PGCPS Pay for Performance for administrators and teachers program funded by a USDE Teacher Incentive Fund Grant.

10. Our experience suggests that decisions related to administrator evaluation be made collaboratively between district staff, such as the superintendent or the director of administrative professional development, and building administrators and their representative bodies wherever possible.

11. Charlotte Danielson, *Enhancing Professional Practice: A Framework for Teaching* (Alexandria, VA: Association for Supervision and Curriculum Development, 1996).

12. Genevieve Brown and Beverly J. Irby, *The Principal Portfolio* (Thousand Oaks, CA: Corwin Press, 1997).

13. Tina Blythe, David Allen, and Barbara Schieffelin Powell, *Looking Together at Student Work* (New York: Teachers College Press, 1999).

Chapter 6: Compensation

1. Laura Goe and Leslie Stickler, "Teacher Quality and Student Achievement: Making the Most of Recent Research" (Chicago: National Comprehensive Center for Teacher Quality, March 2008); Eric A. Hanushek, John F. Kain, Daniel M. O'Brien, and Steven G. Rivkin, "The Market for Teacher Quality," Working Paper Series (Cambridge, MA: National Bureau of Economic Research, February 2005); Steven G. Rivkin, Eric A. Hanushek, and John F. Kain, "Teachers, Schools, and Academic Achievement," *Econometrica* 73, no. 2 (March 2005): 417–58; Michael J. Podgursky and Matthew G. Springer, "Teacher Performance Pay: A Review," Working Paper 2006-01 (Nashville, TN: National Center on Performance Incentives, 2006).

2. Goe and Stickler, "Teacher Quality and Student Achievement," Hanushek et al., "The Market for Teacher Quality"; Rivkin et al., "Teachers, Schools, and Academic Achievement."

3. Allan Odden and Marc Wallace, *How to Create World Class Teacher Compensation* (Lake Bluff, IL: Freeload Press, 2008).

4. David Figlio and Lawrence Kenny, "Individual Teacher Incentives and Student Performance," *Journal of Public Economics* 91 (June 2007): 901–14; Elena Silva, *The Benwood*

Plan: A Lesson in Comprehensive Teacher Reform (Washington, DC: Education Sector Reports, April 2008); Podursky and Springer, "Teacher Performance Pay: A Review."

5. Bureau of Labor Statistics. *Current Population Survey* (Washington, DC: Bureau of Labor Statistics and the U.S. Census Bureau) [Data File]. Available from Census Bureau Web site http://www.census.gov/cps/

6. Odden and Wallace, *How to Create World Class Teacher Compensation.*

7. N. Fredric Crandall and Marc J. Wallace Jr., *Work and Rewards in the Virtual Workplace* (New York: AMACOM, 1998)

8. Odden and Wallace, *How to Create World Class Teacher Compensation.*

9. Ibid.

Chapter 7: Compensating Educators in the Absence of Value-Added Assessment

1. "Performance-Pay for Teachers" (Hillsborough, NC: Center for Teaching Quality, 2007); Working Group on Teacher Quality, "Creating a Successful Performance Compensation System for Educators" (Santa Monica, CA: National Institute for Excellence in Teaching, July 2007).

2. Additional information is available online at http://Denverprocomp.org.

3. Space limitations have prevented us from discussing the full range of districts experimenting with pay for performance. Other noteworthy examples include Florida and Chattanooga, Tennessee.

Chapter 8: Integrated Assessment

1. Gary Williamson, *Student Readiness for Postsecondary Options* (Durham, NC: MetaMetrics, Inc., The Lexile Framework for Reading, July 2004).

2. Paul Black and Dylan Wiliam, "The Formative Purpose: Assessment Must First Promote Learning," in *Towards Coherence Between Classroom Assessment and Accountability: 103rd Yearbook of the National Society for the Student of Education. Part II ,* ed. Mark Wilson (Chicago: University of Chicago Press, 2004), 20–50.

3. *Benchmarking for Success: Ensuring U.S. Students Receive a World-Class Education,* a report by the National Governors Association, the Council of Chief State School Officers, and Achieve, Inc. (Washington, DC: National Governors Association, 2008); David J. Hoff, "National Standards Gain Steam: Governors' Embrace Rooted in Competitiveness Concerns," *Education Week* 28, no. 3 (March 4, 2009): 1, 20–21).

4. These principles draw from best practices developed by the Assessment Training Institute.

5. W. James Popham, Roger Farr, and Mary Lindquist, "Crafting Curricular Aims for Instructionally Supportive Assessment" (self-published, September 2003).

6. Ibid.

7. Rick Stiggins and Jan Chappuis, "What a Difference a Word Makes," *JSD* 27, no. 1 (Winter 2006): 10–14.

8. Rick Stiggins, Judith Arter, Stephen Chappuis, and Jan Chappuis, *Classroom Assessment for Student Learning: Doing It Right—Using It Well* (Portland, OR: Educational Testing Service, 2004).

9. Stephen Chappuis, Richard J. Stiggins, Judith Arter, and Jan Chappius, *Assessment FOR Learning: An Action Guide for School Leaders* (Portland, OR: Educational Testing Service), 78–79.

10. Ibid., 64–77.

11. Listing is based on Ibid., 71.

12. Ibid., 87–93, provides a school district assessment self-analysis tool.

13. Lauren B. Resnick, *Education and Learning to Think* (Washington, DC: National Academies Press, 1987).

14. Chappuis et al., *Assessment FOR Learning*, 74–77.

15. Ibid., 62.

16. We recommend that districts interested in establishing a professional learning community approach access the model developed by the Educational Testing Service (ETS), where teachers can work together throughout the school year to analyze data and improve practice. For more information, go to http://www.assessmentinst.com/.

Chapter 9: Value-Added as a Classroom Diagnostic

1. S. Paul Wright, William L. Sanders, and June C. Rivers, "Measurement of Academic Growth of Individual Students Toward Variable and Meaningful Academic Standards," in *Longitudinal and Value Added Models of Student Performance,* ed. Robert W. Lissitz (Maple Grove, MN: JAM Press, 2006).

2. Jennifer Booher-Jennings, "Below the Bubble: 'Educational Triage' and the Texas Accountability System," *American Educational Research Journal* 42, no. 2 (2005): 231–68.

3. Joshua S. Wyner, John M. Bridgeland, and John J. Dilulio Jr., "Achievement Trap: How America Is Failing Millions of High-Achieving Students from Lower-Income Families" (Lansdowne, VA: Jack Kent Cooke Foundation, 2007), available online at www.jkcf.org/assets/files/0000/0084/Achievement_Trap.pdf.

Chapter 10: Value-Added Training

1. Kerry Patterson, Joseph Grenny, David Maxfield, Ron McMillan, and Al Switzler, *Influencer: The Power to Change Anything* (New York: McGraw Hill, 2007), 50.

2. More information on this program can be found at http://battelleforkids.com/home/toolkit.

Chapter 11: Mentoring and New Teacher Induction

1. National Commission on Teaching and America's Future, "No Dream Denied: A Pledge to America's Children" (Washington, DC: NCTAF, January 2003); The Teaching Commission, "Teaching at Risk: A Call to Action" (New York: City University of New York Graduate Center, The Teaching Commission, 2004).

2. Michael Strong, "Mentoring New Teachers to Increase Retention: A Look at the Research," *Research Brief No. 1* (Santa Cruz: University of California, Santa Cruz, New Teacher Center, 2005); Michael Strong, "Does New Teacher Support Affect Student Achievement? Some Early Research Findings," *Research Brief No. 1* (Santa Cruz: University of California, Santa Cruz, New Teacher Center, 2006).

3. Richard Ingersoll, "Teacher Turnover and Teacher Shortages: An Organizational Analysis," *American Educational Research Journal* 38, no. 3 (Fall 2001): 499–534.

4. National Commission on Teaching and America's Future, "The High Cost of Teacher Turnover" (Washington, DC: NCTAF, June 2007).

5. Districts interested in developing their own mentor training curriculum can access explanation of the content for each of the sessions at www.newteachercenter.org/ti_mentor_pro_development.php.

6. For additional information, go to www.newteachercenter.org/ti_continuum_of_teacher.php.

7. To learn more about the thinking behind NTC's formative-assessment system, district leaders may review the material found at www.newteachercenter.org/formative_assessment.php.

8. Anthony Villar and Michael Strong, "Making a Case for Policy Investments That Make New Teachers Succeed" (Santa Cruz: New Teacher Center, University of California, Santa Cruz, 2007).

9. For a detailed discussion of the calculations supporting these costs and benefits, go to http://newteachercenter.org/newsletters/ReflectionsW08.pdf .

Chapter 12: Peer Assistance and Review and Mandatory Remediation

1. Steven G. Rivkin, Eric A. Hanushek, and John F. Kain, "Teachers, Schools, and Academic Achievement" *Econometrica* 73, no. 2 (March 2005): 417–58; Eric A. Hanushek, John F. Kain, Daniel M. O'Brien, and Steven G. Rivkin, "The Market for Teacher Quality" (Washington, DC: National Bureau for Economic Research, February 2005); William Sanders, "Value Added Assessment: Linking Student Achievement to Teacher Effectiveness" (Upper Saddle River, NJ: Pearson Education, Inc., 2005), available online at www.pearsonschool.com/live/assets/200727/2005_11Sanders_546_1.pdf.

2. National Commission on Teaching and America's Future, "No Dream Denied: A Pledge to America's Children" (Washington, DC: NCTAF, January 2003); The Teaching Commission, "Teaching at Risk: A Call to Action" (Washington, DC: The Teaching Commission, 2004).

3. Ann Bradley, "Peer-Review Programs Catch Hold as Unions, Districts Work Together," *Education Week* 17, no. 38 (June 1998): 1–7.

4. Pamela D. Tucker, "Lake Wobegon: Where All Teachers Are Competent (Or, Have We Come to Terms with the Problem of Incompetent Teachers?" *Journal of Personnel Evaluation in Education* 11, no. 2 (1997): 103–6.

5. Available online at www.tft250.org/ten_questions.htm.

6. Ann Bradley, "Peer-Review Programs Catch Hold as Unions, Districts Work Together"; Karen Gutloff, "You Be the Judge," *NEA Today* (November 1997): 1–9.

7. Julia E. Koppich, "Peer Assistance and Review: Enhancing What Teachers Know and Can Do" in *The Peer Assistance and Review Reader,* eds., Gary Bloom and Jennifer Goldstein (Santa Cruz, CA: New Teacher Center, 2000), 31.

8. Philip P. Kelly, "Teacher Peer Review Recommendations" in *The Peer Assistance and Review Reader,* eds., Gary Bloom and Jennifer Goldstein (Santa Cruz, CA: New Teacher Center, 2000), 40.

Chapter 13: Strategic Professional Development Review

1. More detailed instructions and methodology can be found on the Education Resource Strategies Web site, www.educationresourcestrategies.org.

2. A full list of all interviews and data-collection needs are listed on the ERS Web site.

3. This coding tool is available on the ERS Web site.

4. More detailed information on coding professional development activities in each of the areas can be found on our Web site.

5. Karen Hawley Miles and Matthew Hornbeck, "Reinvesting in Teachers: Aligning District Professional Development Spending to Support a Comprehensive School Reform Strategy," *New American Schools Strategy Brief No. 3* (2000).

6. Richard F. Elmore, "Getting to Scale with Good Educational Practice," *Harvard Educational Review* 66 (1996): 1–26; Milbrey McLaughlin and Joan Talbert, "Reforming Districts: How Districts Support Reform" *Document R-03* (Seattle: University of Washington, Center for the Study of Teaching Policy, September 2003); James P. Spillane, "School Dis-

tricts Matter: Local Educational Authorities and State Instructional Policy," *Educational Policy* 10, no. 1 (1996): 63–87; James P. Spillane, "A Cognitive Perspective on the LEA's Role in Implementing Instructional Policy: Accounting for Local Variability. *Education Administration Quarterly* 43, no. 1 (1998): 31–57.

7. Note that this does not include contracted teacher time and education salary increments.

Pilot Overview

1. In Denver, by a 2 to 1 margin, voters approved a surcharge on their real estate taxes that generated a $25 million increase in teacher compensation.

2. The OPE framework determines the amount of starting salaries and percentage increases beyond the minimums set for each rung in the career ladder, and defines the meaning of *significant* when it comes to bonuses and salary levels for hard-to-staff and hard-to-serve positions.

Chapter 14: Communications

1. Joan Baratz-Snowden, *The Future of Teacher Compensation: Déjà vu or Something New?* (Washington, DC: Center for American Progress, 2007).

Chapter 15: Evaluation

1. Carol H. Weiss, "Theory-Based Evaluation: Past, Present, and Future," *New Directions for Evaluation* 114 (2007): 68–81; Patricia J. Rogers and Carol H. Weiss, "Theory-Based Evaluation: Reflections Ten Years On," *New Directions for Evaluation* 114 (2007): 63–67.

2. Paul Holland, "Statistics and Causal Inference," *Journal of the American Statistical Association* 81 (1986): 945–60.

3. Daniel McCaffrey, Daniel M. Koretz, J. R. Lockwood, and Laura S. Hamilton, *Evaluating Value-Added Models for Teacher Accountability* (Santa Monica, CA: RAND Corporation, 2004).

4. Nancy Love, "Taking Data to New Depths," *Journal of Staff Development* 25 (2004): 22–26; Eva Chen, Margaret Heritage, and John Lee, "Identifying and Monitoring Students' Learning Needs with Technology," *Journal of Education for Students Placed at Risk* 10 (2005): 309–32.

5. Amanda Datnow, Vicki Park, and Priscilla Wohlstetter, *Achieving with Data* (Los Angeles: University of Southern California, Center on Educational Governance, 2007).

6. Julie A. Marsh, John F. Pane, and Laura S. Hamilton, "Making Sense of Data-Driven Decision Making in Education," RAND Corporation Occasional Paper Series (Santa Monica, CA: RAND Corporation, 2006); Victoria L. Bernhardt, "No Schools Left Behind," *Educational Leadership* 60 (2003): 26–30.

7. Ellen Foley, Jacob Mishook, Joanne Thompson, Michael Kubiak, Jonathan Supovitz, and Mary Kaye Rhude-Faust, *Beyond Test Scores: Leading Indicators for Education* (Providence, RI: Brown University, Annenberg Institute for School Reform, 2008).

About the Editors

THEODORE HERSHBERG is a professor of public policy and history and the director of the Center for Greater Philadelphia at the University of Pennsylvania, where he has taught since 1967. He is the founding director of Operation Public Education (OPE) and holds MA and PhD degrees in American history from Stanford University. He was acting dean of Penn's School of Public and Urban Policy and served as assistant to the mayor of Philadelphia for strategic planning and policy development. He has written and lectured extensively in the fields of urban-industrial development, regional cooperation, and education policy.

CLAIRE ROBERTSON-KRAFT is associate director of the Center for Greater Philadelphia and Operation Public Education. She graduated from the University of Pennsylvania in 2004 with a double major in urban studies and philosophy. Prior to joining the OPE team, she worked with Teach For America in Houston, first as a third-grade teacher and then as a program director for corps members teaching in elementary and special education placements. She is currently pursuing her PhD in education policy at Penn.

About the Contributors

VIRGINIA ADAMS SIMON, a lecturer and policy analyst at the University of California, Davis, School of Education, holds her MA and EdD degrees in educational leadership from the University of Pennsylvania. She is also a senior associate for Cross & Joftus, LLC, an education policy consulting firm, where she serves as project manager for a best practices Web portal being developed for the California Department of Education. Prior to moving to California in 2005, Adams Simon spent five years as the associate director of the Center for Greater Philadelphia, helping to develop the OPE framework.

JACQUELYN ASBURY is an education consultant at Battelle for Kids. With vast experience in standards-based education, professional development, instructional design, value-added analysis, leadership development, and formative assessment, she has served in urban, rural, and suburban school districts as an assistant superintendent, principal, counselor, and teacher. She also works as a coach for the Ohio Appalachian Educator Institute sponsored by the Voinovich School for Leadership and Public Affairs at Ohio University in Athens, Ohio. She earned her PhD in counseling and educational administration at The Ohio State University and her MS and BS degrees in education from Youngstown State University.

CHRISTOPHER T. CROSS is chairman of Cross & Joftus, LLC, an education policy consulting firm. He has been a Senior Fellow with the Center for Education Policy and a Distinguished Senior Fellow with the Education Commission of the States. Cross chaired the National Assessment of Title I Independent Review Panel on Evaluation for the U.S. Department of Education from 1995 to 2001, and the National Research Council (NRC) panel on Minority Representation in Special Education from 1997 to 2002. He also was a member of the NRC panel on International Education and Foreign Languages in 2006-07. He has written numerous scholarly and technical publications.

CHARLOTTE DANIELSON is a former economist and an educational consultant based in Princeton, New Jersey. She has worked as a teacher and administrator in school districts in several regions of the United States. In addition, she has served as a consultant to hundreds of districts, universities, intermediate agencies, and education departments in virtually every state and in many other countries. Her work has ranged from the training of practitioners in aspects of instruction and assessment, to the design of instruments and procedures for teacher evaluation, to keynote presentations at major conferences. She is the author of a number of books supporting teachers and administrators, including *Enhancing Professional Practice: A Framework for Teaching, Enhancing Student Achievement: A*

Framework for School Improvement, and Strengthening the Profession Through Teacher Leadership, all published by ASCD.

JOHN DEASY has extensive experience and a successful performance record in the administrative, organizational, operational, and communicative areas of educational organizations. He has used his skills to implement whole-school and systemic reform initiatives as superintendent of the Prince George's County Public Schools in Maryland, the Santa Monica-Malibu Unified School District in California, and the Coventry Public Schools in Rhode Island. These initiatives have led to record advancements in student achievement. He was an Annenberg Fellow, a Broad Fellow, and was named State Superintendent of the Year in Rhode Island.

JOEL GIFFIN is the former principal of Maryville Middle School in Maryville, Tennessee, an educational consultant, and Milken Award winner. As a principal, he used the value-added system to diagnose and evaluate each individual student's needs and incorporated the Multi-Grade Level program at Maryville, which allows students in grades 6–8 to grow at their own pace using a combination of hands-on, nontraditional, traditional, and technology-based instruction. He created a program called Academic Intervention, which provides at-risk students from low-income, single-parent families with supplementary instruction during the school day. Students in the program have demonstrated considerable academic improvement, earning Maryville recognition as a Blue Ribbon School.

JOHN GROSSMAN served as president of the Columbus Education Association from 1978 to 2004, and continued to assist the staff after his term ended. He was also a governor and faculty representative and served on numerous association committees, including the NEA Legislative Committee, the NEA Committee for the Revitalization of Urban Education, and the NEA Committee on Peer Assistance and Review. He was appointed to the Ohio Governor's Education Management Council and the Columbus Mayor's Educational Advisory Board. He was a charter member of the Teacher Union Reform Network and a founding member/past cochair of the Ohio 8. John Grossman died on July 28, 2008.

LAURA S. HAMILTON is a senior behavioral scientist at RAND and an adjunct associate professor in the Learning Sciences and Policy Program at the University of Pittsburgh. She conducts research on educational assessment, accountability, instructional practices, and school reform implementation. Much of her work focuses on the validity and effects of large-scale achievement testing and on the development of measures of instructional practice. She has served on several national and state panels, including the joint committee to revise the Standards for Educational and Psychological Testing.

MARGARET JORGENSEN is CEO of Measure2Learn, LLC. She was previously senior vice president for product research and innovation at Harcourt Assessment, where she was responsible for the development of the tenth edition of the Stanford Achievement Test Series, the eighth edition of the Otis-Lennon School Ability Test, and many of the state custom development programs. Before joining Harcourt, Jorgensen was assistant vice president for development at ACT, Inc., a nonprofit testing company known mainly for its college admission test. She earlier held several positions at Educational Testing Service and was responsible at various times for test development for the K–12 market, new business development, and continuous process improvement in test development.

BRAD JUPP is the senior academic policy advisor to Denver Public Schools (DPS). In that role, he has shaped district direction in a wide range of fields, including school and district performance and accountability, new school development and school choice, and the management of educator human capital. Before taking on that assignment, he taught in the DPS for nineteen years and worked as an activist in the Denver Classroom Teachers Association (DCTA). Jupp led the joint district/union effort to develop and implement Denver's Professional Compensation System for Teachers and volunteered as a member of the negotiations team for the DCTA. In his most recent classroom assignment, he held his dream job of lead teacher at the Alternative Middle School of the DPS Contemporary Learning Academy, working with at-risk sixth, seventh, and eighth graders. Jupp has been a teacher in the DPS since 1987.

JULIA E. KOPPICH is a San Francisco–based education consultant and President of J. Koppich & Associates. She holds a PhD in educational administration and policy analysis from the University of California, Berkeley, and has been a consultant to the U.S. Department of Education, the National Commission on Teaching and America's Future, the National Governors' Association, the National Board for Professional Teaching Standards, the National Alliance of Business, the American Federation of Teachers, the National Education Association, and the National Science Foundation. She is the coauthor of two books: *A Union of Professionals* and *United Mind Workers: Unions and Teaching in the Knowledge Society.*

JAMES W. MAHONEY is executive director of Battelle for Kids, an independent nonprofit organization committed to improving student learning. Over the last thirty years he has served as a superintendent, assistant superintendent, principal, teacher, and professor. He has published numerous articles, has served as a keynote speaker in many school districts, and has made presentations throughout Ohio and across the United States, Canada, and China. He has been the recipient of numerous awards for his leadership in education, including the Ohio Friend of Education Award from the Ohio Federation of Teachers and the prestigious President's Award from the Ohio School Boards Association, an award given annually to an individual who has greatly influenced public education.

PATRICIA MARTIN is a development associate at the New Teacher Center. Her recent publications include "Novice Teachers: Meeting the Challenge" in *Principal Magazine,* and "The Ubiquitous Art of Bluffing" in *TESOL Magazine.* She has taught elementary and secondary ESOL students and produced educational television programming for WGBH-TV in Boston. She has also held senior positions in high-tech venture capital, market analysis, and business consulting operations. Martin holds an MPA from Harvard.

KAREN HAWLEY MILES is executive director and founder of Education Resource Strategies (ERS) a nonprofit organization in Boston, Massachusetts, that specializes in strategic planning, organization, and resource allocation in urban public school districts. She has worked intensively with urban districts including Atlanta, Los Angeles, Chicago, Albuquerque, Boston, Baltimore, New York, Providence, Rochester, and Cincinnati to deeply analyze and improve their funding systems, school-level resource use, and human capital and professional development systems. Miles has taught school leaders at Harvard University and in school districts, with New Leaders for New Schools and the Broad Insititute for School Boards. She is coauthor of *The Strategic School.*

JULIE A. MARSH is a policy researcher at RAND who specializes in research on district-level educational reform, policy implementation, and accountability. She recently completed studies of the instructional improvement efforts of three urban school districts, working in collaboration with the University of Pittsburgh's Institute for Learning, literacy coaching in eight large school districts in Florida, and on the implementation of the No Child Left Behind Act in three states. She has authored numerous publications and is coeditor of *School Districts and Instructional Renewal.*

JEFFERY H. MARSHALL is an associate social scientist at RAND. His research focuses on teacher quality, decentralization, parental involvement in schools, and school dropouts. While at RAND, he has worked on formative evaluations of school reform projects, including New Leaders for New Schools. Prior to joining RAND, Marshall conducted program evaluations of educational interventions in developing countries. He has published a number of articles in education, economics, and development journals.

DANIEL F. MCCAFFREY is a senior statistician and the PNC Chair in Policy Analysis at RAND. He conducts research on education, health, and drug policy. Much of his recent work has focused on the value-added modeling for the estimation of teacher effects from student achievement data. McCaffrey is currently working with the National Center on Performance Incentives to conduct two randomized experiments to estimate the effect of performance-based pay for teachers on student achievement. He is also interested in statistical methods for estimating causal effects from observational studies.

ELLEN MOIR is founder and executive director of the New Teacher Center based in Santa Cruz, California. For over twenty years, she has pioneered innovative approaches to new teacher development. She has received national recognition for her work, including the Harold W. McGraw, Jr., Prize in Education and the Distinguished Teacher Educator Award from the California Council on Teacher Education. She has authored several articles and book chapters and has produced video series related to teacher development. Her work has been supported by foundations, including the Ford Foundation, the Carnegie Foundation, and the National Science Foundation.

SHEPPARD RANBOM is cofounder and president of the Washington, D.C.–based public affairs firm, Communication *Works*, LLC. He has focused on increasing the visibility and power of ideas and institutions through leveraging research, the media, issue-driven campaigns, grassroots advocacy initiatives, and marketing techniques. His clients have included many of the nation's leading foundations, corporations, nonprofits, and national commissions. An award-winning writer and strategist, Ranbom is a former staff writer for *Education Week* and has written or edited dozens of reports on education and civil rights issues. He was assisted in preparing this chapter by Sofia Rivkin-Hass of Swarthmore College.

JUNE RIVERS is the manager of the SAS EVAAS for K–12 group at the SAS Institute. She has collaborated with William Sanders on teaching effectiveness research. She was previously with the administration of Tennessee's K–12 mandated testing program and is a former math teacher and K–12 administrator.

WILLIAM SANDERS is senior manager of value-added assessment and research at the SAS Institute. Over the past decade, he has refined and applied value-added assessment using complex, mixed-model methodologies, which has revolutionized the use of test data for educational assessment. School districts across the nation are adopting his statistical approaches to explore the effects of schools, school districts, and teachers on the academic growth of students. He formerly served as director of the Value-Added Research and Assessment Center at the University of Tennessee. In addition to his work in the area of education, he has been a statistical consultant to the agricultural, manufacturing, engineering, and development industries.

REGIS ANNE SHIELDS is a director at Education Resource Strategies (ERS), responsible for the human capital practice area. She holds a JD degree from New York University Law School and an MPA from the Kennedy School at Harvard University. Prior to joining ERS, she served as director of high school reform and special assistant to the superintendent for the Providence Public Schools in Rhode Island. At ERS, she has partnered with numerous urban school districts across the country to develop professional development strategies. She is also the coauthor of the recent report, "Strategic Designs: Lessons from Leading Edge Small Urban High Schools."

BRIAN M. STECHER is a senior social scientist and the associate director of RAND Education. His research focuses on measuring educational quality and improvement, with an emphasis on assessment and accountability systems. During his nineteen years at RAND, he has worked on a range of educational projects, including evaluations of the National Longitudinal Study of No Child Left Behind, the California Class Size Reduction initiative, the Vermont Portfolio Assessment system, and high-stakes testing programs in Kentucky and Washington. Stecher has served on a number of expert panels for the National Academies and has published widely in professional journals.

MICHAEL THOMAS is the senior director of innovative solutions at Battelle for Kids and has led the development of several Battelle for Kids innovative learning and leadership tools and solutions. Such resources include the *Understanding & Using Value-Added Analysis: Toolkit for School Leaders* and the Ohio•Learn, an online system that gives educators access to personalized professional development, instructional leadership planning tools, and more. Prior to joining Battelle for Kids, he served as a program manager at The Ohio State University, where he coordinated elementary and middle school programs and designed professional development activities for teachers.

MARC J. WALLACE JR. is a founding partner of Teacher Excellence through Compensation. He is based in Lake Bluff, Illinois, serving clients by bringing to bear his extensive consulting and research experience in compensation, workforce effectiveness, human resource strategy, and labor relations. He has pioneered the adaptation of proven compensation strategies and techniques in the field of education. His work has resulted in the successful introduction of teacher pay for performance in a variety of schools, school districts, and states. Wallace has coauthored over seventy articles and twelve books on management and human resources.

Index